BRIAN F, PENDLETON

Reviews of Current Research

LONGITUDINAL STUDIES & THE SOCIAL SCIENCES

BRIAN F, PENDLETON

SOCIAL SCIENCE RESEARCH COUNCIL
Reviews of Current Research

1. Research in Political Science
2. Research on International Organization
3. Research in Social Anthropology
4. Social Research on Automation
5. Research on Poverty
6. Comparability in Social Research (*with the British Sociological Association*)
7. The Population Census
8. Longitudinal Studies and the Social Sciences
9. Research in Economic and Social History

W. D. Wall and H. L. Williams

Longitudinal Studies & the Social Sciences

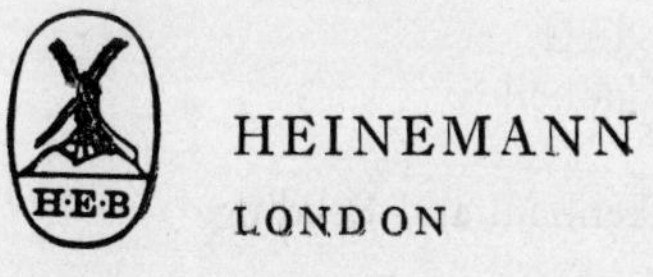

HEINEMANN
LONDON

Heinemann Educational Books Ltd
LONDON EDINBURGH MELBOURNE TORONTO
SINGAPORE JOHANNESBURG
AUCKLAND IBADAN
NAIROBI NEW DELHI

ISBN 0 435 82847 9

Published by Heinemann Educational Books Ltd
48 Charles Street, London W1X 8AH
for the Social Science Research Council
Printed in Great Britain by
Cox & Wyman Ltd, London, Fakenham and Reading

Contents

Foreword

In 1967, the Social Science Research Council (SSRC) commissioned the National Foundation for Educational Research (NFER) to carry out a review of longitudinal studies and to identify the distinctive contribution that studies of this kind could make to the development of the social sciences. The NFER was also asked to make suggestions about the way in which longitudinal studies could be most effectively organized and financed.

The study was carried out by Dr W. D. Wall, who was Director of the NFER at the time, and Mr H. L. Williams. The SSRC has decided that it should be published because it is a unique guide to longitudinal studies in the U.S., Britain and elsewhere and because its appraisal of the advantages and constraints of the longitudinal method should be of great help to social science research workers. The time that has elapsed since the review was prepared has made it possible for the authors to include in the Selected Bibliography references to later work in this field.

The opinions and recommendations about the organization of longitudinal studies are, of course, those of the authors and not of the SSRC.

JEREMY MITCHELL, series editor

Preface

This work had a wide circulation in its early draft, which was prepared in haste to meet the needs of the sponsoring body, the Social Science Research Council. In its final form it has greatly benefited from the criticisms, suggestions and additions proposed by colleagues working in all the social science fields. It could not have been undertaken at all without the co-operation of a very large number of social and medical scientists who, often at no more than a few days' notice, attended meetings, produced written evidence for us, criticized rough drafts, and generally gave most generously of their time and knowledge. The help they have given cannot be acknowledged in the detail it deserves: at almost every page the manuscript has gained in balance, accuracy, and depth from those who helped us. A list of participants in the Symposium is given in Appendix I. A number of the participants, and of those who could not take part in the meeting, have been laid under exceptionally heavy contribution, among them Dr Wanda C. Bronson, Sir Cyril Burt, Professor N. Butler, Mr R. Davie, Dr J. W. B. Douglas, Dr Joan Faulkner, Dr W. H. Hammond, Dr C. B. Hindley, Professor G. Jahoda, Dr N. P. Masse, Mr T. Moore, Dr David Morley, Dr J. Newson, Mr G. F. Peaker, Dr M. Rutter, Professor J. Tizard, Miss Thelma Veness, and Dr A. T. Welford. It is a pleasure also to record our thanks for the invaluable assistance so generously provided in the way of documentation by the directors of all the major U.S. centres of longitudinal research, and our lively appreciation of their readiness and promptness in answering our inquiries.

We are deeply grateful to those who helped us in this way, and to the secretariat of the Social Science Research Council, who did all they could to facilitate the task, providing us with contacts and information at every turn. The faults which still remain are ours, but while we accept full responsibility for the report and its conclusions, we believe that it represents a reasonable consensus of knowledgeable opinion in the behavioural sciences.

The terms of reference given to us by the Social Science Research Council were as follows:

> To review the most important longitudinal studies of the past with special reference to the contributions they have made to knowledge which could not have been gained so well in any other way.
>
> To define the objectives of longitudinal studies in the future in the fields and disciplines to which they are appropriate, and their reference to current discussions in Government Departments on linking educational, health and other such records maintained by them of individuals over the whole or part of the life-span.
>
> To make proposals, in the light of past experience, for methods of organization that will ensure the most effective and economical conduct of longitudinal studies.
>
> To make recommendations for the policy the Social Science Research Council should pursue over the next 25 years on the research objectives to be sought through single or multiple longitudinal studies, the administrative means to employ, and the financial assumptions to be made.

W. D. WALL

Slough, 1968   H. L. WILLIAMS

I. Methods of Collecting Data in the Social Sciences

INTRODUCTION

There is no way of sampling or of collecting data which is uniquely appropriate to the research problems of the social sciences, or is the preferred approach of any one of them. By and large, however, there do seem to be discernible trends and associations between specific kinds of problem or specific disciplines and particular ways of tackling them. Some – like the tendency towards broad sampling surveys in sociology, education, and epidemiology – have been determined by the scarcity of resources and the need to get information which is statistically reliable. In contrast, workers trained in such disciplines as medicine or clinical psychology tend to be interested in the complexities and uniqueness of the individual. Sometimes, however, it is ignorance or distrust of statistical techniques that determine their preference for intensive case studies of limited numbers of individuals, who may in fact often be unrepresentative. So, too, those whose training or tastes incline them to the experimental methods of the natural sciences, tend to adopt modified laboratory methods, with the painstaking assessment of simplified treatments and comparative studies of experimental and control groups.

The obvious may be stated at the outset: the mode of approach chosen, and often the problem itself, are likely to remain largely a function of the training, experience, and predilections of the research worker. Even so, to a large extent the research design must be determined by the question we want to answer. Yet, so far as concerns those aspects of the social sciences which deal with human beings, we may venture a few generalizations.

I

CROSS-SECTIONAL SURVEYS

Whenever we are concerned solely or mainly with the relative prevalence of some characteristic, or with norms and with variation, the *cross-sectional*[1] *sampling survey* is likely to be the cheapest and most effective way of securing the necessary descriptive data. Such surveys also make possible the estimation of associations between continuously or discretely distributed characteristics. If retrospective information is sought, as well as some accurate measurement of present status, hypotheses as to possible causes may be inferred, though not conclusively tested. Examples of such cross-sectional surveys abound in the literature, ranging from those concerned with education, like Burt's (1917) study of the relations and distributions of educational ability, or the NFER (National Foundation for Educational Research) national surveys[2] of 1955 and 1960, to the surveys of journal and magazine readership, market research or opinion polling, and the census.

A greater degree of elaboration and of power for some purposes derives from the *cross-sectional survey repeated after an interval of time* employing the same or closely similar instruments and sampling directly comparable populations. Such repeated cross-sectional samples will display population trends and may make it possible to predict future trends by extrapolation. If major events likely to influence trends are

---

[1] The definition employed by recent Harvard studies is worth noting here: 'A cross-sectional study is one that deals with *Status*. It may relate to an individual or to a group or groups at a comparable period, usually of the same age. One may therefore refer to cross-sectional data to distinguish them from those which are concerned with progress or change.' Stuart et al (115). For full bibliographical references see Appendix IX.

[2] Pidgeon, D. A., 'A national survey of the ability and attainment of children at three age levels.' *Brit. J. of Educn. Psychol. 30*, 124–33 (1960).

monitored between surveys, then associations and even 'causal' inferences become possible. Partial examples of this can be drawn from the work of the Home Office on 'Delinquent Generations'[1] and the surveys of reading levels[2] carried out by the Department of Education and Science. Each of these has demonstrated trends of change and has tended to show for example that the general disturbance of the war years affected generations of children differently according to their age during the critical period 1939–45.

One elaboration of the cross-sectional survey makes it possible to generate hypotheses about changes with increasing age. This is the survey of samples of differing ages. For example, if we are interested in changes in weight, growth in ability, absences from work, or the like, over a decade of years or longer, we can apply our measurements simultaneously to a series of samples of subjects covering the age range in question, and compare the means and variations of the factors studied in each successive age sub-sample. Providing the sampling techniques are adequate, a valid curve of mean growth should be obtained. This method rests upon the assumption that, apart from differences in age, the subsamples are comparable. This will hold if the sampling is properly random at each age level and if the characteristics studied are unaffected by factors related to age in indirect ways, such as a change in school systems or in the values and expectations of society. Studies of this kind will tell us little of *individual* departures from the pattern of average growth. Information on the average value of a characteristic at each age tells us nothing of the route by which individuals reach

---

[1] *Delinquent Generations*: a Home Office Research Unit Report (H.M.S.O., 1960)

[2] *Reading Ability* (H.M.S.O., 1950) and *Standards in Reading* (H.M.S.O., 1957).

it.[1] In some cases and with some easily identifiable variables, it is possible to include in such cross-sectional studies retrospective data – for example, presence or absence of evidence of separation from the mother, hospitalization, surgical treatment, type of education – which allow a longitudinal element and enrich the growth-predictive element. From the present point of view, the chief values of properly conceived cross-sectional studies are that they are likely to throw up hypotheses for longitudinal verification, while at the same time making it possible to decide whether a longitudinal study will be really worth while, and that they permit us to test methods about whose validity we may have doubts.

RETROSPECTIVE INDIVIDUAL STUDIES

In contrast to the survey, the *retrospective individual study* (case history) seems likely to bring us nearer to theories of causation. The main advantage of the case-study approach lies in the greater detail and greater precision of information, particularly of a qualitative kind, which it permits compared, for example, with the retrospective and contemporary quantitative data usually obtained in large-scale surveys, which depend upon questionnaires, structured interviews and group measures. Many, if not most of the hypotheses about the causation of human behaviour – and particularly that of deviant personalities – are based upon such retrospective individual studies of special groups, sometimes with, sometimes without a comparative matched control group drawn from the general population and studied along similar lines.

---

[1] See, for example, the graphs of Shuttleworth (109) on the growth of stature in girls. The curve for increments averaged by ages 'misses the drama' that is evident in the curves plotted for individuals: in every case, menarche occurred at or near the time of greatest gain in height. Only a longitudinal study could have revealed such a finely-tuned relation.

4

The classical examples in psychology and education are the studies of backwardness and delinquency, conducted in the 1920's by Sir Cyril Burt,[1] which combined detailed case studies with the technique of the control group and the broad sampling survey. Few subsequent studies have been as thoroughly designed.

PROSPECTIVE STUDIES

Apart from longitudinal studies of normal groups, which will be discussed later, most *prospective studies* have been concerned with deviant individuals of one kind or another, and the majority with the outcome of some particular form of treatment or intervention, sometimes with a control group, sometimes not, even where such a group might be considered scientifically necessary. The method is a routine procedure in medical research, especially in trial of new drugs or new surgical operations. It is more difficult to use in the social sciences, largely because of the problems of defining criteria, of analysing initial status and of rigorously controlling the experimental intervention. It has, however, been applied in remedial education, in therapeutic treatment, and in studies of teaching methods. One very successful and valuable example is the study made by Skeels[2] of children in orphanages, some of whom were given special nursery education, and some of whom were adopted. In the relatively brief early period of his study, striking differences in levels of intellectual functioning were demonstrated; and in the follow-up thirty years later (194) it was possible to obtain what looks like

---

[1] *The Young Delinquent* (1925) and *The Backward Child* (1937). It should be pointed out that these studies were also prospective in that cases were followed up for forty years or more.

[2] Skeels, H. M. and Dye, H. B., 'A study of the effects of differential stimulation on mentally retarded children', *Proceedings and Addresses of the American Association of Mental Deficiency*, 44, 114–36 (1939).

conclusive evidence of the long-term effects of early differences in treatment.

Evidently this form of prospective study is of the same general nature as the more or less rigorously controlled experimental study in which a hypothesis is set up, various alternative forms of experiment or observation are devised to test it (so called 'treatments'), groups of equivalent initial status are assigned randomly to 'treatments', and the various outcomes measured and compared. Biological and especially agricultural research provide examples of a relatively precise and rigorous form analogous to work in the social sciences, and it was within the ambit of the former sciences that the basic concepts of design and statistical analysis were developed in a form applicable to small samples under strict experimental conditions.[1] However, in the real and somewhat confused situations of human life it is rarely possible to match groups with the same degree of precision as one can match plots of soil, seeds, and so on; nor are 'treatments' either simple or always ethically acceptable; still less are they likely to be homogeneous and comparable if they involve human intervention.[2] The investigator nearly always has to fall back on groups imperfectly matched,[3] and on attempts to randomize errors or irrelevant factors by the use of special methods, such as covariance analysis. What is perhaps even more important is that, as a rule, in practical situations, such as

---

[1] Fisher, R. A., *Statistical Methods for Research Workers* (Oliver & Boyd, Edinburgh, 1947). Much of the bearing of Fisher's work on the design of studies of all kinds in the social sciences seems to be imperfectly appreciated. One constantly comes across cases where the analysis of the data appears to be an afterthought and has not been decided upon before the experiment was attempted.

[2] Such, for example, as the 'teacher variable' in studies of educational methods.

[3] The task of matching individuals is finally impossible, even if we restrict ourselves to a few variables. Twenty variables each with only five classes define nearly a hundred billion classes!

6

those of children at school, old folk in various forms of care, and factory workers, the more rigorous the design and the matching, and the more controlled and extensive the treatment, the shorter must be the lapse of time involved in the experimental period: otherwise severe losses occur through individuals ceasing to participate.

Studies of this kind have an important place in the social sciences, especially in the attempt to verify theories of causation and to evaluate the relative effectiveness of different forms of provision, training, treatment and the like. They are likely to be of greater value when arrangements are made for successive follow-up studies over lengthening periods of time. The real pay-off of Skeels' study came thirty years later, just as Terman's studies of children of high ability are now after forty or more years reaching their full effectiveness (200). Similarly in the educational field, the work of J. M. Morris has shown that changes after one or two years associated with particular methods of teaching reading may not last over a decade (385).

LONGITUDINAL STUDIES: A BRIEF HISTORY[1]

A longitudinal study may be defined as one which is based upon repeated measurements of the same individuals over time. Cross-sectional or 'conspective'[2] studies are 'psycho- or socio-static', providing a simultaneous and synoptic study of the situation as it is at the time of the enquiry. Longitudinal or prospective studies are 'socio- or psycho-dynamic' and are interested in change. In the words of the Colloquium

---

[1] In this section, and throughout, we have drawn heavily upon the account of a three-day *Colloquium on Longitudinal Studies* convened by the National Institute of Child Health and Human Development (U.S.A.) in 1965; and upon Kodlin, D., and Thompson, D. J. 'An appraisal of the longitudinal approach to studies of growth and development' (42).

[2] The word is Burt's. See *The Young Delinquent*, op. cit.

convened in 1965 by the U.S. NICHHD (National Institute of Child Health & Human Development)(15a) 'Only the longitudinal method can show the nature of growth, and trace patterns of change in an individual. Only the longitudinal method can give a true picture of cause and effect relationships over time.' It might be argued that retrospective studies will do this also and are simpler and cheaper to operate – besides lending themselves more readily to precise definition of hypotheses. However, human memory is fallible, and events which subsequently prove to be critical in their long-term effects may, at the time of occurrence, appear trivial, and be quickly forgotten. Human beings naturally seek for causes and may unconsciously fabricate or exaggerate something to account for the present state of affairs – such as a fall down stairs which many parents advance as a reason for the mentally subnormal child.[1] Where events are recent, or can be verified by means other than the unsupported evidence of the respondent, the retrospective study may be adequate.[2]

---

[1] To say nothing of the doctor who delivered an infant after he had been to a party!

[2] A recent appraisal considers the principal disadvantages of retrospective studies to arise from biased selection of criterion and control groups for study, and the deliberate or unconscious distortion of information inherent in viewing the past through a 'retrospectroscope': Gregory, 'Anterospective data following childhood loss of a parent', *Arch. Gen. Psychiat. 13* (1965). In 'remembrance of things past' the cultural stereotype as well as the personal reason can be a source of adulteration. The New York University Study provides an illustration of distortions effected by 'social levelling'. After a two-year interval parents were asked to recall important details of their child's behaviour in the first year of life which had been obtained from the same parents at the time of occurrence. 'Fifteen per cent of the mothers who had never used a pacifier stated they had, and only six per cent who had used it failed to recall this. Twenty-eight per cent whose children had sucked their thumbs stated this had not happened and no parent in 100 recalled thumb-sucking when it had not previously been reported. This

8

This is true only for very few events – and mostly those which have little emotional tone or can be readily identified by other means – for example, lengthy periods in hospital. Where earlier status is variable – for example, height, weight, general ability, vocabulary – or where forms of behaviour are difficult to recall and describe accurately – for example, aggressiveness, shyness and withdrawal – retrospective information is of little or no value; and it is peculiarly liable to distortion in the light of subsequent knowledge.

Longitudinal studies abound in the literature of the social, biological, and medical sciences. They have a long history, going back to the records kept from 1759 by de Montbeillard[1] of his son's growth to the age of 18, and the biographical studies of Tiedmann and Shinn.[2] In the U.S.A., in the late 20's and early 30's, many long-term studies of children were

---

[1] Buffon, 'Sur l'accroissement successif des enfants; Gueneau de Montbeillard mesuré de 1759 à 1776', *Oeuvres complètes* (Furne et Cie, Paris, 1837).

[2] Shinn, *The Development of the Senses in the First Three Years of Life* (University of California, Berkeley, 1907).

---

opposite direction of distortion corresponds, moreover, to the attitude of the most widely accepted authority on child care for this group [not difficult to identify] who approves of the use of a pacifier but frowns on thumb-sucking. The pattern of distortion in recall is one which causes uniqueness in individual functioning to disappear and to produce information which approximates the socially acquired concept of optimal functioning.' Chess, S., et al. (229). 'But if the while I think on thee, dear friend . . .' A report, however, made by a mother when her perception of a situation is distorted by deep anxiety may be far wider of the facts than one made later when the anxiety has passed. Brekstad, A., 'Factors influencing the reliability of anamnestic recall.' *Child Development*, 37, 603–612 (1966). An observation made by Schaffer & Emerson is pertinent here: 'Validity of interview data is, after all, to a considerable extent a function of the relationship between interviewer and interviewee, and it is one of the advantages of a longitudinal study that a greater opportunity is held out to put this relationship on a proper footing.' Schaffer, H. R., and Emerson, P. (270).

begun.[1] Many of them – like the earlier work of Baldwin (76), the Brush Foundation Growth Study, and that of Wingate Todd, concentrated particularly on physical characteristics, and have contributed enormously to our knowledge of individual patterns of growth, of the phenomena of critical growth periods, and of 'catch up' – all three matters on which no evidence can be obtained from cross-sectional studies of any kind. At the same time, and subsequently, longitudinal studies of children, of great complexity were begun at Berkeley, Harvard, Minnesota, and elsewhere. One of the earliest (1929) was the Harvard Growth Study.[2] This accumulated more than 200,000 mental and physical measurements on the same children over a period of eighteen years, with a follow-up 'maturity study' of health and social development between the ages of 25 and 34.[3] It involved an interdisciplinary team of medical, biological and social scientists.

Bloom conducted a thorough study[4] of eight major (American) longitudinal development researches, and of a large number of shorter and more limited ones. He presented the results in his book *Stability and Change in Human*

---

[1] A list of the principal ones will be found in Appendix II.

[2] A fuller account of this study is given in Appendix IIA. The subjects of this study are currently being reinvestigated by the Population Research and Training Center of the University of Chicago (124). The emphasis is on changes of I.Q. with age in the adult range, on occupational status now as related to childhood, etc., on social mobility, and on the relations between measurements of the original Harvard subjects and of their offspring.

[3] As in the project of the Child Research Council (U.S.A.) which aims to continue study beyond the growth period and contribute to an understanding of adult life and old age.

[4] Supplemented, of course, by a great variety of related studies of a longitudinal and survey kind, as well as experimental investigations specifically related to them, conducted by his graduate students.

Characteristics (12). This is probably the most compendious synthesis of the bearing of longitudinal studies on our knowledge of child development in the physical, cognitive, affective and educational domains. From his analysis he advances a variety of conclusions which may be regarded as being as certain as any of our knowledge in the human sciences. He is able to demonstrate, for example, the critical nature of the early years, especially those up to the age of four, in determining ultimate physical and intellectual status, to show that there is a growing irreversibility of adverse effects due to deprivation which is largely proportional to the earliness of its incidence, to suggest where different critical periods may lie, to throw some light on the 'catch-up' phenomenon, and to suggest how the 'overlap hypothesis'[1]

---

[1] Basically this assumes that the correlation between measurements of height at two different ages is a correlation between a part and a whole, and the measurements of height and other characteristics are additive, i.e., that the measurement at age 18 consists of the measurement at age 2 plus the gains made in between. There may or may not be a correlation between status at point A and the *rate* of gain between point A and point B. In the case of height, Bloom points out that the data fit the hypothesis of a zero correlation between initial status and gains, except for periods of unusual or rapid growth – such as birth to age 2, and puberty. In terms of age – where the centimetre measurement may be regarded as an absolute scale against which to check relative gains – fairly precise statements can be made about percentage of adult height gained at each period.

Applying the same line of reasoning to measurements of intelligence (where there is no absolute scale such as that of height) Bloom shows a similar set of relations, and, using a set of theoretical predictions from early estimations to final status, infers an ideal growth curve for general ability, and estimates the proportional effects of normal, defective and enriched environments.

The hypothesis seems less true for achievement and least true for values, interests and personality variables – as one would expect since these are heavily affected by environment. Even, however, with personality characteristics like intellectual interests, may be important for prediction and consequently for remedy if this is necessary.

In his preface, he enunciates three propositions which bear quotation:

1. The relation between parallel measurements over time is a function of the levels of development represented at the different times.
2. Change measurements are unrelated to initial measurements but they are highly related to the relevant environmental conditions in which the individuals have lived during the change period.
3. Variations in the environment have greatest quantitative effect on a characteristic at its most rapid period of change and least effect on the characteristic during the least rapid period of change.

So far as we are aware, no comparable body of longitudinal studies exists to cover adulthood or the problems of ageing.[1]

---

dependency, and aggression, Bloom is able to show similar patterns to those of physical and intellectual growth.

The importance of this simple hypothesis is that it enables periods of rapid growth, of increased sensibility to environment, to be identified from longitudinal data, and permits the establishment of a clear relation between longitudinal and cross-sectional studies.

[1] A number are instanced in a contribution to the Symposium on Longitudinal Studies held in Moscow in 1966: 'Since the early years of life stamp the entire subsequent history of the individual, it is understandable that attention has long been directed towards the study of childhood. While population samples of school age children can be obtained with relative ease through co-operation of educational institutions, no comparable community resource exists in the United States and many other countries for the ascertainment of mature individuals, other than the highly selected groups of institutionalized aged persons.' Special handicaps also are the 'lack of standardization data on old-age samples for many tests', 'the deficit of measures specifically designed for that age-group', and 'the inapplicability of concepts, such as the full-scale I.Q., that have proved valuable in child research'. Jarvik, L. F., and Erlenmeyer-Kimling, L.(37a).

For good practical reasons, research in ageing has been slower to adopt the longitudinal method, while of the fifteen longitudinal studies known by Damon (16)[1] to be in progress in the U.S.A. in 1964 the majority centred on cardiovascular disease. 'Since', he observed, 'longitudinal studies in adult life are so new, most of our knowledge – or perhaps "notions" would be a better term – of age changes rests on cross-sectional findings'. 'Longitudinal studies of ageing', he concluded, 'are not merely desirable – they are mandatory' – a proposition that found echoes in contributions to the NICHD Colloquium[2] (15a). Even puberty and adolescence are relatively unexplored except as a by-product of studies on infancy and childhood, and these are richest in the physical and biological field. Here the work of Tanner (116, 117, 118) is classic and has contributed enormously to our knowledge of differential patterns of physical and sexual development,

---

[1] The American longitudinal research on ageing considered by Damon to be the most extensive in terms of areas encompassed and age-span (it includes the adult offspring of the subjects) is the Framingham (Massachusetts) Heart Study of the U.S. Public Health Service. In addition, he notes the Tecumseh (Michigan) Community Study of the University of Michigan, and the Thousand Aviator Study of the U.S. Naval School of Aviation Medicine begun in 1940.

[2] In his contribution to the Colloquium's session on ageing, Streib noted that 'a recent book by Berelson and Steiner (*The Behavioral Sciences Today*, Harper & Row, 1964) which sums up knowledge on the behavioural sciences, has only a few points on ageing, relating to such areas as religious activity, political activity, or family life. Longitudinal research is not mentioned at all in the index'. In the discussion on areas for future longitudinal research in the social sciences Streib advocated the value of larger 'social book-keeping' studies involving the several agencies of government concerned, citing as an example a Canadian study of the effects of ageing on socio-economic condition, health, work activities and certain other basic characteristics. Begun in 1959 with 2,000 males aged 45, it will continue for twenty years.

and of the way these are related to social class, ability, and school progress.

CRITICISMS OF LONGITUDINAL STUDIES

It would be otiose to list in further detail the findings concerning human development which can only be (and have been) demonstrated by longitudinal studies.[1] The utility of the procedure for many problems one would think requires little demonstration. However, as recently as 1966, Professor Réné Zazzo (74) presented a characteristically Cartesian analysis of the problems to a Symposium on Longitudinal Studies. Was developmental psychology, he asked, pursuing a mirage? It was not the techniques that exercised his mind but the possibility itself of truly longitudinal study.

He began by distinguishing longitudinal from cross-

---

[1] The NICHD Colloquium (op. cit. p. 10) reached no consensus on a definition of *longitudinal study*. 'There were very nearly as many definitions as there were participants.' Viewpoints of more general acceptance would seem to find succinct expression in Terence Moore's definition: a study 'in which information is collected concurrently on one or many individuals over a time span long enough to encompass a detectable change in developmental status' (1951). For Burt, the longitudinal is synonymous with the *prospective* study, which he distinguishes from the *retrospective* study by its aim: the former seeks to verify *predictions* based on antecedent hypotheses, and the latter to ascertain *causes* (*The Young Delinquent*, 1925, op. cit. p. 3). For Moore the concurrence of observation with development and change is crucial: 'The term *follow-up* is sometimes applied to retrospective studies . . . but when the subjects are observed before or during' a particular experience in the past, 'and then again later, the follow-up is essentially longitudinal, although the data on the intervening period may be missing'.

The span of time over which observations are made depends on the issue investigated and its rate of change – e.g. studies such as that of Ambrose (215) on the smiling response in infants.

sectional work, and proposed that the type of study which re-examines the same population at recurring intervals should be called 'évolutive transverse' (cross-sectional-developmental). As it is at present used, he suggested, 'longitudinal' is a blanket term and does not describe a method but a wide variety of methods.

He then went on to distinguish the two very broad and radically distinct types of problems with which all longitudinal studies appeared to be concerned: on the one hand those of prediction, and on the other those of *'genesis'* – the stages, sequence, rates, in brief the laws of growth. The predictive study, he argued, is concerned with monitoring the stability of defined characteristics of a defined population over time, with the object ultimately of exploring how far such character-istics may be modified by environmental or other change or by therapeutic intervention. Genetic change is quite a different matter. Human beings accomplish their growth at different rates and hence arrive at the same growth stage at different ages. The essence of the longitudinal method is to discard chronolog-ical age as a definition of a population and to replace it with the quest for developmental sequences and their inter-relations. Its doctrine was born in the '20s of criticism of the cross-sectional method and of a conviction that for growth to be explained and understood it had to be followed over its duration. This, he objected, is a profound illusion in the light of the difficulties that have never been resolved when a study has been extended over the whole span of childhood and with several variables. Research has been hobbled not so much by a failure of ingenuity and by inadequacy of instrumentation as by the absurdity or at least the inherent contradiction in methodology that we have failed to recognize as such. In spite of defining longitudinal as the antonym of cross-sectional, the former has been shackled by the procedures of the latter method – large samples when a few subjects would suffice for the discovery of a developmental sequence, and standardized tests, that is to say, rigidity in theory and in instrumentation when the essential is freedom in the search of the unknown. The misapprehension has been fostered by the success held out by longitudinal analysis in the study of physical growth, with its calculations of rates and velocities for a known, definable, and directly measurable variable. Psychological variables cannot be measured like stature. The most perverse of illusions, in that it touches the very principle of longitudinal study, is the imperative that length of observation and of development cannot be coincident and coterminous if the nature and rhythm of the latter are to be revealed – the ancient fallacy that confounds the reality of what is observed with the process of observation.

The support for this thesis was the work of Wallon, and of Piaget, who dispensed with the procedures, sampling or other, of longitudinal and cross-sectional methods and simply 'picked out', for case-study and not to establish norms, children at their disposal of various ages, but paying no regard to the exactness of the latter, 'to discover by trial and error and by successive approximations, the significant response, the reference point, and marking post for plotting the trajectory of development'.

Wallon insisted that the 'rigorous formulation which Piaget has provided of the growth of intelligence owes absolutely nothing to longitudinal methods' and the techniques he used were 'observational and experimental techniques open to an unanticipated reality. They were never fixed or standardized'. Standardization, he suggested, and the construction of tests, should come only when the realities have been discovered and the variables defined, and when we wish to compare one child with other children. This is the proper starting-point for exploring individual differences, though this was never an aspect that attracted either Wallon or Piaget, whose concern was always the general laws of development, neither more nor less. However, if problems of development can be solved with such economy by their methods it is proper to ask what is left for the longitudinal approach. The answer, argued Zazzo, is quite simply the proposition just formulated: the study in individuals of variations in development, but with this distinction – and herein lies its originality – that the study is one conducted over time (*une differentielle longitudinale*). Only when a law of development is known, and a sequential order of growth established, should we be concerned to compare children or populations and to see how the law works out in each child or population, with age as a variable – not as a parameter defining a population for study.[1]

This definition, he observes, owes its origin to Binet's concept of mental age, while a contemporary and practical illustration is to be found in the work of Hindley and his collaborators which, in effect, is the comparison over time of several populations using a common basis of methods.[2]

The second and oldest ambition of longitudinal research is the study in depth of the development of behavioural patterns in all the delicacy and complexity of sequence and causality. It is, in his view, very doubtful if this can be realized with large numbers of children and variables, or over a long period. In practice every study with this aim must be short, and limited to a clearly defined segment of growth, its starting-point a clearly formulated problem. Furthermore, its solution is dependent not on a single method but on a wide variety of approaches (clinical, experimental, longitudinal, cross-

---

[1] Cf. Bromley's observations on the 'age-factor' in studies of ageing (137): 'In psychology, the age variable is not a single distinguishable factor but the vehicle for a wide range of interacting influences. Psychologists are not studying the effects of "pure ageing" but exploring the ways in which human performance and capacities are *associated* with chronological age. The psychology of ageing is a natural extension of developmental psychology.'

[2] See Appendices IV and VI.

sectional) and 'on their rational co-ordination'.[1] Certain phases only of a study will make it necessary to employ a longitudinal approach – at the outset perhaps to clear the ground and specify the proper question to be asked, at a later one possibly to study the application of a general law to a particular case.

There is of course much force in this argument, and it certainly clarifies the relationship between various kinds of longitudinal study and points to criteria of appropriateness for the different methods available. Perhaps the crucial points are the distinction between predictive studies – which by and large demand carefully defined and adequate samples – and genetic studies which, if they are to be undertaken at all, demand that the measures and hypotheses used should have some pre-existing basis of growth theory and be sufficiently open-ended.

Other objections have been advanced[2] which are partly

---

[1] This is a point made by Dr Bronson, of the University of California Institute of Human Development, in discussing with the authors an earlier draft of this report.

This seems a convenient place for citing the observations of Escalona (see ref. (a) p iii) – not in opposition to the views of Zazzo and Bronson but rather for their relevance to them: 'As the total design of a study is separated into such components as "aims", "methods", "rationale", and "procedure", an impression may be given that these components are independent, and can be grouped at will into a great variety of combinations. Actually, methods determine aims quite as much as the reverse, rationale finds expression in procedures, and extraneous "chance" factors influence a study quite as much as does deliberate design.'

[2] Almost all of those generally advanced apply only to the long-term study lasting many years. The longitudinal method is of course at least as applicable to enquiries over much shorter periods of time, as, for example, the study of the *immediate* effects on development of various environmental influences. Other objections apply in such cases; notably, that we do not know how permanent an effect may prove to be.

administrative and partly methodological. They may be summarized as follows:

1. Individuals for longitudinal study often have to be chosen in terms of their accessibility and co-operativeness, which renders them unrepresentative and makes generalization[1] suspect. Over long periods of time attrition of the sample occurs, and it is often difficult to state precisely the comparability of the initial and final groups.[2] In this connection, too, we should note the objection that continued study of the same individuals carries with it the risk of modifying their behaviour in unknown ways.

2. Maintaining contact with and sustaining the motivation of the subjects is difficult and costly, even with the groups of 300–500 of most longitudinal studies. Nor is it easy to continue a complex testing and measurement programme on the same individuals time after time without considerable administrative and technical resources.[3]

---

[1] But generalizations are, of course, permissible from replications of findings from different, and often very small, longitudinal samples; for example, the congruence of the results of inquiries into behavioural consistencies through childhood into the adult years – see Kagan & Moss (320); Bronson (302) – and, again, the closely similar correlations emerging independently from the different samples of the five European studies collaborating through the International Children's Centre and using a common basis of methods.

[2] Especially in studies of geriatric groups 'with their quickening mortality rate': for which the corollary is measurement at short intervals, not only as a safeguard against gradual depletion but as a means of getting 'a more thorough picture of psychological

[3] 'Research on ageing is a late arrival in science, trailing the fields of growth and development by several decades' – Birren, J. E. (134). Nevertheless, the periods of growth and decline are the periods of most rapid change – physiological, intellectual, emotional and social –

3. The passage of time leads to changes in the hypotheses and in the questions raised, and to unforeseen and unforeseeable changes in instrumentation and theory. The tendency is to start out with a comprehensive and mixed bag of variables and measures, to add to these as time goes on, and to accumulate so much information that frequent analysis becomes impossible and, indeed, that much, even most of the material is discarded. In particular, the magnitude of the task of concurrent analysis precludes a systematic re-evaluation of the study in the light of its own interim findings.

4. In the course of a longitudinal study carried on over many years, it is likely that new hypotheses will arise either from the study itself or from general advances in the relevant fields of social science. There is a reasonable chance, say the critics, that the refutation or verification of these will depend upon anterior data which were not collected because their possible significance was not perceived.

5. 'Someday' or 'Methuselah' research, as Garn (28) calls it, forces a research worker to choose between professional immobility or the abandonment of many years of

---

in the life-span, and confront the investigator with a variety of common problems – for example, sex differences in rates of maturation and deterioration, the evaluation of continuous and relatively rapid change, and the factors of motivation and stress in assessment procedures. 'Older people, like young children, are relatively delicate organisms that cannot be subjected to some of the more stressful experimental procedures tolerated by middle-range subjects. . . . Old age . . . is a time of gradual sensory and social isolation. The differences engendered by such contradictional changes are reflected by alterations in the emotional life of the subjects, as well as in the motivational level brought to successive test sessions. Methods specifically fitted to follow-up investigations with the aged must therefore be devised.' (Jarvik and Erlenmeyer-Kimling, op. cit. p. 9.)

work without evident result.[1] Indeed, it is held that only the mediocre will accept the restriction of their professional interests to the collection of similar kinds of data on the same individuals.[2] Particular difficulties may arise if the programme of data collection is so considerable that no time is allowed for concurrent analysis and feed-back, and if changes in the research staff automatically produce a change in the direction of the research or even the abandonment of earlier work.

6. The kinds of data collected range in objectivity and reliability from measurements with a high degree of consistency like height and weight, to those which are extremely difficult to free of error, such as aspects of behaviour, temperament, personality and character. This leads, critics say, to one of two decisions – that of

---

[1] It is worth pointing out that Lewis Terman had continued over thirty or more years to direct his study of the highly able, that Harold C. Stuart has maintained over twenty-five years his association with the Harvard study, and that L. W. Sontag, who began the Fels Study in 1929, is still director of the Institute.

[2] This seems to us something of a slander. One might put it the other way and say that only the shallow-minded would accept the restriction which the short-term study of children or animals imposes. The career aspect of this problem is one which depends largely upon the provision made for professional advancement within a project.

H. E. Jones (317) has made the point that the very richness of possibilities that are vested in the long-term longitudinal study for examining concomitant trends, the interaction of variables in a changing environment, and the lags and precocities in individual traits at a point in time, have their repercussions on continuity of staffing. 'The scientific worker who likes to move swiftly from one hypothesis to the next may feel frustrated in such a slow research milieu. This hazard is a serious one; it suggests that we must be concerned not merely with the personalities of our subjects but also with the personality attributes needed in maintaining a long-term staff.'

confining attention to what is easily and accurately measurable; or that of accumulating observations by different observers which are so unreliable as to be practically valueless. It is also argued that we cannot be sure that a complex characteristic such as 'intelligence' measured at (say) age 8 corresponds with the characteristic called 'intelligence' measured at (say) age 15; even when the measures used are themselves highly reliable, they represent relatively small samples of a considerable universe.[1] In other words – for example, the ability to read the printed word – we can be reasonably sure that the nature of the process has changed, and the functions measured at ages 8 and 15 are intrinsically different.

These are objections of substance, but to most there are satisfactory answers, which, if they do not allay all disquiet, at least are as adequate as can be expected in the present state of the social sciences.

Objections 1 and 2
The most damaging criticism relates to sampling.[2] However, British experience, particularly that of Douglas, shows that, even over a period of twenty years, it is possible to maintain the interest and participation of 90 per cent of the initial sample,[3] even when this is large (5,000) and representative.

---

[1] See Bayley (5). Again it requires longitudinal studies, such as Bradway and Thompson's (136) to demonstrate the complexity of adult intelligence, its incapacity for meaningful expression in a simple index, and the degree of constancy of different kinds of ability through life: a pre-school test heavily weighted with verbal items seems to be a more valid predictor of adult abilities, both verbal and non-verbal, than one using many performance items.

[2] This is only an objection – according to Zazzo (74) – if we are concerned with predictive studies.

[3] Maxwell, in a publication of the Scottish Council for Research in Education, now in the press, quotes a very similar figure (92 per cent) for the 1947 national sample followed from age 11 to age 24.

Other gaps may occur in the data – owing to the absence of subjects at particular sessions: these can, as the Douglas study has shown, be minimized by efficient administrative follow-up. Furthermore, the reduction of the total of dropout allows the investigator to look at his incomplete arrays and to determine from previous data whether or not there be anything systematically causing the gaps.

These difficulties of sampling and of gaps in data are by no means confined to longitudinal work. Several techniques are open to the same objections. In the most favourable conditions – those of sampling children in schools – absence on the appointed day of testing, absence from just one of the tests, unwillingness or inability to co-operate on the part of the school or teacher, will lead to biases which may be difficult to allow for. House-to-house surveys or interview surveys in public places are open to similar objections. Here certainly the sample may be rendered representative in terms of such variables as age, sex, and social class, and gaps due to non-responders can be filled by substituting a more willing member. Nevertheless, there is little chance of detecting or allowing for bias.[1]

Objections 3, 4 and 5
The problems of a change in the hypotheses studied, arising

---

[1] One of the most difficult groups to sample satisfactorily are adolescents in the second half of the second decade. This has not deterred research-workers from the attempt.

Again, the discrepancy between the findings of cross-sectional and longitudinal studies on intellectual deterioration as a characteristic of ageing is partly attributable 'to cultural changes in intellectual attainment and general exposure to intellectual stimulation which favour the younger groups tested in cross-sectional studies'. Longitudinal studies reveal that a general trend appears only on tests with speed and psychomotor components. Kuhlen, R. G. and Thompson, G. G. (Eds.), *Psychological Studies of Human Development* (Appleton, Century, Crofts, 1963).

from a change in staff or in their interests, and the possibility that new knowledge may invalidate the previous rationale, are real ones. The longer the enquiry continues the more likely is change to occur and diminish the value of what has already been done. This, however, will depend largely on the nature of the data. Height, weight, general ability, social class, educational attainments, the diagnoses of disease, for example can be precisely assessed. Data on these collected for one purpose may be re-examined in the light of new ideas. Changes in our notions of general ability (intelligence) and its measurement have not invalidated the *data* obtained from tests like the Terman-Merrill or the American Army Alpha, although they may lead to reinterpretation.

More difficult to allow for are new views about the importance of particular periods or events, such as retirement or growth spurts – or of unanticipated causal factors, such as smoking, or separation from the mother. It is therefore unwise to set out – as some have done – without clearly stated hypotheses which provide a recognizable rationale for the selection of the sample, and the variables to be studied. As well as this, a well-designed longitudinal study anticipates the possibility of spotting the unpredictable influence, the critical period – and any worthwhile definition of the process of research must include the occurrence of insight along the way, unforeseen and arising from living with the data obtained. Too restrictive a set of hypotheses may in fact produce rigidity and actually prevent the sudden illumination.

Objection 6
The final objection – that not all data are 'hard', and indeed that much of what is most interesting to the behavioural scientist is not yet susceptible of reasonably objective assessment – is one that affects all work in the social sciences. Measurements of physical characteristics, of general ability,

and of educational attainments can be made with a considerable degree of precision by different workers, and with definable margins of error (reliability coefficients of such measures are all about $+$ 0·95 or better). Methods of assessing economic and cultural status, income, housing standards, and the like, are almost equally reliable. The difficulties occur where the variable measured is composite and complex and does not express itself in reasonably standard ways which can be clearly and objectively defined, and for which adequately constructed measures do not exist. Personality, character, attitudes, behaviour patterns, speech, vocational satisfactions, and such like – all matters of absorbing interest to those concerned with the behavioural sciences – are very difficult to analyse meaningfully, to define and consequently to measure, at least in any way which can be regarded as reasonably free from observer error and bias.

This has led many investigators planning cross-sectional or longitudinal studies to exclude all but strictly physical and cognitive measurements, thus risking the omission of what could be most relevant to their problems. Others have adopted the opposite procedure and tried to be all-inclusive, multiplying the assessments in the hope that errors of observations and the like will cancel out and leave something of value behind.

Two things can however be said. The first is that techniques for assessing interests and attitudes, and estimating, suppressing or allowing for errors of observation, have greatly improved during the last few decades.[1] The second is complementary and to some extent more important. We can

---

[1] *See*, for example, Vernon, P. E., *Personality Assessment – a critical survey* (Methuen, 1964).
Warburton, F. W., 'The measurement of personality', *Educational Research*, Parts 1–3, Vol. 4 (1961/2).

distinguish varying degrees of 'power' in variables:[1] some – for example general ability – are extremely useful as predictors in a variety of fields; others – for example speed of reaction as a predictor of scholastic success – are extremely poor. If a variable is 'weak' in this sense, then any association it may have with another will be obscured when there are large errors in measurement. If, on the other hand, it is an influential factor – for example, parents' interest in their children's school progress – even relatively crude measures of it, such as those initially used by Douglas (teachers' estimates), will exhibit significant associations.[2]

To quote Kodlin and Thompson (42):

> ... there is considerable disparity between the soundness of the ideas which underlie the longitudinal approach and the methods by which this approach is carried out. It is this disparity, in some cases obvious to all, that gives rise to uncertainty regarding the value of longitudinal studies. It is well to remember, however, that similar and other shortcomings could be listed for any research be it concerned with the test tube or with human populations. The shortcomings exist because there is

---

[1] Baldwin (4) points out: 'The introduction of any variable into a longitudinal study that will last for several years is expensive in time, money and personnel ... To set up a new longitudinal sample for every new experimental and control variable is out of the question. ... So a major problem is to pick out likely variables whose effects will be so strong that they will show up even when the error term contains all of the variations introduced by uncontrolled events in the child's life.'

[2] Kagan and Moss (320) have been able, on the Fels data, to show considerable continuity between forms of behaviour exhibited by children between 6 and 10 years and those of adulthood. (See Chap. IX and passim.)

Stone and Onqué (340) provide nearly 300 abstracts of longitudinal researches reported up to 1955, giving evidence that for many traits, forms of behaviour and attitudes, sufficiently objective assessments were obtainable to demonstrate significant continuity and something of the mechanisms of change.

considerable disparity between our conceptualization of how problems should be solved and the adequacy of methods which we can employ to solve them.

Nevertheless, however great the methodological difficulties, the longitudinal approach is essential if we wish to determine the influence of conditions, acting over a period of time, on the same individuals.[1] This, however, is not to say that elaborate studies over decades are invariably necessary, and still less that 'sperm to worm' studies should be the rule. Considerations of cost, of the likelihood of attrition in the sample, and the staffing and administrative problems involved, should lead us to make sure that a longitudinal study is really necessary, and to determine the most economical form for it – the basis of sampling, its duration, and the kind of information to be gathered.

SAMPLING AND DESIGN

The hypotheses we choose for investigation will largely determine the basis of our sampling. For example, if we are interested in the influence of particular kinds of institution – such as schools, universities, foster homes or factories – we would probably be wise to take a sample of institutions according to the nature of the hypotheses we have in mind, and to sample subjects randomly within them. Our minimum of two sets of measurements of the same individuals over time can be regarded as 'input' and 'output', and we shall be concerned with the measurement of the institutions or of some aspects of their influence. If, on the other hand, we are

---

[1] When the concern of such studies is to relate environmental to personality change their effectiveness patently depends on the adequacy of the personality constructs employed and their operational definition – dependent in turn on an adequate theory of personality derived from 'information on the entire process of development from birth to maturity' which only longitudinal studies can supply. Schaefer (336).

interested in the broad predictions that can be made about children's growth from a knowledge of their pre-school circumstances, then our sampling may well be by date of birth, sex, and possibly by region or social group.

Similarly, the duration of a longitudinal enquiry depends upon hypotheses about change and its rate. For example, we might predict behavioural disturbance if a child is suddenly separated from a parent by death or going into hospital. Whether this occurs can be checked by a relatively brief study: whether the effects observed are permanent demands a longer period of follow-up.

An alternative consists in a modification of the procedure, by combining a number of short-term longitudinal studies in an overlapping age-pattern, so that it becomes possible to study a considerable age-span within a limited period of years. The effectiveness of this method depends upon comparable sampling and upon choosing the appropriate overlap points in the light of knowledge of critical periods of growth.[1] Ideally, each of the longitudinal periods should begin and

---

[1] Recent studies cast doubt on the existence in social learning and personality growth of critical periods in the special sense of the term which, stemming from embryology, has been used in the literature of developmental psychology, viz: that 'there are certain *limited* time periods in development during which a particular class of stimuli will have particularly profound effects, and that the same stimulation before or after this interval will have little, if any, effect upon the developing organism.' See Denenberg (285) for references on Critical Period Hypothesis. Here, however, the term is used somewhat loosely to include periods of rapid growth and stages in life – such as starting school, transition from primary to secondary education, starting work, marriage, and the like – where cultural or societal demands may strikingly affect the individual. For human growth an *optimal* period, rather than a critical period, hypothesis is advanced by Deutsch (395) as of wider generality and assuming a more optimistic position. It is a clear derivative of Bloom's proposition that environmental influences are greatest on a characteristic during the period of its most rapid growth.

end just before and just after a known or surmised phase of rapid change – for example, the first two or three years after birth, puberty, or retirement.[1]

CRITERIA OF SUITABILITY FOR LONGITUDINAL STUDY
The upshot of this discussion is to suggest two conclusions. Much of the criticism levelled against the longitudinal studies begun thirty or forty years ago is justified – but justified mainly by hindsight. Many, in fact most, of the defects attributed to them can now be avoided by more carefully thought-out sampling and experimental design, by allowing for more rapid data-analysis and feedback, by advances in measurement techniques. In spite of their defects, in spite of the accumulation by some, but by no means all of them, of unanalysed, and in many cases un-analysable, data, they have been productive of new insights and new and more powerful theories which could not have been gained by other means – even if we now know they might have been obtained somewhat more economically and less equivocally.[2]

The fact does, however, remain that even modified forms of longitudinal study involve a heavy commitment of

---

[1] See Kodlin and Thompson (42), Bloom (12), and Bell (8), who suggest a combination of longitudinal and cross-sectional research. Schaie (57) carries the matter much further. He points out that cross-sectional studies and longitudinal studies or even conventional combinations of them rarely allow us to separate conclusively the three sources of developmental change – maturational, change within the environment, and the changes operating in the culture differentially affecting different generations. He proposes three models for variance-analysis and a design for developmental studies which permits their application. See also Appendix V.

[2] Recent years have seen an increasing flow of reports summarizing the results of particular long-range projects on specific aspects of growth, and a number of syntheses of knowledge derived from longitudinal work – see, e.g. Bayley (129) and Jones, M. C. (319).

resources over a lengthy period of time. It should also be said that actual unit costs are probably no higher (and may be less) than those of a similar number of cross-sectional studies.[1] The difference lies in the commitment of funds more or less irrevocably and the consequently greater risk that a weakness in design or excessive attrition of the sample will be more expensive.[2]

This leads us to suggest that the decision to mount a longitudinal study of any magnitude requires the fulfilment of certain conditions. These may be expressed (not exhaustively) as follows:

1. The stated objectives of the study demand measurement of change in individuals through time.[3]
2. Some ('causal') relation can be postulated between an early and a subsequent event.

---

[1] 'Longitudinal studies will not increase in cost in direct proportion to the frequency of interviewing or the length of the time period covered. Long periods of repeated observations of a small sample will produce as many observations as one-stop interviews of a much larger sample.' Lawrence & Tibbitts (44).

[2] Kodlin and Thompson (42), provide a cost-effectiveness model comparing cross-sectional with longitudinal sampling as a means of arriving at estimates of *mean growth*. This suggests that for equal precision of estimates of means, longitudinal sampling is likely to be cheaper.

This paper has been sharply criticized in some of its aspects by Healey, M., *Hum. Biol.*, *30*, p. 245 (1958).

[3] It is suggested that these two criteria take account of the argument advanced by Zazzo – that differential or predictive longitudinal studies should succeed the establishment by clinical means of hypotheses about the laws of growth, and concentrate upon individual or group differences and upon the prediction and analysis of change or stability.

See also Netchine (52). The author, a colleague of Zazzo's, employs the results of a study with a Parisian sample aged 5 to 11 years to illustrate what he considers are the two principal courses

3. The measurement of the traits, characteristics, or events proposed are meaningful and of reasonable validity.
4. The results of the study will permit generalization.[1]
5. The analytic technique proposed will permit the rapid exploitation of the data gathered at intermediate ('feedback') stages and at the end of the enquiry.
6. The design takes into account the possibility of economy in time and effort of overlapping 'short-term' and cross-sectional studies.

---

open to longitudinal study for 'integrating' the ubiquitous and 'manifestly important entity of time': the first seeking to eliminate, by statistical means, variations introduced by time so as to reveal interrelations between simultaneously evolving phenomena – and 'what, so to speak, in development transcends it' (as in studies of stability and change in a characteristic); the second treating time 'as the sole mediational process between phenomena which are distinct in character but capable of acting one on the other'. The latter course is most successful in problems of discovering causal relations in a series of events in separate sectors, e.g. the econometric models of Tinbergen (65) showing how the cost of a product X at a given moment can be determined by features of production and consumption at an earlier one and operate as a determinant of phenomena later in time. The models are appropriate when rapid variation in one area takes place against a relatively stable background in other areas and not, as so frequently in child study, when several areas present symptoms of change simultaneously and 'the existence of a general maturational factor interferes with the apprehension of specific relations'. Nevertheless, in investigating relations between variables that differ widely in character, such as EEG records and psychological findings, the maturational factor can be minimized, especially when the former are more allied to subsequent than to contemporaneous behaviour – always assuming that repeated examinations are sufficiently close in time. A course midway between the two principal ones described would be the longitudinal study of variables in terms of their concomitant variation over a period – which, notes Netchine, Hindley adopts – and not of positions reached on a scale at a point in time.

[1] This is a key point. See next section.

2. Large-sample Longitudinal Surveys (Cohort Studies)

AN UNSUCCESSFUL ATTEMPT AT DEFINITION

Most of the longitudinal studies begun in the late 20's and 30's were based upon small numbers of subjects, chosen on the more or less fortuitous bases of contiguity to the research centre concerned, and willingness to co-operate. Thus, the Harvard School of Public Health (1929) study began with a group of 309 births only, and the Berkeley (Tuddenham and Snyder) study begun in 1928 had complete physical data from birth to the end of the second decade for 66 boys and 70 girls (119). Many involved varying dates of enrolment as well as relatively small numbers, and most report attrition rates higher than 30 per cent over the period. Few match up well against criterion no. 4 enunciated above. As Schaie (57) points out, not only is generalization dubious, but the design adopted provided no means of disentangling the influences of maturation, immediate environment, and general cultural change. They were not, of course, concerned to do so.

Studies of physical growth suffer less from these defects of design and sampling than those concerned with psychological, social, and cultural variables. For most practical purposes in social and educational policy we are concerned to predict outcomes in which the family and social environments play a considerable part, and we would like to know how differences in 'treatment' – such as different types of schooling, different kinds of vocation, earlier or later retirement, affect outcomes of all kinds; and we are concerned to determine, if we can, how a likely course may be influenced for the better – for example, how a child who is 'delinquency-prone' may be handled to minimize the likelihood of overt delinquent acts in adolescence or adulthood. Thus, the study of the immediate environments of home, school, factory, and so on, and of broad trends of change in society become as important as the study of individual characteristics.

To some extent – though here the argument approaches the circular – we may define what are sometimes called 'cohort studies' in the above terms.[1] They tend to take a statistical sample (either random or stratified in some way) of a considerable group of subjects who can be defined as a group by

---

[1] Although the word 'cohort' may prove to be a convenient label for a particular kind of longitudinal sample. it is in fact very imprecise and somewhat pretentious. Sir Cyril Burt points out (in a private communication) that the word seems to have arisen in something like its present use in the course of discussions of a committee called by Beveridge in 1935, and in relation to the planning of certain statistical surveys. Among its members were Beveridge, Bowley, Burt, Fisher, Hogben, and Nunn. Fisher proposed that the minimum number required for the intensive study of specific social problems could be arrived at as follows: there are two sexes; socio-economic classes can be reduced to three; the minimum number for the smallest sub-group should be 100. Hence, 100 males and 100 females in each of three socio-economic classes amounts to 600; and such groups could be taken at – for example – birth, age 10, 20 . . . 90. This yields a three-way classification readily amenable to analysis of variance along standard lines, and if the individuals are chosen according to some random procedure the error variance should be small enough to yield statistically reliable results. Beveridge drew attention to the fact that the unit of the Roman army was a *cohort* of 600 men, and that a legion at full strength contained ten cohorts, i.e. 6,000 men, a figure which would be arrived at by studying ten cohorts separated in age by intervals of ten years. In current use this term no longer has any reference to the figures of 600 or 6,000, and is often synonymous with age group or some other criterion by which the group to be sampled is defined. All studies using the term 'cohort' of which we are aware are longitudinal and based on specifiable samples of fairly narrowly defined groups; but not all longitudinal studies employ random-sampling techniques, and not all are based on narrowly defined groups. In what follows we shall only use the term 'cohort' where it forms part of a study title or where it occurs in a specific quoted context.

having a small number of characteristics in common – age, for example, and place of birth; or entry to an institution, e.g. a school, hospital, university, or factory, within a limited period of time. They are concerned with estimating the probabilities of different kinds of outcome in relation to certain initial conditions (for example, conditions of birth, socio-economic class, previous education or training, medical history, etc.) and in relation to intervening events or continuously acting variables (for example, change of workplace, change of domicile, level of parental interest, influence of a given reference group, and so on). Provided the measures used are made at sufficient intervals and are of sufficient sensitivity and detail, they may also aim at securing detailed information about the growth of individuals. In fact, the chief distinction between a cohort study as the term seems to be used and the usual form of longitudinal study lies in the adequacy of the initial sampling, in the size of the sample, and in the consequences which usually very much larger samples have for the kind of data sought and the means by which they are collected. No hard and fast lines of definition can be drawn.

However chosen and sampled, a single group cannot by itself give information on the influences of social change; and, in times like the present, this confounding of two kinds of environmental influence may conceal the very matters of most practical interest.[1] Hence, as was argued in the case of

---

[1] This is a subject we shall return to. The objection applies equally to the isolated cross-sectional survey and to most enquiries designed without specific cross-reference to existing data or measures. The study made by Douglas though concerned with a single narrow age group, allows of extrapolation and generalization in some important respects, because many of the measures used – e.g. the measures of ability and attainment – had been standardized on other groups, and cross-sectional surveys conducted by the DES, the SCRE and the NFER provide information on trends through time. The same is true of the NCDS 1958 Study.

the longitudinal studies discussed earlier and may be even more strongly urged in the case of longitudinal studies of large samples, the design most likely to provide the maximum of information is one which incorporates several groups overlapping in time, and which will yield information of a longitudinal kind on each group, cross-sectional incidence and prevalence studies across groups, and knowledge of trends over time. This pattern is simply described in Appendix V.

Administratively and economically such a design usually requires data to be collected at specified intervals, and since the samples have to be large, much data will have to be gathered by means of interview schedules, behaviour ratings, record sheets, and group tests of the simple kind which can be used by parents, teachers, nurses, and medical officers, without specific training in the methods employed. More intensive and rigorous studies demanding a high level of professional skill on the part of the investigator must be restricted to relatively small samples, or the costs become astronomic.[1]

---

[1] The NIH Collaborative Project, which involves follow-up studies of 50,000 children had cost $60,000,000 up to 1966 (when the oldest children were 7 years). The design of the study required 'the prospective observation of 50,000 pregnancies to assure the availability for intensive follow-up of at least 40,000 liveborn children' to the age of 7. Its prospective nature and simultaneous evaluations of many factors are essential elements in the study. 'Retrospective studies, because of the limitations of existing records, do not permit us to make the extensive evaluations of factors that the problem of pregnancy wastage requires. Nor is the controlled study more than a partial answer, and then only when we can formulate strong hypotheses. . . . Information regarding pregnancy and labour must be obtained prior to any knowledge of the outcome thereof, in anticipation of the probability that a certain percentage of the pregnancies will in fact lead to unfavourable outcome. Experience has demonstrated the essentiality of such a procedure, if reliable data are to be obtained; but the method requires the study of many normal pregnancies for the sake of

There is in the literature a considerable number of longitudinal studies of sizeable samples of age or other groups in the United Kingdom. None combines into one pattern the use of successive age-groups, the overlap of groups to shorten the overall time, and the inclusion of individually studied subgroups. They are found in the medical field,[1] in the field of human physical and physiological growth,[2] in education,[3] and in what might best perhaps be called the field of child development, embracing psychological, social, educational and medical aspects.[4] A very restricted number are national in their sampling,[5] most are restricted to a geographical area,[6]

getting information on those which eventually have proved to be abnormal.'

For the significance of the Study's title: 'If representatives of any participating unit are involved in decision-making, if the participants share in the design, development, conduct, analysis and publication of the investigation, the research is collaborative; if one unit is primarily directing others in their work, if final authority rests with this one unit, the research is co-operative.' 'The structure and scope of the Collaborative Project on cerebral palsy, mental retardation and other neurological and sensory disorders of infancy and childhood': *Papers presented at the Conference on Research Methodology, University of North Carolina, Sept. 1963,* by Heinz W. Berendes, Chief, Perinatal Research Branch, National Institute of Neurological Diseases and Blindness, National Institutes of Health, Bethesda, Maryland.

[1] e.g. Stewart, A. M. and Russell, W. T., Interim report on the Oxford Child Health Survey. *Medical Officer, 88,* 5–8 (1952).

[2] References to major longitudinal studies in this field appear in section B of the bibliography.

[3] e.g. The N F E R Reading, Streaming, and French inquiries.

[4] e.g. The Isle of Wight studies conducted by Rutter, Tizard and Whitmore.

[5] The Scottish Mental Survey, the National Child Development Study, and the P I C National Survey of Health and Development.

[6] Miller, F. J. W., Court, S. D. M., Walton, W. S. and Knox, E. G., *Growing Up in Newcastle upon Tyne* (Oxford University Press, 1960).

or even to a group of institutions.[1] Most are concerned with subjects between birth and age 20; there is a scattering concerned with family units,[2] and a slightly larger number which focus on aspects of ageing.[3]

THE PIC (POPULATION INVESTIGATION COMMITTEE) 1946 AND NCDS (NATIONAL CHILD DEVELOPMENT STUDY) 1958 STUDIES

Each of the two national studies (Douglas 1946, and Kellmer-Pringle and Butler 1958) arose out of perinatal surveys conducted in 1946 and 1958. The 1946 perinatal data were gathered with no overt intention of using them to embark on a long term follow-through. The more comprehensive perinatal survey of 1958[4] was expressly designed as the starting point for longitudinal work. The difficulty of finding financial support delayed a start on follow-up until 1964–65, when the children were in their infant schools. Both studies have been managed with a very small[5] full-time research team, and depend for the collection of data mainly on the voluntary participation of a multitude of public health, social service and educational staff;[6] both have been remarkably successful in tracing and maintaining the participation of their sample; both have an excellent record in the swift

---

[1] e.g. Brooke, E. M. (1964). A cohort study of patients first admitted to mental hospitals in 1954 and 1955 (H.M.S.O., 1964).

[2] e.g. The clinical and sociological studies of disturbed children and their families conducted by Rutter at the Maudsley Hospital.

[3] e.g. Young, M., Benjamin, B., and Wallis, C., 'The mortality of widowers,' *Lancet*, 31 August, pp. 454–6 (1963).

[4] Conducted by the National Birthday Trust and directed by Professor N. R. Butler.

[5] Rarely more than 3–4 professional workers.

[6] In consequence, their directly measurable costs have been modest, certainly compared with American studies.

analysis and publication of data,[1] partly because of excellent planning, and partly because they enjoy and exploit to the full modern facilities for data analysis.

Both have been interdisciplinary in conception, and have recognized the importance of the inter-relations of physical, cognitive, and affective aspects of the individual, of the interactions of immediate and more remote environments. Each has had an interdisciplinary guiding or consultative committee. Both are unparalleled in the comprehensiveness and adequacy of their sampling, the success with which they have maintained co-operation over a very wide area, and the richness of the information which they are yielding.

Of the two, the later (NCDS) survey has the more ambitious and potentially the richer schedule of data. Profiting by experience gained in the first enquiry, the 1958 perinatal

---

[1] The first complete and fully longitudinal report of the PIC enquiry appeared in 1958, after two surveys of the population in 1948 and 1950. Prior to this the team published the results of the perinatal survey (*Maternity in Great Britain*, B.U.P., 1948) and eight papers mainly but not exclusively concerned with cross-sectional data. In 1964, Douglas published the results – longitudinal and survey – of two further follow-ups made in 1954 and 1957. Some twenty-five further papers recording aspects of the normative and longitudinal data had also appeared up till then. The NCDS (1958) has been going for a much shorter time. The perinatal survey of the National Birthday Trust Fund, which was its point of departure, concerned 17,000 children born in England, Scotland and Wales in one week in March 1958. A follow-up study became possible in 1964, and had to be prepared in haste to catch the subjects in their last infant school year. Within eighteen months of starting the operation, all but 10 per cent of the children had been traced, and a thorough medical, social, psychological and educational survey had been mounted. The results were analysed for publication of a first interim report (*11,000 Seven Year Olds*, Longmans Green, 1966) two years after work was commenced. This is in the main a report of cross-sectional data on children in England and Wales.

survey covered a great many more important pre- and post-natal conditions,[1] and the first follow-up has covered virtually all the births included in the perinatal study. Thus, whereas the PIC survey deliberately omitted illegitimate children and twins, and selected a stratified sample of about 5,000, the NCDS, retaining the whole group, plans special sub-surveys of groups of various kinds – notably those hypothesized to be particularly vulnerable because of perinatal conditions, adverse social factors, or educational difficulties declaring themselves in the early school years. The social and educational data are also more elaborate for the whole group and are planned to be so for any intensively studied subsamples for which finance can be obtained. Financial support for the second study was not forthcoming soon enough for surveys to be carried out at age 2 and 4, as with the first, although retrospective data were obtained through parental interview.

While the information gathered in the two studies is not comparable in detail, there is sufficient parallelism – particularly in the medical, educational, and social variables – for comparison to be established, and for information to be obtained as to trends of change over the twelve years separating them. If the new perinatal survey proposed by the National Birthday Trust Fund for 1970 is realized, and the children are followed through in a similar fashion, we shall be in possession of true trend data for a span of over twenty years. If they are considered in relation to such cross-sectional surveys as those conducted by the Scottish Council for Research in Education, the National Foundation for Educational Research, and the Department of Education and Science, we shall be in possession of a body of information

---

[1] 'It would be most helpful if someone versed in the classics could give us a new term to designate the combination of pre-natal, natal, and early neonatal.' Buck (225).

about children from birth to early maturity, unrivalled anywhere in the world.

SOME PRELIMINARY RESULTS OF THE NCDS (1958) STUDY

It is of the nature of longitudinal studies that investment is for the future; the pay-off comes in an accumulating fashion, with the richest and most powerful insights towards the end. Nevertheless, at the time of writing we have some first longitudinal results of the 1958 NCDS Cohort. A preliminary (unpublished) analysis[1] was carried out in 1966 on a partial sample (9,317 children), relating some of the perinatal conditions to the outcome of a reading test (Southgate) and of a social adjustment assessment (Stott Bristol Social Adjustment Guide), carried out on children aged 7. At that time no information had been processed on the incidence of *established handicaps*, nor was it possible to utilize the extensive data on the *post-natal environment*, except for a crude division into two parental occupational groups, non-manual and manual. It was considered important even at that early stage to obtain preliminary information as to which of a large number of children might be 'at risk' of handicap by virtue of an abnormal pregnancy or birth history. It is from information of this type that an education or health authority has to determine which children who have had, say, a perinatal complication should be included on the current 'at risk' register, as requiring special supervision or educational provision. It is, therefore, heartening that in this interim sample a history of any one of the following conditions in pregnancy or labour, taken singly and without reference to each other, did not indicate that a seven-year-old child would be likely to require provision for special reading help (as indicated by a poor, measured reading performance) or for

---

[1] Personal communication from Professor Butler.

40

child guidance facilities (as indicated by an 'unsettled or maladjusted' score on the Bristol Social Adjustment Guide): maternal hypertension in pregnancy; maternal bleeding after the 28th week of pregnancy; breech presentation; forceps delivery; emergency or elective Caesarean section. These preliminary findings are of course subject to confirmation from more detailed analysis now going on, but they are perhaps equally encouraging for educationalists, obstetricians and parents, and also show the sort of valuable information this type of longitudinal analysis can produce. They should, however, not lead to complacency, as all these complications carry an increased risk of perinatal mortality and therefore require a high standard of care before, during and after birth.

An interesting preliminary finding of practical importance from this study is the association of a departure from a normal gestation of 40 ± 2 weeks with reading ability and social adjustment scores at age 7. In fact, gestational maturity appeared to be a better predictor of reading ability and social adjustment at seven years than the more commonly accepted birth-weight measurement. The lowest proportions of poor readers and the highest proportion of well-adjusted children were found among those born at full-term (39–41 weeks), and there were poorer average performances from those born more than three weeks early (pre-term) or more than three weeks late (post-term). A practical application of the latter finding, if confirmed, may well be an extension of the present widespread obstetric practice of inducing labour for 'post-maturity', when pregnancy is prolonged for two or three weeks after the expected date. Subnormal weight at birth, defined as less than $5\frac{1}{2}$ lbs (2,501 grams), was also confirmed in the NCDS to be significantly associated with poor reading later, and also poor social adjustment.

It is worth remarking that there have been conflicting conclusions about the relation between the foregoing (and other) perinatal variables and later educational ability and physical ability, health and strength. This is largely because studies have been retrospective, based on selected samples or without means of checking on the differential influence of socio-economic status; these difficulties have been minimized in the NCDS as they were in the PIC investigation.[1]

RESULTS OF THE PIC (1946) STUDY

Apart from the studies of a somewhat different character reported further on in this paper, the only study sufficiently near to completion to show the striking nature of the results obtained in the very long term is the PIC 1946 study, whose subjects are now young adults. Of the 73 principal conclusions listed by Douglas in his first report (*Children under Five*, pp. 145–51), at least 18 could not have been reached except by longitudinal methods. Briefly, they show:

1. that the effects of social mobility and increasing material prosperity have differential effects according to the educational levels of the parents and the number of children in the family. (Conclusions 3, 4 and 5.)
2. that a relatively poor social environment is cumulative in its effect on children's height, girls being more sensitive to this than boys. (Conclusions 15 and 16.)
3. that separation from mother, as well as being much more prevalent than had been thought, seems (in the period from birth to five years) to provoke less serious permanent disturbance than might have been expected from clinical studies of a post-hoc kind. (Conclusions 48, 49 and 50.)
4. that by the age of 5, *broken homes* apparently do not provoke more than temporary disturbance (bed-wetting), and this only in non-manual families. (Conclusions 52 and 53.)

---

[1] In Appendix VII will be found a statement of the likely long-term educational and social outcomes of the NCDS study.

5. that the proportions of mothers taking up full or part-time work increased as their children approached the age of 5, but that there was no evidence that their children were less emotionally stable at this age. (Conclusions 54 and 63.)
6. that early potting leads to earlier bowel control, less bed-wetting and less breakdown later. (Conclusions 65 and 69.)
7. that a high proportion of bed-wetters bite their nails and have speech defects, difficulties which persist even after they become dry. (Conclusion 70.)
8. that children prematurely born are more vulnerable physically during their first two years but not afterwards; that although rather smaller than normal children in later childhood, this is not the result of prematurity; and that by the age of 8 they tend to be handicapped in mental ability, particularly in reading. (Conclusions 72–5.)[1]

---

[1] In their report on the Fels data, Kagan and Moss (40) draw attention to what they call 'the sleeper effect'. Certain forms of early experience (for example, maternal acceleration of a child's developmental skills) do not show their influence until many years afterwards.

The corollary for longitudinal studies – Honzik (37) – is the potential yield from more specific documentation 'of the origin of significant behaviours from the cumulative records of the various growth studies'.

'Sleeper effect' appears to subsume two phenomena: the effects of specific early experiences on later development, and discontinuities in personality development. The findings of Kagan and Moss have analogues in other disciplines. The delayed or long-term effects of educational methods, though commonly observed, are rarely reported – Miller (384) – and should serve as a warning 'against pinning all our experimental evaluation of teaching methods on immediate post-tests or measures at a single point in time' – Campbell and Stanley (374). Carroll (375) has made a reasoned and eloquent plea for 'panoramic' and longitudinal as opposed to the

In his second report, *The Home and the School*, Douglas analyses the results of two further surveys of the same children at ages 8 and 11. The results, combined with the earlier data, are less clear-cut and more complex, and consequently more difficult to summarize adequately. We can do no better than quote two paragraphs from D. V. Glass's introduction:

In the primary school years there was a strong association between measured intelligence, school performance and success at the '11+' examination. But the study has shown how, even within the narrow span of years between 8 and 11, measured intelligence responds to environmental factors (including the family environment) and also how, especially in the border zone of 110–120 I.Q., environmental factors affect the allocation of children to grammar or secondary modern schools. These environmental effects demand a critical reappraisal with respect to the question of which aspects are most significant for which groups of children and at what stages in their development. Some of the more powerful aspects of the environment include the condition of the home; the degree of parental encouragement given to the children; the previous academic record of the primary schools (that is, the proportion of their pupils reaching grammar schools); and the 'streams' in which children are placed early in their primary school years. But the relevance of the factors differs with social class and with the age of the children. Housing conditions act cumulatively over time on working-class children; for middle-class children, however, some adjustment appears to be reached as they grow older. The academic record of schools acts differently at different levels.

---

traditional 'snapshot' studies of the learning process in schools, and for taking advantage of the continued presence of children in them. Recent reports on two longitudinal studies in France signal a step in this direction by educational research on the continent (381, 383). In the field of communication and persuasion, Hovland and his associates have repeatedly found that long-term effects differ not only quantitatively but also qualitatively from immediate effects.

Schools with a very good academic record show a continued high success rate even if children receive little parental encouragement; while when there is a poor record, even the children who receive much parental encouragement still do badly. But in the entry to primary schools, a much larger proportion of middle-class than working-class children attended schools with good records, while at the same time a larger proportion of middle-class parents gave strong encouragement to their children. For middle-class children, therefore, school and family environment tended to reinforce each other positively, for working-class children negatively. The 'streaming' of children tended to work in a comparably differential manner.

Beginning with handicaps, in the sense of having a poorer physical and cultural environment, the children (of working-class homes) suffer an intensification of disadvantages, relative to middle-class children, during their primary school years. If they live in poor housing conditions, they may well attend schools with a low record of success at the 11+ examination. Those who are least well cared for may find themselves allocated to the lower streams at school and their school performance will tend to conform accordingly. In general they are less likely to receive encouragement from their parents. Between the ages of 8 and 11 years, the working-class and middle-class children will thus tend to grow further apart in operational ability. If, based on their tests at the age of 8 years, they had had, at each level of measured intelligence the same chances of being awarded a grammar school place as the children of the upper sections of the middle classes, we should have needed fifty-six per cent more grammar school places than were actually available. The gap between the hypothetical and the actual is an indication not only of the continued existence of cumulative inequalities but also of the extent to which our society has failed to encourage the development and realization of ability at various levels.

Later in his introduction, Glass refers to results from subsequent follow-ups of the same children, not yet reported in detail. He writes:

Only a very small proportion of pupils move from secondary modern to grammar schools (20 per cent in the present study) and transfers are more frequent among middle-class than among working-class children. And though secondary modern schools now provide facilities for older pupils, most of them still leave at the age of 15 years. Among the children in the survey – they reached the age of 15 in 1961 – 70 per cent of those in secondary modern schools left school at the minimum age, as compared with only 4 per cent of the children in grammar schools. For the large majority of children in secondary modern schools, the minimum school-leaving age marked the end of full-time education.

The present system of public primary and secondary education is based upon assumptions which, even when they appear to be realistic, give that appearance because the selection mechanisms used act as self-fulfilling prophecies. But even within their own narrow terms, the mechanisms are imperfect. They select out; but they by no means succeed in keeping in, for subsequent entry to higher education, the top layers of measured intelligence. Around 20 per cent of boys and girls have I.Q.'s of 113 and over. But by June 1962, when the survey children were just about sixteen years of age, fifteen per cent of that highly intelligent group of boys and girls had already given up full-time education, almost four-fifths of the leavers being working-class children.

It is not an exaggeration to say that these findings have had considered influence on current thinking about such matters as the reorganization of secondary education, the abandonment of selection, the attack on streaming in primary schools, and the notion of an unrealized pool of ability.

There are, of course, many other results described in the book,[1] and particularly striking is Douglas's more detailed analysis of the interrelations between social class, parental aspirations and encouragement, and the general intellectual

---

[1] In Appendix VII will be found a note by Douglas outlining the future plans of the survey.

46

growth, attitudes and behaviour of children. This exhibits one particularly important methodological point, made earlier in general terms.[1] Parental aspiration and encouragement are clearly influential factors. Hence, although the measure used was relatively simple and open to objections, the observer error did not obscure the relation. Indeed, since the study, as well as obtaining teachers' assessments of parents' interest, gathered a great deal of collateral information on such things as use of medical and social services, and level of home care, it is becoming possible to identify syndromes of parental behaviour likely to carry our knowledge much further and deeper – in spite of the fact that any one measure might be considered subject to criticism on the grounds of a lack of objectivity and of the errors inherent in the use of large numbers of observers.

The two studies mentioned concern national samples and amply demonstrate that co-operation of the subjects, their parents, and a multitude of education, social and health staff can be maintained over a long period – in one case as long as twenty years. They show that, though some of the information has to be gathered by persons not specially trained, this method can nevertheless be adopted with enough reliability and objectivity for the purposes of a broad research, provided the tests, schedules and questionnaires used have been carefully designed with this in view. In both enquiries there was only a very small loss of data.

CONCLUSIONS

Perhaps as a result of the discussion of the two national studies about which the term 'cohort' has been used, we are somewhat nearer to a series of clarifications. We should of course reiterate that the form of longitudinal study chosen, the nature and size of the sample, and even whether longi-

---

[1] p. 20.

tudinal study is necessary at all, will depend upon the problem chosen for study and the hypotheses set up. Accepting this, we may say that the study through time of samples of children defined either as complete narrow age groups, or as narrow age groups within a region, or as a random or stratified sample of them, is probably an essential method of studying the effects of broad social, economic and cultural factors on growth. Similar 'flow studies' of groups taken at ages considerably after birth would be helpful in the study of adolescence, adulthood, and old age. The fact that both the national studies described began in sociological, medical and biological perinatal surveys and have continued to concern themselves with the various services (social, medical and educational) and their effects on particular groups of individuals, is indicative of the practical problems on which they are designed to throw light. Their value in terms of knowledge of *individual* growth patterns is considerably less than the kind of broad predictive and prognostic information they yield. Essentially they are, as it were, 'tracer' groups. Their results point to questions on which more intensive studies should be made, they set up a series of bench marks by which we can map change, and they provide banks of data, particularly on the normal population, which can serve as a reference for comparison with special groups much more intensively studied, and with a much more restricted sample.

3. Practical Considerations and a Suggested Organization

INTRODUCTION

From the foregoing discussion we reach the conclusion that the type of study represented by the PIC (1946) and NCDS (1958) is essential for many purposes in the social sciences, but that the precise details of organization, of problems for study, and above all of the relation between such work and other, especially but not exclusively, longitudinal studies, require careful thought.

At the risk of repeating ourselves, we will recapitulate some of the considerations which we believe have emerged from the earlier discussion, as they apply to longitudinal surveys of substantial groups through a considerable period of time. They are as follows:

1. The more interest is focused upon the effects of environment on specified groups of persons, the more essential it becomes to have adequate and comprehensive sampling, and the more likely is it that it will be necessary to sample groups closely defined by age or by one or a combination of other simple criteria.

2. Single longitudinal studies, though of great value in themselves, are less powerful and their conclusions less capable of generalization than (i) a combination of longitudinal studies with cross-sectional surveys, and (ii) a sequence of longitudinally studied groups starting at intervals of time. Only in this way is it possible to avoid confounding the effects of cultural and secular changes with changes in the individuals and in their immediate environment. This becomes increasingly important when the main interest turns on the effects of social policy.

3. Both local[1] and national studies are valuable and necessary. Local groups have certain advantages, particularly of proximity to the research team, and they allow a more intensive examination of a sub-culture. Generalization, however, is less certain. National studies will usually reveal gross regional differences only. With careful planning, regional and national groups could be complementary.

4. Both broad statistical studies and detailed individual studies of a longitudinal kind are required for many problems. Each would gain immeasurably if they were closely related.

5. Experience has shown (i) that it is possible to maintain a large age-group sample in being over one or two decades without serious attrition, and (ii) that the cooperation of a wide range of local-authority staff can be gained and held, and that careful design of survey instruments results in data which are adequately objective and comparable for most purposes.

6. In the social sciences, sufficient knowledge exists to enable us to set up hypotheses concerning the growth of children and adolescents which will make future longitudinal studies in this age range more economical in their design and in data collection than some have been in the past. We may also expect developments in psychometrics and sociometrics to provide more means of measurement and assessment which can be objectively applied by staff not specially trained in the social sciences. The two British examples (PIC and NCDS) have shown marked advances in these respects. Because of their design and their exploitation of modern

---

[1] Included in this term are studies based on a town or a region, and those which take institutional groups as their basis.

methods of data processing, they have been rapid in reporting – the most recent one remarkably so – and considerably cheaper in terms of direct costs than their U.S. counterparts. We should not, however, allow ourselves to fall into the error of rigidity in design. While such studies must be based upon a general theory of development, of environmental influences and the like, insistence on a narrowly formulated series of initial hypotheses could preclude the possibility of new theories, unforeseen generalizations, or alternative interpretations arising en route or at the end. Some considerable element of the drag net should be included.

7. When it can be achieved, the method of overlapping age-group samples in such a way as to telescope the time scale and to provide periodic cross-sectional studies to give time trends and mean curves for groups seems highly desirable on practical as well as theoretical grounds. The distance between age-group samples in such a pattern has to be carefully determined in terms of what is known or surmised about critical periods – of growth, of administrative, or of social change, for example.

8. In terms of what is done and what is achieved, the cost of conducting a long-term study of a sufficient sample may not be greater than that of repeated surveys of different samples of similar size. A longitudinal study, however, implies a long-term commitment, and the pay-off is least in the beginning and greatest at the end. A defect in the initial plan is therefore more costly and disappointing. This implies careful planning at the outset and continuous feed-back and flexibility. It implies also that the approach should be used only when (i) the information can be better gained by no other means; (ii) there is reasonable likelihood of a

pay-off increasing with time; (iii) that contact and collaboration can be maintained, and (iv) that the variables chosen for study are sufficiently powerful to 'penetrate' any defects in the measures used. For some problems at least, a cross-sectional study would provide a useful feasibility exercise and could be used to test the efficiency of new instruments prior to longitudinal work.

9. In spite of the many positive things which can be said about longitudinal studies, there remain great methodological problems to be solved. Notable among these are: (i) as in all the social sciences, the question of improving the methods of collecting data and the measurement of what are now regarded as 'soft' variables, among the potentially most interesting – e.g. value systems, role perceptions, attitudes, etc.; (ii) the question of devising statistical techniques, particularly those related to the measurement of growth on an absolute scale; (iii) the problem of finding ways of monitoring, describing and measuring changes in the immediate and total society and culture.

10. There is also a variety of administrative problems. These concern the maintenance of continuity in design and planning over long periods of time, the organization of tracing and maintaining contact with the subjects, interdisciplinary collaboration, and ways of reconciling the legitimate career interests of staff with the essential continuity of the study.

DATA LINKAGE

Since the start of most of the studies mentioned earlier, there have been the beginnings of change in official attitudes to the gathering and use of population statistics. Moreover, the Social Science Research Council Data Bank has been set up at the University of Essex; and data banks of other kinds, having become feasible because of developments in storage and retrieval, are now under discussion. Some large local authorities have set up their own research and statistical services.[1] It is not surprising then that the question of data linkage between official collecting agencies and present or future longitudinal studies should have loomed large in the discussions of the group of social scientists called together by the NFER.

In the time at our disposal, no thorough study could be made of the nature and availability of official statistics nor of the feasibility of linkages among them or between them and specially mounted follow-through studies. The majority of official statistics are not available on an individual unit basis, and their principal value is that of helping to determine sampling frames and in giving broad indications of the kinds of factors which have to be taken into account. They can be used to check for bias in particular samples, and particularly in checking how far regional or local samples differ from national ones.

The collection centrally of cumulative data on individuals would be one of the greatest steps forward in making longitudinal studies of many kinds both more economical to conduct and more effective. Some government departments have already begun such schemes, and others are contemplating them. Like all statistical inquiries, they raise questions of consistency of definition and classification between different sets of statistics – a problem particularly difficult to resolve once one gets away from simply factual data like chronological ages, and into such areas as educational or physical handicaps, or the classification of institutions. Not unnaturally, and in view of the costs of collection and analysis, all the

---

[1] e.g. The Greater London Council Research and Intelligence Unit under the direction of Dr Benjamin. Incidentally, this Unit is currently involved in three studies of a longitudinal kind.

existing schemes for collecting individual data are partial, and directed to quite specific problems. The Home Office collects such data on institutions (prisons, Borstals) and on offenders. The Ministry of Health keeps statistics relating to individual admissions and discharges for all mental hospitals and most major mental homes, but little effort is made to collate input with output – for example, a patient who enters a mental hospital three times in one year is counted as three admissions.[1] The General Records Office keeps statistics of 10 per cent of all hospital admissions, and is proceeding to an analysis of hospital activities.

A project of at least limited use (in terms of direct linkage with longitudinal studies) is the proposed *Individualized Data Scheme* of the Department of Education and Science. It has the characteristics of an overlapping series of age groups which will provide flow data and cross-sectional sweeps at different points of time. It is based upon a 10 per cent sample of annual groups of school leavers (those whose birthdays fall on the 5th, 15th and 25th of any month) for whom such data as school history, area of residence, institution of further education, occupation, and examination results are to be collected. In addition, the teachers' records already maintained are to be integrated into the scheme. A main reference file will collate all the information on the educational record of the 10 per cent samples.[2] At present this work is confined to school-leavers and, so far as the professions are concerned, to teaching. There is no *inherent* reason why it should not be extended backwards in time and broadened to include other professions. The actual data collected also are very limited, a

---

[1] The Ministry of Health is conducting one special study for 1964–7 linking admissions and discharges.

[2] We are indebted for this information to Mr P. Redfern, Chief Statistician, Department of Education and Science.

fact which severely restricts its usefulness unless it be supported by other studies.[1]

Data of all kinds are collected by a great variety of institutions for their own specific purposes. Some of the information is eventually analysed; much, even most of it, is lost when its immediate usefulness is past. Even when data are preserved and made available for research, we frequently find that, for example, data collected for similar purposes by similar institutions cannot be collated and used because they are not comparable. All too often the sheer clerical task of digging out the information and preparing it for analysis and collation is greater than that of collecting the same data afresh for the specific purposes of the research.

At this stage it is probably unrealistic to hope that such things as *ad hoc* medical examinations, case-histories taken by social welfare institutions, internal school records, vocational guidance advice, employment histories, and such like, could be fully standardized to the point of usefulness as research material and made readily identifiable for tracing purposes. A major break-through would be achieved in research in the social sciences if *samples* of various kinds of institution (schools, colleges, clinics, hospitals, social service agencies) would undertake to record certain kinds of information in standard categories according to a national plan. This does not seem impossible, though it would be difficult to organize and is beset with problems of identification and tracing. The projected scheme of the Department of Education and Science (which involves the co-operation of

---

[1] A closely similar scheme which has been in operation in Sweden since 1961. This scheme which, although financed by the Swedish Board of Education, is under independent auspices, has a much wider schedule of data and seems more genuinely educational in its intentions. Links with other longitudinal work are more feasible as well as likely to be more useful.

a great variety of educational institutions) suggests that it is feasible.

The linkage of data on even the most modest scale between individual longitudinal studies and official statistical sources obviously also presents formidable difficulties. Apart from those mentioned above, there are the problems of preserving the privacy of the individual. In some cases – as for example with Census data – the confidential nature of the information is recognized by Act of Parliament. In others – as, for example, with medical and prison records – there are professional barriers. The third and largest category is governed by the written or unwritten assurance given by an inquirer that respondents will not be identified – for example, assurance is given that the details of expenditure gathered by the Social Survey's Family Expenditure Survey will not be disclosed to the Inland Revenue. The preservation of confidence and privacy, particularly in relation to subjects voluntarily taking part in an inquiry, is immensely important. Any steps taken here must be extremely prudent since, once public confidence is undermined and privacy appears not to be respected, the whole possibility of conducting many of the more valuable kinds of research would be prejudiced.

Another form of linkage seems, however, less difficult to achieve. We have been struck by the number of longitudinal studies of various kinds in progress and contemplated in this country – and by the apparent lack of communication between them. The customary processes of scientific interchange through journals and the meetings of learned societies do not seem sufficient to ensure that each proceeds in full awareness of the intentions, successes, and failures of the others – and this is particularly true across disciplines. Each study tends to develop its own instruments, and not infrequently makes similar demands for information on the same institutions. There are, of course, registers of current research in the social sciences[1] and in education.[2] The British Psychological Society and the NFER maintain libraries of tests. There is no clearing-house for information on instruments for collecting data and methods other than psychological and educational tests; nor is there any means whereby those concerned with longitudinal studies can rapidly exchange information.

INTER-STUDY LINKAGE: A BANK OF DATA

There is a further aspect of data linkage to be considered. It arises from longitudinal studies themselves, and particularly from the cross-sectional surveys made en route. As has been pointed out, the yield of any longitudinal study increases with each successive collection of data.

We now possess perinatal data on two age-groups of children, numbering some 13,000 from the PIC (1946) study and 17,000 from the NCDS (1958). Quite apart from the use of these data in the main longitudinal follow-ups, they provide an excellent (and unusually reliable) quarry of retrospective information for studies of sections of the adolescent and adult population throughout their lifetime – a quarry which can be all the better exploited if contact is maintained with the subjects at regular intervals. Similar use, too, could probably be made of the *Scottish 1947 Mental Survey* data and of the information gathered in the various regional longitudinal studies, notably those of Newcastle and the Isle of Wight.[3]

A special case is inherent in the objectives (and to some

---

[1] *Scientific Research in British Universities and Colleges, Volume III: Social Sciences* (H.M.S.O.).

[2] List of Current Researches in Education, NFER, and the DES list of projects it sponsors.

[3] This is not as simple as it sounds. We still have a long way to go in developing a technique of data storage and description which makes it possible for a later investigator to use anything other than tabulations from an earlier inquiry.

extent the conduct) of the NCDS (1958) study. From the outset two main lines of inquiry were intended. The first is the more usual – common to most longitudinal studies – that of following the development of a sample of normal children. The second is that of relating data about hypothetically vulnerable groups – premature, perinatal 'at risk' groups, illegitimate, separated from parents, physically abnormal children, etc. – to their subsequent educational, sociological, psychological and physical progress. It is proposed to exend the studies of exceptional children to include categories whose terms are applicable to individuals in their schooldays exclusively, and are defined by features which are commonly supposed to characterize vulnerability to environmental hazards: viz. the educationally subnormal, those who have marked difficulty in adjusting to school, the severely retarded readers, and so on. In the study of problems of this and similar kinds, while much can be done by regular survey methods, individual studies in some detail are manifestly necessary. They become the more so if we are interested in the reasons why certain likely consequences – such as delinquency, maladjustment, social inadequacy, heightened physical vulnerability, job instability, and so on – occur in relation to earlier apparently predisposing factors, in a proportion of cases only. By examining why breakdown does *not* occur in some manifestly unfavourable cases, whereas in others it does, we can begin to infer ways by which the environment can be positively manipulated.

Similarly, there is no reason why – in relation to the 1958 study and certainly in relation to any similar later ones – the method of the research should be one of detached observation exclusively. As soon as we have positive hypotheses to suggest effective intervention – and we do have some already in terms, for example, of the importance of pre-school conceptual enrichment, of the value of remedial work with late readers, of the necessity for support and interpretation

58

when children have to be taken into care – experimental studies of considerable power and rigour become possible.[1]

REGIONAL VERSUS NATIONAL STUDIES: STUDIES OF SPECIFIC GROUPS VERSUS STUDIES OF SUB-SAMPLES

There are limitations to the kind of information which can profitably be collected from a national study. Both the major child-development studies mentioned so far have been restricted to one week's births; and there is no guarantee that any one week of the year will be strictly typical. It will be recalled that the DES Individualized Data Scheme proposes to take children born on the 5th, 15th and 25th of any month, and the Scottish follow-through of eleven-year-olds took births on six days distributed evenly over the year. The concentration on one week is administratively much simpler, and precludes the complication of having to make age-allowances in any tests or similar measures that may be used. Douglas proposes as a suitable compromise the taking of a Spring week sample and an Autumn week sample in the same year, and thereby doubling the sample.

This does not entirely solve the other problem, that posed by the fact that a national sample is inevitably spread thinly over the country. In turn, this makes for a multiplicity of local agents gathering information, for difficulty in making any but the broadest regional comparisons and, if any special

---

[1] This point has been made by J. W. B. Douglas in a paper prepared for the Home Office Research Advisory Committee (Mimeographed: HORAC 66/3, Home Office, 1966).
A recurrent theme in the NICHD Symposium was the reciprocal relationship between prevention and prediction, and the contribution that longitudinal research through its unique ability to predict individual change and development can make to refining clinical skills. 'We can make life so much more effective by projecting for an individual at any age the outlook and prognosis not only with reference to disease but to behaviour and to his whole life.' op. cit. p. 13.

examinations conducted by the research team are required, for higher travel costs and time lost in travelling. It is also true that even in a sample of 17,000 some at least of the special groups we should like to study intensively are present in numbers too small for our purpose.

These arguments have force. Experience has, however, shown that health, welfare and educational staff can gather reasonably accurate and objective information if they are well briefed, if the instruments used are properly constructed and validated, and if the data sought consist so far as possible of observable facts. If – as seems likely – such staff participate increasingly in social research (and if some understanding of research methods is given them in their training) we may expect considerably greater skill and reliability over the next years.

One cannot, of course, expect from such staff the ability to conduct kinds of detailed interviews and specialized examinations of individual children outside their professional competence. Thus the second disadvantage remains. However, the additional time and cost involved in travel by specialized staff out from the centre to the regions can be exaggerated. Use can be made of local specialist facilities, and in any case the main cost in time and money is that of the journey from base: the regional journeys will be the same for a local institution as for a visitor.

Certain conditions – for example, cerebral palsy – have an incidence so low that even in 17,000 births the numbers are too small to provide an adequate sample. For such, the one-week national study does not provide a suitable sampling frame. For many other conditions – and those among the most practically interesting – it does. Children taken into care (3 per cent), adoptions (2 per cent), and premature and post-mature births (5 per cent and 10 per cent respectively) occur in sufficient numbers to warrant their use in intensive individual longitudinal studies which can only gain by comparisons with data from the normal group. Similarly, categories like mental subnormality, severe reading retardation, markedly superior ability, or maladjustment, which are definable by a combination of statistical and operational criteria, also provide sub-samples of adequate size. Moreover, since many of these conditions overlap, the actual numbers to be studied intensively are less than the crude sum of separate samples. Incidentally, the cost per child of a field team, whether from a national centre or from a local institution, will be proportionately less the greater the numbers of subjects studied.

This is not to say that regional groups do not have their value and advantages. They reduce the number of persons gathering data and make careful briefing easier; they lend themselves to a more thorough examination of regional peculiarities, and, for the same sample size, it becomes possible to get more readily a spread over the whole year – or to have two or more age-groups. For certain of the rarer conditions, the groups appearing in the sample can be supplemented by other cases to be found in the local population as a whole, and studied by comparable methods. Hammond[1] has argued – and we believe correctly – that it should be possible to arrange for local facilities such as clinics, hospitals, university departments, and the like, to be brought into a close co-operative relationship, thus increasing the facilities available, with no more than a marginal increase in costs.

The principal disadvantages of local or regional groups are that they are not nationally representative, and are highly vulnerable to losses by migration.[2]

---

[1] See paper previously cited. Hammond proposes, as ideal, the combination of national and regional studies. This suggestion is taken up in the section concerned with proposals, see Appendix VII.

[2] The PIC (1946) study found that the families of 15 per cent of children had moved across administrative boundaries in the first four years, and 4 per cent had moved across regional ones.

A POSSIBLE MODEL

From the conclusions stated at the beginning of this section, and from the succeeding discussion, a pattern of what one might hope to achieve, and of the kind of practical design most likely to achieve it, seems to us to emerge.

Before attempting to outline a model, however, we should state unequivocally that the study of samples of children or adults over time is a method suitable for certain important purposes, and we believe indispensable for some: it does not provide a portmanteau solution to all problems in the social sciences. Indeed any problem area is likely to require a considerable variety of methods for its solution, some of them based on the intensive longitudinal study of a few individuals, some depending upon the follow-through study of large samples of an age-group; and the widespread use of various kinds and sizes of longitudinally studied groups suggests that this is so. Much, too, is being done and much more could be achieved by large and small sample surveys of a cross-sectional kind. Thought along these lines would suggest that any institutions set up for research in the social sciences should be problem- rather than method-oriented; and with this we would in general agree, though as we argue below, there seems to us a very strong case in favour of an organization to sustain and foster a specific pattern of longitudinal studies of representative samples based upon wide co-operation.

Similarly, the existence of a considerable number of longitudinal studies set up for special purposes within the medical and social science disciplines suggests that there should be no sort of monopoly; though there is considerable evidence of the need for some kind of central organization to provide for cross-fertilization, the systematic exploration of scientific and administrative techniques, the stimulation of data-linkage, and such linkage as may prove possible among ongoing and, particularly, projected studies, and finally for storing longitudinal and survey information in such a way as to provide a resource for later exploitation. Such an organization would become essential if the present national longitudinal studies are to prove the starting point for a series of related cross-sectional, overlapping age-group, and long-range studies.

The studies of the PIC (1946) and NCDS (1958) birth groups cut across the social, biological, and medical sciences. This is important. Although the main focus of interest may shift in a longitudinal study from medical and biological factors to educational and social ones, studies of human behaviour and growth suffer if they are undertaken exclusively from the standpoint of a single discipline or group of cognate disciplines. Whatever decisions are taken as to the finance and affiliation of future national studies, their interdisciplinary nature should be sustained. In view of the co-operation given by the staff of the various public services in the pre-school and school periods and, in the case of the PIC (1946) study, into the early years of working life, it seems relatively easy and practical to maintain this. There are, however, certain financial and administrative problems which would have to be resolved: the PIC (1946) study began with assistance from private trusts and is continuing under the aegis of the Medical Research Council; the NCDS (1958) Cohort has been financed in the main by funds from individual Government departments, and now has a grant from the Social Science Research Council, although support is forthcoming from private foundations for more detailed analyses of some of the present data and for individual case studies.

For any organization of the kind suggested, it will be necessary to find a formula which not only permits the maintenance of the main programme or substantial parts of it over a lengthy period of time, but which does not preclude the financing of particular aspects from private and central government resources. In work of the kind implied in long-range studies, what cannot be accepted without severe inefficiency is *ad hoc* finance with no guarantee of continuity.

RECOMMENDATIONS

A suitable organization could take either of two forms – that of an independent or university-based institute, or that of an active committee set up to plan and organize through a variety of institutions the prosecution of the various tasks set out below. Either form would need substantial and long-term support from the Social Science Research Council, and would be a considerable innovation.

The tasks of such a committee or institute might be as follows:

1. It should explore the feasibility of setting up data-linkage schemes, and particularly of some form of individualized data-collection, making use of modified forms of existing records. This is obviously a major task, the organization of which, even in a simple form, will take some years and necessitate preliminary and continuous studies of the formidable problem of what data to collect and store, and in what detail.

2. It should explore and if possible exploit the possibilities of linking the data of any longitudinal projects with such cross-sectional statistics-gathering as the Census, Births and Deaths Registration, the Social Survey Family Expenditure Surveys, the records kept by the Home Office and the Department of Education and Science. This will involve some delicate negotiations at the highest level concerning the release of confidential information.

3. It should act as or provide a clearing-house for information on the sampling and design of longitudinal studies and on research on the many biometric, psychometric,

sociometric and statistical problems involved. It should undertake or stimulate studies to validate data-collection instruments and techniques of all kinds for use by volunteer and not specially trained workers.

4. It should arrange for the storage of longitudinal data, making them available to bona fide research workers.

5. It should attempt to organize co-operation between those concerned with longitudinal studies of all kinds, endeavouring to bring about at least minimum comparability.

6. It should either itself, or through existing agencies, conduct major studies of representative population samples, and aim over the years to develop a pattern covering the more important periods of the life-span of human beings. These studies should be in the fullest sense interdisciplinary. Their principal aim being to chart the effects of broad environmental differences and social change on individuals as members of groups, and thereby provide reference data for other studies, such projects should in the main be based on relatively few (and carefully chosen) sets of data.

No gloss is perhaps needed on items 1 to 4. Items 5 and 6 require elaboration.

It is suggested that any future applications for funds for studies of a longitudinal kind coming before the Social Science Research Council should be carefully considered in the light of possible linkage with work in progress, and that the committee or the institute should be able to recommend support for studies in progress which might be brought into relation with this programme, without entailing, it need scarcely be said, close organization within it.

The two major national studies which exist – PIC (1946) and NCDS (1958) – are reasonably comparable, and could be made more so. They are separated by twelve years. This suggests that a third perinatal survey should be mounted in 1970.[1] It would be highly desirable if the PIC (1946) study could come into scientific association with the proposed Committee or Institute and provide the first long-range probes into adulthood. The situation of the 1958 group is different, in that it seems likely to be dependent for its further support on SSRC funds. It might well, therefore, become the first central activity of the committee or institute.

RESEARCH PLANNING

Just as the pay-off of a well-planned longitudinal study increases with the lapse of time, so the value of each study increases if it is associated with others beginning at intervals of time. A pattern of overlapping age-groups providing comparisons over time to indicate broad change in the social and cultural environment, longitudinal data to detect individual patterns of growth, and cross-sectional surveys, seems therefore to be the best.[2]

---

[1] At time of going to press preparations had been completed for mounting the third perinatal study in 1970.

[2] See Appendix V. In a further personal communication, Peaker says – 'All individuals pass through the diagram of cohorts, stages and epochs by moving diagonally upwards to the right, but they have different points of entry across the vertical boundary to the left or the horizontal boundary at the foot. Any individual may be followed across a single column, which also entails following him across a single row. Or he may be followed across several columns, and rows, with measurements either at each boundary, or at every other boundary, or at the first and last boundary, and so on. Each measurement, or derived combinatorial statistic, may be regarded as an ordinate above the diagram, and the general object of the inquiry is to get at the shape of the surface defined by these points when due allowance is made for errors of measurement by more or less plausible methods of smoothing. This surface can be regarded as rolling on to the diagram from the left hand vertical in the same way that tomorrow will roll on to the surface of the earth from the international dateline. As the epoch advances it gradually covers

66

The problem of a design which is financially economical remains. This turns in part upon whether the group is to be a nationally representative one or whether it is to be regional or local. To us, the best formula seems to be a combination of regional and national groups. A system of what Douglas has called 'national bench marks' is necessary if we are to interpret the more intensive information which we can obtain by local and regional studies. The regional and, even more, the local study has the advantage of greater homogeneity in data collection, the possibility of utilizing locally available specialized resources for more thorough examinations, and of augmenting samples of the comparatively rare categories (of handicap, for example). The national group can be used for monitoring the effects of legislative or social change (such, for example, as a radical change in the kind and distribution of social services, or the effects of economic recession), and for the standardization of instruments; the regional or local group for action studies. One should, too, note the limitations. For many kinds of problem – for example, a study of the effects of comprehensive education – sampling by institutions and then by individuals would be a more economical and certainly a more effective way of obtaining information. The design suggested for the institute is adapted for certain purposes only, and is neither comprehensive nor exclusive – one of its principal functions

---

more and more of the diagram. Initially we can only measure it across the first vertical column, but as time goes on we have more choice, and either cover succeeding verticals or restrict ourselves to following a single diagonal band. The latter may be the more economical when there are very strong grounds for believing that one diagonal band (cohort) is very like those that came before and will come after. Otherwise it is better to spread the sampling over the whole diagram as it is gradually revealed. In both cases we are following individuals, but in the second case we are not confining our attention to those individuals born in a particular short interval of time.'

would be in fact to serve as a kind of linking system, useful in itself, but valuable also because it is related to other studies.

Hammond[1] has proposed an attractive model of combined regional and national studies. He suggests that all the births recorded on one day (approximately 2,500) should be used as the national framework for England, Wales and Scotland. In addition to this, a ten-day sample should be taken of all children born either in large centres such as the London Boroughs, Aberdeen, Manchester, and Birmingham, or in the major conurbations recognized by the Registrar General (Tyneside, W. Yorkshire, S.E. Lancashire, Merseyside, W. Midlands, Greater London, and Glasgow). He calculates that this procedure would add 9,000 children to the sample, and of course considerably increase the number in any special group for detailed study.

Such a pattern would require devolution of organization. The structure could be that of a central organization in London charged with the conduct of the national study, with the Greater London regional study on its doorstep, and with the clearing-house and other functions suggested in 1-4 above; and five or six regional offices concerned with the regional studies. An attractive alternative would be to rely for the regional studies on existing institutions, supported in their work by a direct financial grant. The likelihood is that the pattern would be mixed: some of the centres being based on universities, others set up *ad hoc*.

A certain complication is introduced if, as we believe, it is necessary to work with groups overlapping in time. The pattern of overlap would have to be applied to the main national groups and to some at least of the regional ones if, in addition to knowledge about the development of children and young people, we wished to gather, within the next decade, some information on young adulthood, adults in

---

[1] HORAC 66/6, 1966, op. cit.,

middle life, and the problems of retirement and ageing. It is difficult to determine priorities here – and considerations of cost dictate that all cannot be done at once – but we would venture to suggest that the period of pubescence might, next to childhood, be among the more urgent problems.

4. Concluding Summary

We started out on our task with some scepticism about the practicality of the kind of long-range study of human growth and behaviour begun between the wars, and with serious doubts about the cost-effectiveness of longitudinal survey studies as currently conceived. We did not fully share the pessimism of many of those whom we consulted, but we were and are still aware that unbounded optimism as to the outcome of continued study of representative national or regional samples of the same individuals over time is not now and probably will never be justified.

Many of the criticisms currently voiced apply particularly to the intensive studies started in the 1920's and 1930's. These studies tended to be based on small samples which were unrepresentative to start with, and rendered more so by attrition. A great deal of data was collected with no very clear hypothesis in mind, little concurrent analysis was done, and directions changed for no better reason than a change of fashion or of staff. There was a great lag between their inception and the emergence of anything in the way of findings more than could have been obtained by well-conceived cross-sectional enquiries.

In spite of this, these studies have contributed increasingly with the passage of time to our knowledge of patterns of individual growth, more particularly in the physical development of children and adolescents, but also in cognitive abilities, and of the degree to which early behaviour predicts later personality. We have the beginnings and some of the detail of a map of stability and change in human characteristics over at least the first two decades, and, in the case of some attributes, over forty years or more.

Great progress, too, has been made in devising objective measures of the more important psychological, educational and sociological kinds. Generally in the behavioural sciences we can be more wary of soft data and, at least for the more powerful factors, methods now exist which enable us to assess their influence.

Apart from longitudinal studies themselves, the great variety of follow-through and survey studies which have been carried out, though by no means providing us with a comprehensive and agreed body of theoretical conclusions, nevertheless put us in the position where a longitudinal study can start with a reasonable array of testable hypotheses. Experience has proved that in this country it is possible to follow a large national age-sample without severe attrition over twenty years: this reduces our anxiety about sampling and the generalizability of the findings.

The studies which we have, and mainly the PIC (1946) enquiry, suggest that the reward of studies of this kind, especially in terms of the limited number of times one can return to the sample and the use of a variety of field staff to collect information, lies most of all in the study over time of the differential effects of differences in environment on groups with differing initial characteristics; and in predicting likely outcomes of forms of 'vulnerability' (medical, psychological, and social) in terms of the presence or absence of intervention (for example, special protection, action by social services, remedial education). Properly designed, they can, in addition, provide a reference sample for more intensive individual longitudinal studies which give richer information on individual growth.

A single age or other group does not in itself enable us to monitor the effects of broad social and cultural change, and the study of a considerable number of subjects from birth to old age seems likely to tire the most patient of investigators, and indeed of sponsors. Our inquiries suggest that a pattern of overlapping age-groups and of successive studies begun at appropriate time intervals – say, a decade – will provide the

F

most effective and economical compromise; and that practically this will be best achieved by lightly sampled national groups combined with more fully sampled and studied regional ones.

We have been struck by the recent tendency of government statisticians to think increasingly of flow statistics, by the possibilities of data-linkage, both with official data-gathering and with records kept by at least a sample of classes of institutions, and by the opportunity offered for future exploitation of well-archived data. If the possibilities held out by these can be actively explored and a minimum standardization and co-ordination achieved, we believe that the costs of a pattern of overlapping national and regional studies such as we propose could be considerably lightened, and its effectiveness greatly increased.

Since the main work of drafting this report was concluded, a suggestion has arisen of a rather different kind to anything suggested. Briefly, it is concerned with the attempt to follow through a population sample in the decade separating two Censuses, and to attempt to account by longitudinal methods for some of the changes which occur.

The idea is an attractive one, and appears to offer a considerable economy in both time and finance. The initial and final surveys would be conducted and financed by the GRO. The intermediate ten year follow-through would be based on a relatively small population sample.

There are however, some obvious difficulties. The secrecy of the Census data is guaranteed by law, and this might provide a formidable obstacle to its use in identifying individual sub-samples and in keeping the follow-through data linked with the initial and final surveys. If this proved impossible to overcome, it would then be necessary to include an initial and final census-type survey in the study of the chosen sample – and much of the economy of resources would be lost.

The second difficulty concerns the nature of the sampling unit. The Census is based on households: only some of these will be families; and only some families will have – for example – children of school age. If one considers such simple but essential variables as age, economic status, sex, family size, age and sex of children, it becomes immediately apparent that even a sample of 5,000 households would provide only very small numbers in some of the most interesting cells. Thus either the sample decided upon would have to be large, or the kind of hypotheses studied very restricted. Such a sample would in fact be ill adapted to the longitudinal study of individuals, and best adapted to that of specifiable groups. To the writers it does not seem to constitute an alternative to the follow-through of samples of individuals, but a design for a different type of study.[1]

We are led therefore to suggest that there should be a strongly supported central activity, either in the form of a permanent co-ordinating committee responsible for the development of a programme, or in the form of an Institute for the Study of Human Development and Social Change. The terms of reference of such a body include the exploration of the possibilities of data-linkage, the attempt to achieve co-ordination and collaboration with longitudinal studies in being or planned, and the development of clearing-house activities concerned with data-storage, methodology and techniques. A research programme based on lightly sampled national age-groups with restricted data, combined with regional groups and some thorough individual longitudinal studies of special groups, seems an essential activity. Any such committee or institute should be fully interdisciplinary and manifestly independent.

We should like to say, in conclusion, that in the course of our inquiries we have become convinced of the feasibility of

---

[1] See Appendix IA.

such an enterprise and of the immense possibilities which it offers for the development of our knowledge of the working of our society as it affects individuals and groups of individuals. In addition, we believe there will be returns which are at present not fully foreseeable in the stimulus it will give to other studies in the behavioural sciences; in the building-up, within the social, medical and educational services, of a capital of knowledge and experience in accurate data-gathering; and in the spread of attitudes among field-workers favourable to an understanding of the value of research to their tasks.

APPENDIX I

MEETING ON COHORT STUDIES

*held at National Foundation for Educational Research,
79, Wimpole Street, London, W1, 20th February 1967*

PARTICIPANTS

Mr M. R. Alderson, M.R.C. Social Medicine Research Unit

Dr J. A. Ambrose, Paediatrics Department, St Mary's Hospital
Medical School

Mr A. Brimer, Institute of Education, Bristol University

Mr J. M. Brynner, The Social Survey, Central Office of Information

Professor N. R. Butler, Department of Child Health, Bristol
University

Mr Ronald Davie, National Bureau for Co-operation in Child
Care

Dr J. W. B. Douglas, Director, M.R.C. Unit, London School of
Economics

Dr C. M. Drillien, Department of Child Life and Health,
Edinburgh University

Dr Victor Dubowitz, Department of Child Health, Sheffield
University

Mr E. Ll. Evans, Department of Education and Science

Dr C. B. Hindley, Director, The Centre for the Study of Human
Development, London University

Mrs R. C. Hollins, Ministry of Health

Mr B. Howlett, Research and Intelligence Unit, Greater London
Council

Mr M. G. W. Jewkes, General Register Office

Dr M. L. Kellmer–Pringle, National Bureau for Co-operation in
Child Care

Dr J. S. Korn, The New York Longitudinal Study of Child
Development

Miss G. F. Cox, Wessex Regional Hospital Board

Dr E. R. Leach, Provost, King's College, Cambridge

75

Dr W. Hammond, Home Office
Dr R. Mackeith, Guy's Hospital
Mr J. F. McClellan, Scottish Education Department
Mr J. Madge, Political and Economic Planning
Dr F. M. Martin, Department of Social Medicine, Edinburgh University.
Dr N. P. Masse, Centre International de l'Enfance, Paris
Mr J. Maxwell, Moray House College of Education
Mr Jeremy Mitchell, Social Science Research Council
Mr T. Moore, Child Guidance Training Centre
Mr D. Newman, Ministry of Social Security
Mr M. Oakes, M.R.C. Population Genetics Research Unit, Oxford
Mr G. F. Peaker
Mr P. Redfern, Department of Education and Science
Mr R. F. A. Hopes, Ministry of Housing and Local Government
Dr J. K. Wing, M.R.C. Social Psychiatry Research Unit, the Maudsley Hospital
Mr S. Yasin, Social Science Research Council
Mr W. Yule, Institute of Education, London University

NFER STAFF
Dr W. D. Wall; Mr D. A. Pidgeon; Mr A. N. James; Mr H. L. Williams

The following research workers who were unable to attend gave advice by letter or personal interview: Dr Heinz Berendes; Dr Bernard Benjamin; Professor B. S. Bloom; Sir Cyril Burt; Mr M. J. R. Healey; Professor G. Knox; Mr T. Lodge; Dr David Morley; Professor J. M. Tanner; Dr D. A. Walker.

SUMMARY OF THE DISCUSSIONS
Purpose of meeting
The Chairman (Dr W. D. Wall) drew attention to the document entitled 'Terms of Reference' which summarized the letter of 23 December 1966, from the SSRC to the NFER. He explained that the object of the symposium was to obtain a reasonably objective consensus of views held in this country for incorporation in a draft report that would be circulated among participants by

the middle of March. This procedure, it was hoped, would allow time for revision in the light of comments received and would meet the deadline for the report to the SSRC by the end of that month. The range of disciplines and fields of interest represented by the participants was an indication in itself that the concern of the SSRC in commissioning the report from the NFER encompassed other fields besides education even in a broader sense that included 'child development'. Experts from at least a dozen disciplines were present – anthropology, biostatistics, child development, clinical psychology, criminology, education, gerontology, paediatrics, psychiatry, sociology, social psychology and statistics.

A number of persons invited who were unable to attend had given their preliminary views in letters from which extracts had been circulated among the participants.

Selected titles deriving from a rapid search of the literature in the NFER library, and from suggestions made by a number of participants and consultants elsewhere, had been hastily classified to form the Bibliography which had been circulated before the meeting. He welcomed comments at the convenience of participants, on the day of the meeting or later, on errors and omissions together with additions from appropriate fields that were neglected or possibly even excluded in the selection of titles so far compiled.

Correspondence had already been initiated for obtaining situation reports of major completed and current longitudinal studies in the U.S.A. and elsewhere. In view of the shortage of time available for making an independent search and review of the published literature, it was hoped that something in the nature of a synopsis could be obtained from most Centres, giving the present situation, future plans, and the principal findings of completed research, with particular reference to findings considered unlikely to have emerged so decisively or successfully had recourse been made to approaches other than the longitudinal.

The purposes served by longitudinal studies
Dr Wall invited a definition of a longitudinal study. Mr Davie volunteered that its purpose was to measure stability and change: a criterion for the fitness of the choice of this approach would be a

problem involving prediction over time either forwards or backwards; the retrospective study of a known group of delinquents provided an example of the latter. Dr Ambrose considered that a distinction should be made between predicting the extent of stability or of change, and estimating the consequences of certain kinds of environmental influence.

On the predictive aspects of longitudinal studies, Dr Douglas cited as examples the studies on continuity in behaviour during early childhood by Birch and his colleagues at New York University, and work in the U.S.A. which aimed at measuring the dimensions of personality over time. He made the reservation that prediction may hold for a particular cohort but that changes in the family circumstances of cohort members introduced complications. In addition, the limitations of retrospective studies should be realized: their data must be 'hard' and measurable, and their samples adequate.

A number of participants pointed to the advantage of longitudinal studies in stimulating hypotheses and in giving the opportunity for including new variables: approaches other than longitudinal can include only variables known at the time of the study. They considered there was no alternative to the longitudinal approach if an issue involved change in the environment.

Mr Peaker used an enlarged diagram of a chequer board to illustrate the changes in design that can be effected and the different strategies adopted during the course of a longitudinal study. (His contribution is expanded in his paper at Appendix V.) Dr Hammond emphasized the advantages in economy provided by Mr Peaker's recommendation of the use of simultaneous cohorts in a study.

Dr Hindley reminded participants that the discussion had so far made no mention of *laboratory studies on animals over time* and their relevance, for that matter, to issues of prenatal and dietary influences on the behaviour of humans. The testing of hypotheses was mandatory for cohort studies and, as a consequence, it was worth while collecting more data than could be handled at the time, despite objections that had been levelled on this score against the early longitudinal studies in the U.S.A.

Dr Masse added that large numbers permitted a combination of cross-sectional and longitudinal approaches: the hypotheses suggested by the latter could be tested cross-sectionally.

Data-collection and measuring change
Dr Kellmer-Pringle made the point that there must be plenty of data to retrospect. An additional recommendation for Mr Peaker's suggestions on *successive cohorts* would be their value in detecting the changes in individuals with changes in circumstances: there must be evidence from other cohorts for monitoring change; she gave patterns of delinquency as an example. The difficulty that participants had found in securing suitable measures for registering changes with age was largely one of ignorance on our part: continued research into the problem would produce better measures. Dr Drillien affirmed the general principle of avoiding undue restriction in collecting original data, but pointed to the dangers of 'reading in' significances in retrospective data: the discovery in recent years of the significance of low gestation periods had sometimes led to looking for this in data where this question had not been properly if at all asked. To ensure accuracy in data it might often be preferable to start the inquiry afresh with a different group.

Data-collection and the duration of a longitudinal study
The volume of data and the cost of their collection to some extent depended on frequency of observations, which in turn appeared to depend on the age and other characteristics of the members of a cohort as well as the nature of the investigation. Was there an optimum length for a longitudinal study? Longitudinal studies, said Dr Korn, need not necessarily be long-term: every learning study was longitudinal in character. They need not be *expensive*: a plurality of cross-sectional studies of equal value might cost even more in terms of time, money and personnel. Dr Douglas felt that the expense of many of the early studies could partly be attributed to the cost of accumulating masses of data that were too unwieldy for analysis and exploitation. His own longitudinal studies had been cheap because financial grants had been supplemented by substantial assistance in kind from a

variety of organizations, and the medical examinations and basic interviewing had been provided free of charge.

Dr Mackeith wondered to what extent the advent of the computer served to answer the problem of digesting accumulations of data. Dr Korn reminded the meeting that changes of staff had often been responsible since every few years at some Centres the same sample had provided longitudinal studies 'de novo'. The same staff, however, had been retained (with additions) at New York for the ten years of the Study of Behavioral Development, and the original formulation of objectives subsisted.

Mr Maxwell gave the Scottish Mental Survey as an example of an experiment that can go on too long: so much data had accumulated that it was impossible to classify them. A series of short studies could give more precise answers to questions.

Mr Moore thought that the 'trawl net' objection need apply only to the early studies, some of which had been initiated forty years ago. Research today was more sophisticated thanks to the pioneers in this field and to advances in data processing. Much of the waste in later studies was the result of not acquiring sufficient information before embarking on a study. To Dr Mackeith's question as to where this information could be found, Dr Wall replied that the review of international literature required by the SSRC was a beginning and that it was the intention of the report to make proposals that would go a deal further in this direction.

Dr Wall felt this phase of the discussion might be summarized by the proposition that questions of the impact of social change called for longitudinal answers, and when these answers were not 'extrapolatable' a series of cross-sectional studies was required. The time-span covered by a study and the length of time anticipated for its completion were determined by its purpose. Cohorts overlapping in time might be the answer to some problems, and delicate points of decision were involved when mounting a study. There appeared to be at least two kinds of longitudinal study: the first, to provide background information for general use, e.g. for intensive clinical studies; the second, to acquire data specific to the purpose of the study.

Attrition

Attrition rate was usually high in studies in the U.S.A., often rising to between 30 and 40 per cent. In England, said Dr Kellmer-Pringle, the rate was relatively small: the NCDS (1928) inquiry had retained over 90 per cent of its subjects over seven years. Throughout the course of her studies on adoption she had been amazed at the ease with which the Courts and such officials as Children's Officers, given proper safeguards, had provided follow-up information.

Mr Maxwell gave examples of his difficulties in getting a body of current information in the follow-up of his samples from the 1932 Survey. He expected to be successful in six cases out of ten, but the same items of information were not procurable for the same persons. The problem was particularly acute in the event of a subject's marrying.

Mr Moore felt attrition was a real problem with no answer. A serious facet of the problem was to determine whether loss was random in its occurrence. Dr Hindley thought it fortunate that often a simple comparison of leavers with stayers was an adequate indication of direction of change in the sample. In the case of intensive inquiries preceding or arising out of large-sample studies, the larger study could give an idea of representativeness. Mr Peaker gave analogies from techniques employed in public finance: the comparison of 'retrievables' with 'irretrievables'.

Dr Masse noted that attrition was an especially difficult problem after school-leaving age and a factor for careful anticipation at the planning stage of an investigation.

Data linkage

Dr Kellmer-Pringle indicated the possibility of expanding Census data into cohort studies, and Dr Douglas of the provision of feed-back information from agencies maintaining official records to control observations from cohort studies, as in the case of the question 'Do children in heavily polluted areas become bronchitic?' Hospitals, also, could supply an automatic feed-back of information. He indicated the advantages of the NHS system of numbering. A prime difficulty, however, was that records are not kept in comparable form. Here Dr Kellmer-Pringle thought cohort studies could help by giving an incentive for better and more comparable record keeping.

Mr Maxwell indicated the value for research of his proposal for a Population Register that would contain more detail than is currently recorded in entries for births, deaths and marriages. Mr Jewkes emphasized the goodwill on the part of the GRO to modify its present recording system. He instanced the record linkage effected for Dr Acheson's Oxford Study as an example of what could be done on an ad hoc basis to meet the needs of investigators. It was essential, however, that the GRO should be consulted at the outset and knew the quality of a project's data recording and the sort of data required from GRO. A prime difficulty lay in conditions of 'confidentiality' – especially in the case of the Census which had statutory sanctions – and these seemed better satisfied by researches in the medical field, possibly because of traditional standards of professional etiquette. A major obstacle, in Dr Hammond's view, was that 'Statistics' in each Ministry so frequently 'lost' the details of information that were relevant to linkages. The representative of another Ministry felt certain that government departments would welcome a recommendation from the SSRC on this problem.

Mr Redfern spoke of the DES scheme that was on the launching-pad for following the careers of students in higher education. Whereas it was limited to acquiring objective facts and would not venture into the difficult territory of motivation, there remained nevertheless the inherent snags of deciding on standard practices for identifying individuals, and of establishing a system for collating at some central point the records obtained from schools, colleges of education, universities and other institutions of higher education. An important by-product, felt Mr Peaker, would be that the scheme would make ratio-estimating possible from smaller samples in research investigations and greater economy in drawing sub-samples.

To a lead from Dr Wall that the discussion so far on data-linkage had implications for national samples only, Dr Hindley observed that two issues should be subsumed: first, the linkage of official and cohort study data, and second, collaboration in data-collection. In the latter connection, he pointed to the success of the Centre International de l'Enfance in resolving the problem of agreement on similar criteria for different investigators. Common methods of collecting data, stressed Dr Wall, could solve problems not soluble by a single study, but pointed to two major difficulties in initiating and conducting the sort of cross-cultural investigations that Dr Hindley had given as an illustration: finance and truly comparable sampling of the ethnic groups investigated; common criteria for such factors as 'social class', were also particularly difficult to establish. Despite the very many difficulties in cross-cultural research, Mr Moore felt that it was defensible to look for similarities in correlational patterns in the data within each sample as indications of what transcended cultural boundaries.

'Cohorts' – their size and nature

Could 'cohort' be defined as a group exposed to the same environment? Was it a sample? Mr Peaker stressed that it was a type of population and should not be confused with 'sampling unit'; by definition it was not a sample but a sub-population: the question of sampling arose at another stage, e.g. '10 per cent of the cohort'. Mr Maxwell agreed that a cohort was a population distinct from other populations, but asked to what extent and in what way the distinction involved the issue of generalizability, and what evidence was required to support the application of findings from a cohort study to other populations. Mr Peaker replied that there was always the internal evidence of the sample itself, its stratification providing one item. But what, he asked, did we rely on for evidence in research? We never started from complete ignorance: what the process of investigation provided were degrees in conviction of the reliability of the views we held at its commencement.

Cohorts worked, Professor Butler interjected. For the N C D S (1958) inquiry he had considered spacing throughout the year children born on selected individual days: administratively this would have been chaotic since it entailed going into action several times throughout the year. (Mr Maxwell considered this procedure a means of keeping staff continuously occupied, if it had no other merit.)

Mr Peaker stressed the advantages of taking children in a particular school, the school being a natural unit: if it turned out to be untypical then the experiment, of a method of teaching, for example, could be repeated in a school 'far away'. In planning a cohort study careful thought should always be given to considerations of replicating it. As for Dr Korn's objection that one could generalize from a negative result, care must be taken in choosing the first school for the experiment. Did those who used the method believe in it or not?

Institutions as cohorts
Might institutions provide cohorts? Mr Redfern replied that industrial firms or organizations had been studied, but it should be remembered that reorganization took place in them. Dr Ambrose instanced developmental studies in work by industrial consultants; a number of reports had appeared in *Human Relations*, for example. Psychology had become sceptical about treating the individual as the unit in behavioural research.

'Industrial firm', in Dr Leach's view, was too vague a term. He referred to the study by anthropologists of the development of cycles. The family was an organism that was self-destructive; it had a life-cycle that did not correspond to the life-cycle of its individual members, but its property of self-termination might make it suitable for longitudinal study. The paramount difficulty, said Mr Redfern, was to find means of identifying a family in records. The GRO would be prepared to maintain records by family groups, but the obstacle was to define 'family' practically. The Scandinavians, rejoined Mr Maxwell, managed to keep records of families.

Might people in a given industry over a period, asked Dr Wall, or with common environmental characteristics, provide cohorts?

National and regional cohorts
How generalizable were findings from the one to the other under the impact of cultural or organizational change? The reorganization of schools under the comprehensive system was

84

cited as an illustration of the latter. Cultures were not uniform over nations, said Dr Leach: the individual was a culturally conditioned creature and, as a consequence, there must be a sampling of 'nests of influence'; in his view the regional matrix had some merit.

Mr Peaker considered region less important than neighbourhood; regions differed with differing proportions of neighbourhood.

Dr Douglas drew attention to the factor of migration, and to continuity and stability in mobility patterns. Regional sampling tended to diminish loss if regions were drawn correctly. Most characteristics were, however, multifactorial, especially if the sample were an occupational group. The choice between national and regional cohorts depended to some extent on whether the project had reliability of data or reduction of cost in mind.

Long-term and short-term longitudinal studies
For examining change over short periods, it was suggested, the requirement was short-term studies, and over long periods, in the case of developmental processes, for example, long-term studies. Dr Leach commented that influences from the outside were constantly changing, and therefore a logical limit, say six to ten years, should be set; things would change even more in thirty years time, so that experiments should be set up with limited numbers of variables.

Dr Hindley replied that it was impossible to build in controls for every aspect of change, and that despite the rapidity of social and cultural change there was considerable evidence at the empirical level for a measure of consistency in certain aspects of the behavioural development of individuals. He cited the work of Kagan and Moss at the Fels Institute, and of Bronson in the Berkeley Guidance Study.

Mr Redfern observed that notwithstanding trends we still wanted to link what happened at 11+, for example, with later events.

Dr Ambrose considered that research was not only concerned with describing but also with understanding the reason for change;

the understanding of processes might require intensive short-term studies – for example, the first year of life with its rapid changes and the complex nature of their underlying variables.

Dr Masse added that rapid changes and wide variation were characteristics also of puberty and required short-term study. She failed to see how a design of overlapping cohorts could answer questions about the association of puberal events with those of the first year of life.

Mr Peaker felt that Dr Leach's recommendation was a counsel of despair. We should study what we could manage, since multiplicity of variables was not so much a complication as the essence of the study of human behaviour. The difficulty could be met by a combination of long- and short-term studies.

Mr Maxwell thought a distinction could be made between experimental and observational studies: the latter should be as long as necessary. The question of time, in his view, obscured the nature of the study. The length of the study, said Mr Moore, should be long enough to measure the change it is desired to measure. He instanced the work of Ambrose on the smiling response in infants; three months had shown marked developmental changes. Dr Hindley added that a longitudinal study was concerned with developmental change over time; there were sensible changes in a baby over two weeks of life, so that a longitudinal study might involve seeing children only twice.

The term 'change', objected Mr Madge, would seem to exclude nothing: might not we limit ourselves to measuring the effects of subjection to single incidents?

Dr Korn felt this was too limited a connotation – a developmental study examined the course of every aspect including the biological: as for duration, a few hours were sufficient for certain developmental changes.

Dr Wall pointed to the refuge provided by the ambiguity of the English tongue.

Intensive studies and large-scale studies providing background data
Dr Hindley was of the opinion that longitudinal studies on smallish samples and large-scale studies were complementary. Only limited control of the observations of social workers, for

86

example, were possible in large-scale studies. When large numbers of subjects and investigators were involved psychological techniques were restricted and only representative information of a crude kind viable. In Dr Kellmer-Pringle's view, however, the answer to this problem was to build the intensive study into the large sample, combine the cohort/longitudinal approach with that of the intensive case-study, and use groups of normals in the large study for controls. The large-scale study, said Dr Wall, must use its scarce resources and inadequate instrumentation to get what it could. The information gathered by Douglas, for example, on the degree of apparent interest shown by parents in the education of their children at its lowest estimate showed that there was 'something there'. More subtle and refined methods were needed to find explanations. Inferences about *causality* were risky in large-scale researches: you got closer to 'intangibles' the closer you got to your subjects. You might at least succeed in identifying groups which required more attention, such as the various types of handicaps. How far would it be true to say that medical research with cohorts was mainly concerned with aberrance?

Mr Oakes thought that perhaps the value of longitudinal research in medicine was to assist in the prediction of disease. He would be apprehensive, however, of the *observer error and bias* in variables like 'parental interest', and was of opinion that this had a greater likelihood when small numbers of observers were employed.

Mr James commented that as a statistician he saw one value of the intensive study to lie in its ability to give estimates of proportions in the larger or general population.

Professor Butler emphasized the value of the long-term study in picking out high risks and following them up. By this he meant children 'with probable diminution in the range of performance', not so much the officially 'handicapped'; he agreed with Dr Douglas that numbers for the latter were in any case small even in a large cohort population, and that abnormality would be picked up anyway without recourse to special investigation. The Medical High Risk Register was clearly linked with longitudinal studies.

On observer error, Dr Wall considered it might be at its maximum in personality studies but that instruments of increased sophistication would help to reduce or to give enough evidence for us to know how much to discount. Teachers, however, commented Dr Kellmer-Pringle, were good informants if given concrete questions to answer.

Dr Wall agreed with Mr Maxwell that bias and prejudice entered into teachers' judgements, but these characteristics were not confined to teachers. The conclusion of the discussion of this topic might be that one should never invest a problem in a single technique: more than one measure should be used and a small sub-sample investigated to see how valid the measures were.

Perhaps, proposed Dr Leach, a broad conclusion was that the neighbourhood/intensive study should come first and a general ideology developed in this small framework. The folklore on maternal employment furnished an excellent illustration of Dr Leach's point, commented Mr Moore: preliminary intensive studies would have helped to kill such notions in the embryo.

Dr Wall observed that sufficient information was available today to provide more than hunches, but that a number of questions would always arise which admitted no satisfactory answer except through intensive studies *within* the large sample. One could go on and on with separate clinical studies of increasing refinement, insisted Dr Kellmer-Pringle, citing the rough figure of 450 for the adoption studies that had preceded hers.

An additional argument proposed by Dr Ambrose in support of the intensive study was that not only did it assist in a decision on what instruments to use, but it made it less likely that variables for measurement would be 'missed'. It was also economically impossible, observed Mr Pidgeon, to visit the homes of all subjects in a large-scale study, so that the reliability of measures within the school could be established by a small number of home visits.

There was clearly a place, in Dr Hindley's view, for both large and small studies, but several small studies could be financed for the cost of one large study. In large-scale inquiries sophisticated techniques were not financially viable – in Tanner's, for example, which required the special examination of urine specimens, highly specialized techniques of photography, etc. Some participants appeared to be speaking as if virtue attached only to the large study, and the small was but its pale imitation.

Could we not envisage, asked Dr Wall, a number of ongoing data-collection agencies, with the long-term data providing anchors? The requirement seemed to be a strategy that would permit the three types of study to go on.

Organizational problems in longitudinal studies
  (a) Interdisciplinary
Few researches in Dr Kellmer-Pringle's experience were continuously multi-disciplinary; the weight of interest changed as the child grew up and must vary at different points in any study. Mr Maxwell considered it preferable for consultants to be called in as required.
  (b) Co-ordination and staffing
Dr Hindley asked to what extent the SSRC would adopt a policy of maintaining semi-permanent units like the MRC – an Ageing Unit, for example, or a Behavioural Development Unit. What would be its policy on career structure, and might each unit have continuing studies over a long period, with *ad hoc* studies in addition?

Mr Yasin replied that the SSRC could give no answer at the moment.

Mr Evans said that the policy of the DES was to allot research grants *(a)* as a pump-primer, and *(b)* in support of long-range work. Its policy might involve rather close control by the SSRC over projects. It would be necessary for the SSRC to persuade the Science side of the DES to embark on something over, say, twenty years.

Dr Wall though it inadvisable for any institution to have a monopoly in the research field. There seemed, however, to be a need for an array of infra-structures, for first-level documentation services, for example. A point to remember in connection with discussion of career structure and personnel was that one learned how to do longitudinal research by doing it.

Mr Madge felt an institution could provide continuity; no lethal blow would be struck if an individual moved out of an institution. The alternative might be some form of servicing centre, a repository of know-how.

Mr Moore outlined his scheme for overlapping appointments of directors should units be established.

Professor Butler gave the Child Development Study as an example of the advantages of private enterprise. What, he asked, would be the future of present ongoing studies, and how was the gap to be filled before any special institution came into being? Would present studies take up so much money that they would stop the development of a special unit? He also wondered how far it was possible to have all disciplines in a working team; there were not only the professional but also the administratively involved groups.

Dr Hindley did not envisage one body but rather a number of units on MRC lines, with different compositions. The SSRC might finance, for example, Ageing, and Delinquency, but there would be a place for different orientations within the scope of specialist units. He would hope also that the SSRC would finance studies that were not in its own administrative structure.

To a question on the policy of the MRC, Dr Mackeith answered that roughly it had two; the first, to back an individual; the second, to promote a topic on which research was needed; though often no individual could be found with the particular interest, he added.

Dr Wall observed that there was a difference between the preoccupations of a Council and those of a government department; between financing a person or investigation and finding the answer to a problem of significance to the administration.

APPENDIX IA

CONSULTATIVE MEETING ON THE REPORT ON LONGITUDINAL STUDIES
held at Slough, 23rd October 1967

At the instance of the SSRC, arrangements were made to hold at the Headquarters of the NFER at Slough, an informal meeting with a small group of consultants who had not attended the February meeting in London on cohort studies. Copies of the report had been sent some weeks beforehand to the consultants, together with sketches of suggested major projects for longitudinal study which the Council had asked us to prepare and submit for its consideration. In addition, a few days before the consultative meeting we received the following notification in a letter from Mr Yasin of the Social Science Research Council secretariat:

> Our office will now prepare a paper for Council recommending the actions which might be taken as a result of your Report. To this end, we expect as a first step to ask Council's blessing for a plan to conduct a multi-purpose longitudinal study during the decade 1971–81 which would be run in conjunction with the census. We envisage a sample of substantial size which would be surveyed at fairly frequent intervals during this period. Its main object would be to observe the dynamics involved in the statistical changes observed by the census during the decade. Obviously the longitudinal study would have potential beyond this. It would not only provide information not now available to the GRO and to population researchers, it will also identify for social scientists a large variety of different groups capable of being intensively investigated by a series of special studies. This probably means that your recommendation to establish a co-ordinating institute for longitudinal studies would be held in abeyance until the research group who would conduct this study has been established and become operational. It might then become the nucleus for an institute along the lines you had in mind in your report.

You promised to present this idea to the experts you are assembling at Slough next Monday and let us have whatever critical comments and elaborations they might have for this scheme.

PARTICIPANTS

Professor G. Jahoda, University of Strathclyde
Dr John Newson, University of Nottingham
Miss Thelma Veness, Birkbeck College, University of London
Dr A. T. Welford, St John's College, Cambridge
Dr W. D. Wall, Director, NFER (at the time)
Mr D. A. Pidgeon, Deputy Director, NFER
Mr H. L. Williams, NFER

Copies of the report had been sent some weeks before the meeting to the consultants, together with sketches of three suggested major projects for longitudinal study that had been requested by the Council and which it had been proposed to submit for its consideration.

Dr Wall outlined the history of the report, the reception it had been accorded by a number of other experts in cognate fields who had been earlier consulted, and its current expression in SSRC policy. The majority had pronounced it a readable and comprehensive review of the rationale, scope, and difficulties of longitudinal work, but a minority had expressed misgivings at the suggestion of setting up a new unit which would be solely or primarily concerned with organizing longitudinal studies of a continuing survey type, and more especially with the possibility that applications for funds for longitudinal work might be considered in the light of the potential linkage with what would seem the primary 'demographic' or 'epidemiological' function of the unit, to the prejudice of the professional freedom of the research worker in the choice and conduct of a study. Dr Wall stressed that the recommendation had arisen from the need that it had been felt existed for a focal point for people concerned with follow-through studies of particular groups of individuals, especially when a number of disciplines was concerned: few studies, on examination, could be termed genuinely interdisciplinary in their conduct as well as their conception, during their progress as well as at their inception.

Miss Veness felt that an Institute was needed if only to provide a forum, and a sense of identity, for researchers in the various disciplines engaged on follow-up studies.

Dr Welford said he concurred with the majority judgement on the report: there had been a need for a balanced report, such as he considered this to be, for clearing the ground for work in this field (a viewpoint with which the other consultants concurred). His own experience in studies of ageing confirmed the necessity for sinking a sufficiency of money into longitudinal work to keep people in it. The real shortage in research, however, was of ideas; the requirement was not so much to define areas of needed research but to produce ideas that needed testing. Nevertheless, it should be possible – indeed it was highly desirable – to set up studies for the collection of basic data that would be sufficiently raw for a variety of processing. This strategy had only become a possibility with the advent of the computer. The data should be got first and ideas would grow out of them; the proposed way of doing this would enable one to find one's way. This proposition was endorsed by Miss Veness: in her view, it implied the re-establishment of inductive thinking.

It would seem, observed Dr Wall, that the demand of the SSRC was rather for a set of hypotheses to investigate, e.g., parental influence and school progress, mental alertness and job changing; but such inquiries were to be carried out against a monitoring background. The Census provided a framework every ten years; sub-samples by family could be taken for intensive annual returns and *pari passu* tell one what to expect in the larger 10 per cent sample of the Census national population. A prime difficulty, from the experience of the Newcastle Study, would be one of tracing individuals – an experience confirmed by the Nottingham and Birkbeck researches.

Mr Pidgeon considered that two major values were inherent in longitudinal studies: (1) the check they could provide on cause and effect relations, and (2) their unique property in monitoring change.

Dr Newson observed that ecological studies by their nature could not set up hypotheses beforehand.

Dr Wall elaborated some of the difficulties of recording events in the lives of individuals that could not be 'timed', the significant 'accident' that could be missed – and the corollary that continuous contact with individuals might be impossible in large samples. Mr Pidgeon felt that data banks provided at least a partial solution for these difficulties, citing hypothetical examples from a possible home/school relationship study. Dr Wall was of the opinion that special experiments should be run to evaluate the difficulties of studying such contingencies in a large and scattered sample. Mr Pidgeon took it that the multi-purpose longitudinal study suggested by Mr Yasin in his letter would first entail drawing a sample from the Census data for a macroscopic view over a decade. In his view a very necessary and difficult pre-requisite was to decide how this sample was to be drawn. Was Hammond's proposal, endorsed by the NFER report, for studying national and regional samples to be adopted? If so, a prime consideration was to decide the size and the basis of selection of six sub-samples, and the costing of the operation in terms of duration of study and the intervals at which observations were to be taken on these samples through the medium of psychological and sociological instruments, interviews, postal questionnaires, specialist examinations, and the rest.

Dr Welford commented that cheaper and less difficult cross-sectional studies would result in reduction of precision with increase of inter-subject variance. A solution might lie in conducting inquiries in terms of long-term panels of investigatees, e.g. the ageing group in the Liverpool study.

Mr Pidgeon wondered if some system of rotating panels would not be an answer. The two-stage sampling procedure employed by the DES in some of their enquiries, e.g. into the standards of reading in schools, might be another solution. Reverting to the problem of the size of the sample to be drawn for a study, he demonstrated from an extempore calculation the consequences of taking one child per family for special studies of children in family context if the SSRC sample comprised, say, 10,000 families, a substantial size: it was probable that only about a half

94

of these families would yield a child of statutory school age, and division of the resultant sample of 5,000 children into ten age-groups only 500 children for each; division by sex reduced the number to roughly 250, while further sub-division into even three broad social groups left very small sub-samples indeed for any study of children on the minimal basis of age, sex, and social grouping.

Another factor, observed Dr Wall, in the logistics of such an operation was that the geographical scatter of a national sample imposed a multiplicity of data collectors and of consequent errors in the data collected. Dr Newson interjected that in his long-term studies within the administrative boundaries of the city of Nottingham it had been found possible to use continuously the same body of trained interviewers at a rough cost of £1 10s. per interview. The real methodological problem, continued Dr Wall, in longitudinal studies might lie not so much in following up subjects but in the kind of observation that can be made on them under the conditions imposed by the sampling design selected. This is to say that a major step forward will be taken when the data-collecting instruments can be brought to the level of reliability and validity reached, say, by tests of attainment or ability in the hands of teachers. This, again, raised the question of the importance of having recourse to an organization like the suggested Institute that could study the variety of problems involved in instrumentation.

Dr Welford made the point that in studies on the industrial aspects of ageing, factories had supplied the first-stage sampling units. He had himself been interested in crucial changes in employment in the fifth decade of life and in verifying or denying the hypothesis that the older workers tended to leave for lighter work. The second-stage sampling had, therefore, been based on employees around the age of 45 years who changed to new employments either within or outside the same organization. He felt that a major function of an Institute would be to make a close and continuous study of data-collecting methods, citing as an example the NIIP study of the design of personnel records kept in industry and commerce. Another proper and first concern of an institute would be a feasibility study of the linkage of various types of records at different points. Research workers, in his experience, were well aware of the sources of the data they required: what was needed was some form of central organization responsible for carrying out an examination in detail of these sources.

Dr Newson observed that unless a sample were sizeable the small numbers in social classes 1 and 2 made generalization impossible. The alternatives were either to ignore social class or to use stratified sampling. The geographical mobility of children and adults was an important area for longitudinal research but might well impose a variety of stratification in sampling. Dr Welford considered the discussion led to the conclusion that where stratification was necessary you should stratify by what you wanted to study: in the case of ageing, for example, you would stratify by age. Any form of sampling, in Professor Jahoda's view, would be restrictive and was dependent on what was to be investigated.

Dr Wall asked if it was possible to inventory the units of basic information for the social scientist; age and sex would be obvious requisites, to which Dr Welford added job, and not social class. Dr Newson said it was not clear whether the family was to be the unit of sampling or the household, as with the GRO Census. The sampling unit gave an immediate bias towards a particular orientation. Sampling by household (which presumably was what Mr Yasin's letter suggested) lost a number of important items of information, e.g. how many children in a family had left the household. Some of the data, Dr Welford thought, could be recovered: the head of household's previous and present marital status could be recorded, his own birth order, and the numbers of children he had had and how many were still at home, etc.

Mr Pidgeon wondered whether Douglas's national sample now aged 21 years could not provide a starting point for a SSRC study.

Dr Welford suggested that the discussion had reached a stage when it could be profitable to give some consideration to questions which could only be answered by longitudinal study. Topics which readily suggested themselves to him were:

96

1. Patterns in job-changing: how far do they reflect true ageing effects as opposed to social and technological change?
2. The stability of personality over the years in relation to social and other circumstances.
3. The effects of family changes, as when children leave home or parents change jobs.
4. Adaptation to critical events.

Dr Newson added:

5. The change in certain child-rearing practices over time, e.g. breast-feeding, the punishment of children: children aged 8 or 9 today appeared more aggressive in public and prone to risk-taking than in the past; would these features change over time, and to what extent would any change be a function of child-rearing, of secular change, of social class, of greater or less dwelling space?
6. The different expectations of students over time.

Other suggested topics were:

7. Changes in families with statutory changes in welfare provision.
8. The relation over time of children's performance in school to parental interest.
9. Delinquency patterns over time.

Professor Jahoda added it was obvious that many topics which had so frequently and naturally been studied as incidence problems were peculiarly problems for cohort analysis, citing alcoholism and coronary conditions as examples.

All these topics, observed Dr Wall, implied the maintenance of contact with the individual subject, as much as did the intensive clinical study over time, if traumatic changes were to have immediate follow-up; other observations could be taken either at fixed points in time or in terms of critical periods in the life-cycle, e.g. leaving school. Dr Welford considered that a return type of study would generally be adequate for the examination of events of normal social incidence.

The discussion, observed Mr Pidgeon, seemed to be leading to the enunciation of another proposition: only through a longitudinal study could you discover why something did *not* happen. It implied additionally, felt Dr Wall, the need for collecting polyvalent data. People, added Dr Welford, should be stopped from jettisoning data after collapsing them for coding: technical advances had made viable the preservation and storage of the original data that might be crucial for other and later researches.

Dr Wall concluded the meeting by once more inviting attention to paragraph 2 of the SSRC letter of 19 October on the Longitudinal Studies Report. Were it possible for the discussion to crystallize around the SSRC proposal to produce a sort of consensus, would the following, he asked, be a reasonable formulation? The favour with which the consultants viewed the proposal to run a multi-purpose longitudinal study in conjunction with the census was subject to a number of provisos: A wide range of data should be collected for the use of workers in the social sciences and might necessarily entail the disclosure of details such as the actual names and addresses of individuals in Census samples. A concerted attempt should be made by the SSRC at deciding precisely what data should be collected and made available centrally for consultation by people doing more intensive specialized studies. At the same time, the SSRC should engage itself in research and development work on data-collection and on instrumentation, paying due regard to the needs of a wide range of potential research in the fields to which such data and instrumentation have application. Necessary preliminaries would be a thorough examination of questions relating to sampling and to the intervals, whether annual, biennial or other, at which observations were to be taken on subjects of the SSRC study, and a close study of the sort of topics that are amenable only to longitudinal treatment.

APPENDIX II

PRINCIPAL LONGITUDINAL STUDIES
IN THE USA

MERRILL-PALMER LONGITUDINAL RESEARCH PROJECT

(We are indebted for the summary to Dr Leland H. Stott, Leader, Longitudinal Studies Program, The Merrill-Palmer Institute of Human Development and Family Life, Detroit)

First of all I should say that up to now there has been no overall report of the findings of the project. In fact there yet remains much work to be done in the way of ordering, analysing and otherwise processing the material in the files before such a report can be made. A terminal monograph of this nature has been projected, but not for the immediate future.

Certain portions of the project data have been used in studies over the years. For example, Dr Norman C. Wetzel of Western Reserve University, author of the well known Wetzel Grid, utilized many of our infant records in the development of his 'baby grid' (Wetzel, N. C. 'The baby grid', *J. Pediat.*, 1946, *29*, 439–54).

More recently studies of Wetzel's Grids and some of the assumptions underlying them have been made by members of our project staff in which project growth data were used. Smillie, D., 'An evaluation of the channel system on the baby grid', *Child Development*, 1959, *30*, 279–88; Baer, M. J., Torgoff, I. H., and Harris, Donna J., 'Differential impact of weight and height on Wetzel developmental age', *Child Development*, 1962, *33*, 737–50). These studies, of course, could not have been made with anything other than longitudinal data.

An early interim report covering the first seven years of the project was published in 1930. The purpose of this monograph was to present age 'standards' in terms of which recorded measurement data, scores on psychological tests, behaviour data, and personality ratings of a particular child could be evaluated. These standards were for the most part presented in the form of percentiles (Wilson, C. A., Sweeny, Mary E., Stutsman, Rachel, Cheshire, Leona E., and Hatt, Elise, *The Merrill-Palmer Standards of physical and mental growth*, Detroit: The Merrill-Palmer School, 1930).

A status study of childhood personality based upon data was published in 1938. The data for this study were obtained by means of a set of check-list behaviour rating scales with statistically derived scoring weights (Roberts, Katherine E., and Ball, Rachel S., 'A study of personality in young children by means of a series of rating scales', *J. genet. Psychol.*, 1938, *52*, 79–140).

In 1957, a limited longitudinal study was made of the personality variable of ascendance-submission in children. The data for this study were also obtained from the behaviour check-list scales. The interest here was the question of change or persistence of the tendency in children to dominate or to be submissive in the social-play situation of the nursery school. The first step was to select those items in the scales that described ascendant behaviour, 'bossiness', leadership, comforting behaviour or dependent submissiveness. The ratings on these particular items of two individual children over a period between ages 3 and 12 years were then tabulated in such a way as to show changes with age. Very briefly, the findings were that, although there was much change in behaviour due to the process of maturing, certain aspects of behaviour representing each child's individuality persisted throughout the period of study (Stott, L. H. and Ball, Rachel S., 'Consistency and change in ascendance-submission in the social interaction of children, *Child Development*, 1957, *28*, 259–72).

A long-term study of personality development is currently under way, designed to span approximately a thirty-year period of the lives of a group of individuals. The check-list ratings of some thirty boys and girls in the Merrill-Palmer nursery school during the early 1920's were re-analysed, and a behaviour profile depicting relative ratings on thirteen 'personality' traits was constructed for each child at age 4 years. Behaviour data and other related data have been abstracted from the records of these individuals covering the subsequent years of our contact with them. Much family information and other environmental data associated with the developmental records were also abstracted. Efforts were then made to locate, and to contact these individuals, by that time adults in their 30's. Considerable follow-up data have been collected by means of questionnaires, self-rating scales, autobiographies and intensive interviews. Most of the work of processing these data yet remains to be done. It is projected that certain of the findings can be presented statistically. Perhaps the most significant aspect of the project, however, will be a series of individual, longitudinal studies of personal development.

STUDY OF THE GIFTED CHILD: DEPARTMENT OF
  PSYCHOLOGY, STANFORD UNIVERSITY

Initiated: 1921 – still in progress.

Aim: The study of the physical, mental and personality characteristics of intellectually superior children. A continuing record has been maintained at approximately ten-year stages on physique, health, nervous tendencies, personal and social adjustment, nature of interests and activities, with detailed educational, vocational and marital histories.

The enquiry is now being followed over a second generation: Stanford-Binet tests have been given to 1,600 offspring of the gifted subjects and data collected on the developmental history in infancy and early childhood of about three-quarters of them.

Subjects: 1,528 (857 males, 671 females) selected from the State of California after a systematic search. Approximately 80 per cent of the parents had been born in the U.S.A., 10 per cent were of Jewish background, 18 per cent Oriental, 2 per cent Negro.

Parental occupation (in 1922): 31 per cent professional; 27 per cent semi-professional and higher business; 24 per cent clerical, retail business, and skilled manual; 7 per cent farming; 10 per cent minor clerical and semi-skilled.

Data: *Mental Tests*

For selection Stanford–Binet (two-thirds of subjects);
purposes: Terman–Group Test of Mental Ability

	(428) National Intelligence Tests or Army Alpha (remainder).
Follow-up:	Concept Mastery Test (to approximately 1,000 subjects or spouses in 1939–40 and in the 1950–52 follow-up).

Personality Inventories

Character, personality and interest tests to subjects. Personality, Temperament and Marital Happiness tests in second and third follow-ups to subjects and spouses. Personality ratings by parents, teachers and field-workers.

Interviews :	with subjects initially and on three later occasions; with parents (at three intervals); with teachers (at two).
Age of Subjects:	on selection for project – mean$=11$ years (9·7 years for Binet–tested subjects and 15·2 years for those selected by a group test).
IQs:	Mean Stanford–Binet 151·5 for boys; 150·4 for girls range 135–200 (with 77 subjects scoring at IQ 170 or higher). The subjects picked out at high school by a group test were as highly selected as the Binet-tested group.

A detailed description of this celebrated study is given in Volumes I, and III to V (inclusive) of the series entitled 'Genetic Studies of Genius' published by the Stanford University Press.

Vol. I   Terman, L. M., *Mental and Physical Traits of a Thousand Gifted Children* (1925).

Vol. III Burks, B. S., Jensen, D. W., Terman, L. M. and others, *The Promise of Youth*: an eight-year follow-up (1930).

Vol. IV Terman, L. M. and Oden, M. H., *The Gifted Child Grows Up : Twenty-Five Years Follow-up of a Superior Group* (1947).

Vol. V Terman, L. M. and Oden, M. H., *The Gifted Group at*

Mid-Life: Thirty-Five Years Follow-up of the Superior Child (1959).

The study began when Professor Terman was in his mid-forties and most of the children around their eleventh year. When he died at the age of 80 the children themselves had reached their mid-forties, and so close had his personal relations been with them over three decades that only 5 per cent of the subjects had been 'lost' to the Study. 'The future promises information of equal importance. . . . On actuarial grounds there is considerable likelihood that the last of Terman's Gifted Children will not have yielded his last report to the files before the year 2010!'[1]

The findings of the earlier stages are here summarized (and the flavour of Terman's admirable reporting sampled) mainly by direct quotation from the chapters drafted by him for the fifth volume which appeared after his death.

1. Despite the recognition since antiquity

> that a nation's resources of superior talent are the most precious it can have . . . a number of factors had operated until recent years to postpone research in this field. Among these are (a) the influence of long-current beliefs regarding the essential nature of genius, long regarded as qualitatively set off from the rest of mankind and not to be explained by the natural laws of human behaviour; (b) the widespread superstition that intellectual precocity is pathological, and (c) the growth of pseudo-democratic sentiments that have tended to encourage attitudes unfavourable to a just appreciation of individual differences in human endowment. . .

---

[1] The preface to the last published volume in the series by Dr Robert Sears, to whom Terman delegated the administrative responsibility for planning continuing research with the group and for which Terman 'assigned funds from his estate that will provide partial support for maintaining the files for several years', mentions that the total sum expended on the study over almost forty years was about a quarter of a million dollars; Professor Terman personally met more than one-fifth of this sum by direct gift. In addition, he and his co-authors assigned to the study all royalties from their publications relating to the study.

The combined results of the medical examinations and the physical measurements provide a striking contrast to the popular stereotype of the child prodigy depicted as a pathetic creature, over-serious and undersized, sickly, hollow-chested, stoop-shouldered, clumsy, nervously tense, and bespectacled. There are gifted children who bear some resemblance to this stereotype, but the truth is that almost every element in the picture, except the last, is less characteristic of the gifted child than of the mentally average. . . .

The interests of gifted children are kept at school tasks two or three full grades below the level of achievement they have already reached.

The interests of gifted children are many-sided and spontaneous. The members of our group learned to read easily and read many more and also better books than the average child. At the same time, they engaged in a wide range of childhood activities and acquired far more knowledge of plays and games than the average child of their years. Their preference among plays and games closely follow the normal sex trends with regard to masculinity and femininity of interest, although gifted girls tend to be more masculine in their play life than the average girls. Both sexes show a degree of interest maturity two or three years beyond their age norm.

A battery of seven character tests showed gifted children above average on every one.

Only on mechanical ingenuity did their teachers rate the gifted as low as unselected children, and this verdict is contradicted by tests of mechanical aptitude.

These facts stand out clearly in this composite portrait: (1) The deviation of gifted children from the generality is in the upward direction for nearly all traits; there is no law of compensation whereby the intellectual superiority of the gifted is offset by inferiorities along non-intellectual lines. (2) The amount of upward deviation of the gifted is not the same for all traits. (3) This unevenness of abilities is no greater for gifted than for average children, but it is different in direction; whereas the gifted are at their best in the 'thought' subjects, average children are at their best in subjects that make the least demands upon the formation and manipulation of concepts . . .

Descriptions of the gifted in terms of what is typical are useful as a basis for generalization, but emphasis on central tendencies should not blind us to the fact that gifted children, far from falling into a single pattern, represent an almost infinite variety of problems.

2. Six Years Later: The Promise of Youth (Vol. III). This composite portrait had changed only in minor respects.

3. Eighteen Years Later: The Gifted Child Grows Up (Vol. IV). Among the conclusions were the following:

That near to mid-life, such a group may be expected to show a normal or below-normal incidence of serious personality maladjustment, insanity, delinquency, alcoholism, and homosexuality.

That gifted children who have been promoted more rapidly than is customary are as a group equal or superior to gifted non-accelerates in health and general adjustment, do better school work, continue their education further, and are more successful in their later careers.

That the intellectual status of the average member of the group at the mean age of 30 years was close to the 98th or 99th percentile of the general adult population, and was far above the average level of ability of graduates from superior colleges and universities.

That in vocational achievement the gifted group rates well above the average of college graduates and, as compared with the general population, is represented in the higher professions by eight or nine times its proportionate share.

That the vocational success of subjects, all of whom as children were found to be in the top 1 per cent of the child population, is, as one would expect, greatly influenced by motivational factors and personality adjustment.

That the incidence of marriage in the group to 1945 is above that for the generality of college graduates of comparable age in the United States, and about equal or superior to that found in groups less highly selected for intelligence, and that the divorce rate is no higher than that of the generality of comparable age.

That the test of marital aptitude predicts later marital success or failure in this group a little better than the test of marital happiness, much better than the index of sexual adjustment, and almost as well as scholastic aptitude tests predict success or failure in college.

That offspring of gifted subjects show almost exactly the same degree of filial regression as is predicted by Galton's Law.

That Jewish subjects in the group differ very little from the non-Jewish in ability, character, and personality traits, as measured either by tests or by ratings, but that they display somewhat stronger drive to achieve, form more stable marriages, and are a little less conservative in their political and social attitudes.

4. Thirty-Five Years Follow-up: The Gifted Group at Mid-Life.

'When the data on general adjustment are reviewed, we find a small but fairly consistent sex difference in the direction of more maladjustment among gifted women than among the men in our group. These sex differences must be interpreted with caution.'

A slightly larger proportion of women than men have suffered a mental disorder serious enough to require hospitalization (3.4 per cent of women and 3.1 per cent of men).

The problem of small numbers confronts us in comparing the sex difference in 'excessive use of alcohol', and in 'evaluating the extent of homosexuality', which showed only a small sex-difference among the gifted. Kinsey, however, 'estimates for the generality that homosexuality is from one-half to one-third less frequent among females than among males'.

The maintenance of intellectual ability
The Concept Mastery Test is so named:

> '. . . because it deals chiefly with abstract ideas. Abstractions are the shorthand of the higher thought process, and a subject's ability to function at the upper intellectual levels is determined largely by the number and variety of concepts at his command and on his ability to see relationships between them. . . .
>
> The data from the retests of the gifted group and of their spouses (also intellectually superior on the average though less highly selected than the gifted) give strong evidence that intelligence of the type tested by the Concept Mastery Test continues to increase at least through 50 years of age.'

Careers

> 'There is no composite portrait to be made . . . for it is in this area that their many talents and great versatility are most evident. . . . But there is no evidence that the men with fewer

vocational achievements are any less able intellectually than those who reach high places. In some instances, the choice of vocation was determined by educational or occupational opportunities, in others by health, and in still others it was a matter of deliberate choice of a simple, less competitive way of life. . . . As for the gifted women, fewer than one-half are employed outside the home. . . . As a group, the accomplishments of the gifted women do not compare with those of the men. This is not surprising since it follows the cultural pattern to which most of the gifted women as well as women in general have succumbed . . . an evaluation of achievement in terms of vocational accomplishment excludes the cultural contributions which the great majority of those women have made in many indirect and intangible ways and which perhaps are never properly evaluated.'

Volume V ends with this comment on answers from the gifted group to the question: 'From your point of view, what constitutes success in life?' 'If we sometimes get discouraged at the rate society progresses, we might take comfort in the thought that some of the small jobs, as well as the larger ones, are being done by gifted people.'

The remaining major areas of inquiry were: avocational and other interests (reading and cultural activities, membership of clubs and organizations, religions and religious affiliations – 'the men report a slightly higher proportion of church memberships'); and political and social attitudes (at mid-life the gifted 'consider themselves close to the centre on a radicalism-conservatism continuum').

Future Plans
The following information has recently been received from Mrs Melita Oden:[1]

'A monograph now in press will bring the research results up to 1960. Part I of the monograph deals with the 1960 status

[1] Private communication. Mrs Oden was Professor Terman's research assistant, wrote six of the chapters of volume V, and is continuing the analysis of developmental trends in the study. The monograph has now been published.

of the total group and Part II presents an analysis of the factors that make for outstanding achievement among gifted men. This study compares the background and development of the 100 most successful and 100 least successful men to 1960 when they were at an average age of 50 years. The title of the monograph is *The Fulfillment of Promise: Forty Year Follow-up of the Terman Gifted Group*, author Melita H. Oden. It will be published by Psychological Monographs and is due to appear in November, 1967.'

INFANCY, COPING, AND MENTAL HEALTH STUDIES
MENNINGER FOUNDATION, TOPEKA, KANSAS

Initiated: 1948 – still active.

Directors: Infancy Study – Drs Sibylle Escalona and Mary Leitch.

Pre-school to Puberty (Coping) Studies – Dr Lois B. Murphy.

Aim: To study the dynamics of personality development from infancy to pre-pubescence 'through the crises of family life and personal trauma as well as through developmental change' – with the focus on the processes contributing to continuity and change and the development of individual styles of adaptation(a)[1]. Strictly speaking the studies are not longitudinal, but comprise a series of independent projects which focus on the children's ways of dealing with problems at each stage of development (a, h). Data collection has not been continuous.

Subjects: 128 volunteers from the Topeka area in the infancy project, selected by Escalona 'for basic normality' and studied intensively during the first six months of life: the study of 32 children (16 of each sex) from this group during preschool and latency years supplies the bulk of the information collected to date, but 50 of the original 128 were re-assessed in pre-pubescence. The occupational grouping of the fathers of the

---

[1] Alphabetical references in brackets are keyed to the list of selected references at the end of the description of this study.

original group is: 25 per cent professional, 34 per cent white-collar or tradesman, and 41 per cent manual. The provenance of the pre-school group of 32 children was predominantly (vocationally) non-mobile working-class families of English stock, in which some economic strain might occur but not amount to severe deprivation. The consistently average to superior IQs of the pre-school children and their good motor skill attest the success of Escalona's predictions in infancy (a, c), active church-going contributes to homogeneity of ideological background, stability of residence promotes continuity in community influences, and the support of the extended family for over half the children helps to stabilize the family in time of stress – all factors calculated to contribute to continuity in adaptational style and not to pressure against the native tendencies of the children (h).

Data: *Mental Tests*

Infancy: Gesell and Cattell during first year of life.

Pre-school: Stanford-Binet and Merrill-Palmer to the thirty-two children. WISC to thirty additional children from the infancy group.

Pre-pubescence: WISC (sixty children).

Projective Tests and Personality Inventories

At Ages: 4 Rorschach, CAT.

7 Rorschach, CAT. Witkin's Field Independence.

10 Rorschach, Thematic Apperception.

11 and 12 Holtzman Inkblots; Mayman (Early Memories); a battery of tests to assess cognitive styles, in particular levelling-sharpening and field articulation.

Paediatric and Psychiatric Examinations

Paediatric: at pre-school (group of thirty-two) and pre-pubescence level (sixty children).

Psychiatric: play sessions with the group of thirty-two at pre-school and latency levels; interviews (sixty children) at pre-pubescent level.

Interviews

With mothers and children throughout.

Behavioural observations

of child: at home, en route to research facility, and on rejoining family; in school setting. A 'parallel observer' recorded behaviour in all testing situations and at parties and trips etc.

More than a half of the sixty children studied from infancy to pubescence changed markedly in one or another aspect of functioning, while some variables showed more persistence than others. A number of factors seemed to make for homogeneity and consistency of experience through time and thereby to contribute to a consistent style of adaptation in some children in the sample. Marked continuity in style of functioning and in appearance was shown either by children at certain extremes of body-build or by certain stable children whose development at every stage had escaped traumatic interference and who had grown up in exceptionally homogeneous and stable environments.

Tendencies with the greatest likelihood of persistence were tempo, vigour, alertness, motor co-ordination and skill, and capacities for delay and for control – outcomes in line with the predictions made by Escalona as well as the findings of other studies (b), and having their source in factors that 'are in part genetically controlled such as smoothness of functioning and of co-ordination, gross aspects of skeletal design, energy and activity level, and responsiveness to the environment as reflected in alertness and alacrity' (h). Continuity was observed also in aspects of cognitive style such as tendency to delay, differentiation versus global perception, and integration in terms of degree of complexity. Some continuity was seen in autonomic variability or reactivity, and in channels of expression; impulse or drive pressure in different zones; and control capacities.

Many children showed persistence in basic coping patterns (such as withdrawal versus protest), in the capacity to accept substitutes, and in style of gratification (contentment versus exuberance) which require further study in terms of the biochemical, genetic, and neurological factors involved and their interplay with the environment. These tendencies were not so prone to change as affective ones like shyness and other expressions of fear or anxiety, affectionateness, anger and destructiveness, or dispositions which are closely related to interpersonal experience such as dominance, leadership, competitiveness, generosity, nurturance. If the environment is in tune with the child's natural development, the expectation is that the genetically controlled tendencies which are closest to body equipment, musculature and nervous system will continue to be manifest in their primary form (h).

Future Plans
In collaboration with specialist psychiatrists and analysts, continuing and more intensive studies of certain aspects of the relation between personality and cognitive development or the assessment of mental health.

SELECTED REFERENCES
(a) ESCALONA, S., et al, 'Early phases of personality development'. *Monogr. Soc. Res. Child Developm.*, *17*, No. 1 (1952).
(b) FRIES, M. and WOOLF, P., 'Some hypotheses on the role of congenital activity type in personality development', *Psychoan. Stud. Child.*, *8*, 48–62 (1953).
(c) ESCALONA, S. and HEIDER, G., *Prediction and Outcome : A Study in Child Development* (Basic Books, New York, 1959).
(d) HEIDER, G., 'Vulnerability in infants, and young children: a pilot study', *Psychol. Issues* (1964).

(e) MORIARTY, A. E., 'Coping patterns of preschool children in response to intelligence test demands', *Genet. Psychol. Monogr.*, *64*, 3–127 (1961).

(f) MURPHY, L. B., 'The child's way of coping: a longitudinal study of normal children', *Bull. Menninger Clinic*, *24*, 97–103 (1960).

(g) MURPHY, L. B., et. al., *The Widening World of Childhood: Paths Towards Mastery* (Basic Books, 1962).

(h) MURPHY, L. B., 'Factors in continuity and change in the development of adaptational style in children, *Vita Humana*, 7, 96–114 (1964).

(i) ESCALONA, S. *The Roots of Individuality* (Tavistock, 1968).

STUDY OF BEHAVIORAL DEVELOPMENT: SCHOOL OF
  MEDICINE, NEW YORK UNIVERSITY

Initiated: 1956 – still in progress.

Project
  Director: Dr Alexander Thomas.

Aim: To study individual differences in primary (and possibly constitutional) reactivity in infancy and childhood, and evaluate the precise relation of initial reaction patterning to psychological growth.

Subjects: Sixty-three boys and sixty-three girls first seen at 2–3 months of age from volunteer parents as homogeneously middle and upper class as those of the Child Research Council's Study in Human Development – the homogeneity being a deliberate choice to ensure so far as possible the independence of individual differences in reactivity of variations in general social or cultural factors. The racial composition is 97 per cent Caucasian and the religious 86 per cent Jewish. Child-care practices were ascertained to be highly similar throughout the sample.

The attrition rate has been remarkably low: only 5 per cent of the subjects had been lost to the study when the oldest children reached 8 years of age, 'a tribute to the co-operativeness and devotion to knowledge of the parents' (e)[1] and, one might add, to the quality of the liaison maintained by the project staff.

Data: *Mental Tests*
Stanford-Binet when the children were between 3 and $3\frac{1}{2}$ years of age, repeated at 6 years and supplemented by a problem-solving situation and interpretation of neutral pictures.

Interviews
Detailed structured home interviews with the mother every three months when the child was 2 to 15 months. At age 3 a three-hour interview with the mother and father separately on discipline and parental attitudes and practices; it included the PARI Scale and a retrospective recall of the child's behaviour during infancy.

Behavioural Observations
Between age 3 and 4 years 80 per cent of the children were observed at nursery school and their teachers interviewed. A major feature of the study are its interview and observational techniques, and the procedures devised for analysing the content of the interview data and behavioural protocols which can be replicated in longitudinal studies of large numbers of children with mental retardation, brain damage and psychopathology. The aim of the Study is to acquire information on as wide a range as possible of the child's responses to features of the natural daily activities of his life 'so that the data sample becomes representative of the child's functioning' (e). A basic assumption is 'that no special advantage derives from constancy of stimuli' which involve testing devices and the strangeness inherent in special

---

[1] Alphabetical references in brackets are keyed to the list of selected references at the end of the description of this study.

manipulation and contrived situations (e). 'The direct longitudinal observation of the child would require a ratio of one investigator to each child. Consequently *serial cross-sectional study has been substituted in many instances for longitudinal inquiry*' (e, g).

A most valuable source of continual direct observation is the parent, and 'parental experience, if adequately assessed, constitutes a basic and economical source of data' (e).

An inductive content analysis was carried out on the interview protocols of the first twenty-two children studied. The analysis established that nine categories were present and scorable for interperiod comparisons of behavioural activity in the first two years of life: (1) Activity level; (2) Rhythmicity of Functioning; (3) Adaptability; (4) Approach or Withdrawal; (5) Intensity of Reaction; (6) Threshold of Responsiveness; (7) Quality of Mood; (8) Distractibility; (9) Attention Span and Persistence. Cluster analyses of these primary reaction characteristics suggest the existence of a limited number of individual types which may well have important prognostic value.

The results have considerable implications for child development and psychiatry:

(i) The effectiveness of parental practice is strongly influenced by the child's primary reaction pattern: what is most effective for one child may be ineffective and even harmful for another (c).

(ii) While it is clear that parental attitudes and practices and other environmental features profoundly influence the course of a child's development, no consistent and direct relation has been found in the specific nature of the personality organization of a given child. Common observation and a number of earlier investigators have suggested that organismic characteristics of the individual infant, which appear to be present at birth and are not determined by postnatal experience, are significant determiners of normality and pathology in psychological growth, but the paucity of detailed developmental data has made it difficult to evaluate the precise relation (a, b). The thesis of the New York Study is that psychological development is the result of the interplay of environmental and organismic forces. 'Children with similar primary reaction patterns may emerge with different personality structures and psychologic contents, depending on the environmental forces to which they have been subjected. On the other hand, children with similar environments may also show differing courses of psychological development, if they start with different primary patterns of reactivity' (e).

Future Plans
The study of development over the first two years of life has been reported in an excellent monograph (f). More complex styles of behaviour and cognition are being delineated for the 6 to 8 years period and will be correlated with the data for the earlier years of life. Children developing behavioural disturbances are being studied and the anterospective data for these cases closely analysed. A parallel study begun with Puerto Ricans will provide a cross-cultural comparison with the New York sample.

SELECTED REFERENCES
(a) ESCALONA, S., et al., 'Early phases of personality development, *Monogr. Soc. Res. Child Developm.*, *17*, No. 1 (1952).
(b) WITMER, H. L. and KOTINSKY, R. (Eds.), *Personality in the Making – Fact finding report of Mid-Century White House Conference on Children and Youth*, pp. 35–6 (Harper, 1952).
(c) CHESS, S., THOMAS, A. and BIRCH, H. G., 'Characteristics of the

individual child's behavioral responses to the environment', *Amer. J. Orthopsych.* *29*, 791–802 (1959).

(d) CHESS, S., THOMAS, A. and BIRCH, H. G., 'Methodology of a study of adaptive functions of the preschool child', *J. Amer. Acad. Child Psychiatry*, *1*, 236 (1962).

(e) THOMAS, A., BIRCH, H. G., CHESS, S., and ROBBINS, L. C., 'A longitudinal study of primary reaction patterns in children' *Comprehensive Psychol.*, *1*, 103–12 (1960).

(f) THOMAS, A., CHESS, S., BIRCH, H. G., HERTZIG, M. E. and KORN, S., *Behavioral Individuality in Early Childhood* (University of London Press, 1964).

(g) MEILI, R., 'A longitudinal study of personality development', in Jessner, L. and Pavenstadt, E. (Eds.), *Dynamic Psychopathology in Childhood* (Grune and Stratton, New York, 1959).

THE STUDY OF ACADEMIC PREDICTION AND GROWTH: EDUCATIONAL TESTING SERVICE

The primary aim of schools is to foster the intellectual growth of children. Nevertheless, there is a surprising dearth of literature on the educational growth of pupils at different times and under different conditions of schooling. This study, sponsored by the Educational Testing Service and the College Examination Board, is an attempt to fill the lacuna, if only partially. Planned to span the period from grade 5 to grade 12, it involves 34,000 pupils from a variety of schools in the U.S.A., and over seventy-five different scores, many of them necessarily obtained on more than one occasion. The study, the planners conceded at the outset, is not large enough or designed in a way to produce national norms of growth, but is calculated to provide reliable pointers to the expected growth of pupils of particular ability levels, interests, sex, home background, etc. in particular kinds of school situations, for administrators, teachers, and guidance counsellors who are vitally interested 'not only in where a child *is* but in where he is likely to *be* in two, four, six, or eight years'. A special feature is the attention given to relationships between scores on two specially constructed instruments – the Test of General Information and the Background and Experience Questionnaire. The former taps learning that is not specific to the usual school curriculum and it 'seems reasonable to hypothesize that the areas in which students acquire the most knowledge of the type indicated are those in which they are most interested'.

The design of overlapping groups adopted for the study has a special interest for readers, in the light of the paper by Peaker in Appendix V. The 'target group' is the 5th grade group tested in 1961 and drawn from the 127 feeder elementary schools for the high schools in the study. As a 'check' on the 5th graders of 1961 an additional testing, on one occasion only, was planned for a sample of 5th graders from the same school systems in Autumn 1963. Final results will not be obtainable until the 5th graders of 1961 have finished high school but 'approximate pictures of the progress of students from grade 5 to grade 12 may be obtained by piecing together results obtained for students tested in 1961 and 1963 in grades 5 and 7, 7 and 9, 9 and 11, and 11 and 12. Even more reliable estimates of growth should be possible by 1965' with the testing of the 5th graders of 1961 in grades 5–7–9, of the 7th graders of 1961 in 7–9–11, and of the 9th graders of 1961 in 9–11–12.

The study is described as 'ambitious', 'expensive', 'demanding', 'difficult' and 'frustrating'. Its difficulty arises from the inadequacy of common-sense notions of educational growth and the necessity to 'appeal to hypothetical constructs in the analysis' – in this connection a reference is made to Lord, F. M., *Elementary Models for Measuring Change* in Harris (34). Its frustrating character is attributed first to anticipations of impatience on the part of 'those who are concerned with results (although the experimental design will make possible interim – and increasingly better – estimates of the total growth picture)'; and second, to a tendency of a project of this magnitude 'to reinforce subsidiary interests in the investigators and interested by-standers' with the inevitable consequence of introducing modifications in the study as it progresses.

Among the technical problems posed by the study for solution are:

(a) the span of time over which measurements are reliable with the type of instruments used in the study;

(b) the proportion of the total variance in test scores that can be accounted for by ability, error, and pupil and environmental change between testings;

(c) discrepancies between score distributions from longitudinal and cross-sectional data;
(d) 'drop-out' and its effects on the nature of school populations at successively advanced educational levels;
(e) the linearity or otherwise of growth patterns;
(f) the significance of background factors for growth and the relevance or otherwise of experience variables to the measuring instruments used.

REFERENCES

(a) ANDERSON, S. B. and MAIER, M. H., 34,000 'Pupils and how they grew.' *J. Teacher Educ.*, *14*, 212–16 (1963). [On which the present account is based, and the source of its quotations.]

(b) MAIER, M. H. and ANDERSON, S. B., 'Adolescent behavior and interests.' Research Bulletin 64–52. Princeton, N. J.: Educational Testing Service (1964).

(c) HILTON, T. L., and MYERS, A. E. 'Personal background, experience and school achievement: an investigatiion of the contribution of questionnaire data to academic prediction', Research Bulletin (Educational Testing Service, Princeton, N. J., 1966).

THE BENNINGTON COLLEGE STUDIES OF PERSISTENCE AND CHANGE IN ATTITUDES AND VALUES IN STUDENTS

Director: Professor Theodore M. Newcomb, University of Michigan

Two reports provide the principal sources of the studies:

(a) NEWCOMB, T. M., *Personality and Social Change* (Dryden, New York, 1943).
(b) NEWCOMB, T. M., et al., *Persistence and Change: Bennington College and its Students after Twenty Years* (John Wiley, 1967).

The first study followed the changes of attitude in Bennington students of 1935 to 1939 towards the variety of burning public issues in a period of rapid change in the U.S.A. – from the Wagner

Labor Act to the end of the Spanish Civil War and the start of World War II. The usual direction of change at Bennington was found to be towards the acceptance of New Deal policies and away from the convictions of the students' parents, and furthermore, of students from very similar upper- and middle-class families attending other American colleges (c).[1]

Such changes can obviously be understood only in the context of the social environment provided by the colleges at the time. Bennington is a small 'unconventional' college for women still widely regarded in the U.S.A., with the Sarah Lawrence College, as a prototype of the 'experimental-artistic' college. 'Its reputation has now crystallized to the point where the stereotyped "Bennington girl" is the subject of cartoons in the *New Yorker*'. Although Dewey had no hand in its founding in the early thirties 'his statue stands prominently in the entrance to the main classroom building'. Its policy is to encourage 'direct experience in learning' through small seminars, individual projects, tutorial sessions, and an annual two-month non-resident term in a job related to the students' college studies. Staff-pupil relations are designedly informal while courses of study are planned by counsellor and student together and tailored to the interests of the individual students.

The limitations and the absence of systematic 'controls' in the original study of the Bennington girl in the thirties left 'considerable uncertainty as to the particular features of the college, as of that time, that were peculiarly responsible for the observed changes'. The second study posed two problems: the fate of the attitudes engendered twenty years earlier, and the difference in Bennington as an institution some twenty years later. The two are complementary in an attempt to acquire a deeper understanding of the processes by which colleges influence their students. The answers entailed an examination of attitudinal change in the current student body of the college also: the hypothesis was that a failure to find changes comparable with those of the thirties

---

[1] Alphabetical references in brackets are keyed to the list of references given at the beginning and end of the description of this study.

could be related to known changes in the world scene and institutional setting, whereas success could be related to whatever constant features, world or institutional, could be detected. 'Without two such comparisons over two points of time (widely separated, preferably) there was no way to distinguish, among all possible influences, those that were from those that were not effective in inducing changes at the earlier time.' An additional aim was to make some contribution, with 'the growth of mammoth universities' in the U.S.A., to testing the assumption that 'the effectiveness of colleges in inculcating values depends rather heavily upon a sense of community that carries with it the exact opposite of impersonality and anonymity'.

The original study in the thirties had taken 525 women as subjects. Despite the expense and the time involved it was decided that a structured personal interview would provide the most information from the largest number of people and that only those for whom the most data had been originally collected should be interviewed in 1961: the graduates of 1938–40. The remainder were contacted by postal questionnaires. Interviews with 129 of a total of 147 whose current addresses were known were generally held at home. Postal questionnaires very similar to the interview schedule were sent to the remainder. In all, 94 per cent of the 147 participated.

The investigation focused on attitudes and behaviour related to public issues and the alumna's identification and involvement with Bennington College. To assess the amount of social support or opposition to her own point of view questions were asked about comparable attitudes and interests of husband and friends, and about friendships maintained with women who had been up at Bennington with her. She also completed two short questionnaires: the Political Economic Progressivism (PEP) scale from the original study, and the items from the Omnibus Personality Inventory (OPI) concerning 'liberalism' and 'non-authoritarianism'. In late September of 1964, some three or four years later, interviewees were asked to indicate, in a follow-up postal questionnaire, their own preferred presidential candidate, and to predict the voting preferences of their husbands and of their own and their husbands' brothers and sisters.

It is impossible to attempt in this short account anything like an adequate summary of the findings. The book by Newcomb and his associates (b) must stand as a model of what such a report should be – in exposition, cautious inference, succinctness, and selection of significant detail. The graduates of the thirties showed greater active participation and involvement in organizations and public causes than a comparable group of women described in Slater's study of the League of Woman Voters (d). The pattern, however, is complex. Sixty per cent had actively furthered the interests of a political party, with 'liberal' groups receiving more help than the 'conservative'. Political attitudes in the thirties predicted well the type of participation twenty years later in the interests of the community but not its amount; both type and amount of participation were also affected by the number and ages of the graduate's children. Student activities, however, were poor predictors of later involvement in the local community. Individual personality characteristics, likewise, were determinants of persistence and change in attitude: change was less likely in women rated as most individualist during their student days, the more 'authoritarian' became more conservative, and those who became less conservative were less so than the ones who did not change. By and large, the alumnae maintained the attitudes developed in the college environment, not 'in vacuo', but by way of supporting environments – including husbands, friends, and co-workers in public or community activities – that were initially congenial to those attitudes and later supportive of them.

The political views of alumnae and students were very similar but more of the former were involved in political activity and more of the latter in aesthetic pursuits. Both generations set a high value on intellectualism, aestheticism and liberalism, showed an equal awareness, 'even to the point of concern', with social and international conditions, and expressed similar points of view.

A feature of special interest is the discussion on the formation of women student subcultures and deviant adaptations, the problem of anti-intellectualism and provincialism in the large American state universities (e), and the conflict between the norms symbolized by the 'feminine mystique' (f) and those maintained by an institution such as Bennington which remain 'rather militantly antihousewifery'.

The authors conclude the report with a suggestion for a programme of research on student peer cultures that might well be transferred to the British scene. This 'inevitably complex' project 'would entail consideration of identity problems among American adolescents; the functions of higher education for different social strata in our society; problems of decision-making and alienation with respect to occupational choice; ethnic, regional, and ecological subcultures in the larger society; and so on'.

REFERENCES
The quotations in the account above, unless otherwise indicated, are from the 1967 report by Newcombe and his associates (b).
(c) JACOB, P. E., *Changing Values in College* (Harper & Row, 1957).
(d) SLATER, C., et al., 'Participation in voluntary associations' (Survey Research Centre, Michigan University, Ann Arbor, 1957).
(e) TROW, M., 'Cultural sophistication and higher education', Unpublished paper (*Center for the Study of Higher Education, University of California*, Berkeley, 1959).
(f) FRIEDAN, B., *The Feminine Mystique* (W. W. Norton, New York, 1963).

THE TRANSITION TO PARENTHOOD: NATIONAL INSTITUTE
OF MENTAL HEALTH, BETHESDA, MARYLAND

Initiated: In 1959 under the direction of Harold L. Raush and Robert G. Ryder.

Aim: To investigate the initial stages of family formation and, on the basis of longitudinal data for the interpersonal adaptation of newly-married couples and their reactions to pregnancy and initial parenthood, to acquire more adequate concepts of preventive psychiatry and thereby better means of identifying the populations at risk in the community (c).[1]

---

[1] Alphabetical references in brackets are keyed to the list of references at the end of the description of this study.

Subjects: Fifty middle-class white couples residing within a
reasonable drive from the Centre who volunteered to
spend, during the fourth month after marriage four
evenings of their time with the 'procedures' of the
Study which entailed 'six interviews of one to two
hours in length, about three hours worth of questionnaires, Goodrich and Boomer's Color Matching Test
and a quasi-role playing procedure called 'Improvisa-
tions'. . . . Husbands were between 20 and 27, wives
between 18 and 25 . . . and not knowingly pregnant as
of three months after marriage.' All couples had completed high school, had not obtained a postgraduate
degree, and neither spouse was a full-time student. The
object of the screening criteria was 'to reduce the
impact on the data of ethnic and socioeconomic differences so that relationships among any other variables
might be more clearly revealed' (c).

The literature of psychoanalysis contains a deal of theoretical
discussion of personality changes during pregnancy and the
assumption of the mother role, and hypotheses on personality
change in both spouses at each developmental phase of the
child (d). No systematic research, however, appears to have been
previously undertaken into the effects of the role change to
parenthood where no clear personality disturbances are involved.
Little work, too, has been done on the longitudinal monitoring of
family defensive and adaptive patterns across stages in the life-
cycle, despite the tendency revealed by clinical experience for
psychological defences to show considerable similarity between
members of the same family and to reproduce themselves in a
very general way across generations (e).
Factor analyses of the NIMH data provided the basis for
identifying eight patterns in the early stages of marriage, corresponding to the positive and negative ends of the four final factors
extracted: I – Closeness to (vs. distance from) the husband's
family; II – Marital role orientation; III – Open conflict (vs.
harmony) in marriage; IV – Closeness to (vs. distance from) wife's
family. Conjunctions of variables and factor loadings suggested that

An eventual psychosocial taxonomy of early marriage may include dimensions of complaints about the husband's or wife's family of origin, marital role orientation, degree of current harmony or disharmony, degree of involvement with the husband's or wife's family during the newly-wed period, and a rational versus affective style of communication between husband and wife. . . . Wives who report problems with their families in childhood or adolescence are to be found in those couples who report unhappiness, doubt, or diffuse marital conflict. Husbands who report problems with their families tend to take a less involved position within the marriage and to be the most striving towards occupational and economic goals. Close family involvement during the early marriage period seems connected with low affectivity in the marital relationship. . . . The developmental timing for the open expression of neurosis in the form of marital problem is likely to be much earlier in the course of the marriage for women than for men. . . . It remains to be seen what functions will show substantial isomorphic continuity and which functions tend to show fairly predictable or unpredictable shifts. . . . A twenty-year follow-up study of these Factor II males, who have awareness of emotional difficulties during childhood and adolescence, might show a higher prevalence of late marital problems and/or late separations than would be anticipated for other husbands in our sample (c).

The report indicates the relevance of Kelly's finding (f) that, over the first twenty years of maturity, attitudes and values about marriage are among the most changeable aspects of personality far more changeable than attitudes towards occupation, politics, or religion.

Follow-up data exists on questionnaire studies of engaged couples (f, g). The NIMH study is the first one on the early marriage relationships of 'average' couples to be based upon combined clinical and experimental methods. The unpublished report by Goodrich (c) which largely forms the basis of our account of the study appears in Judd Marmor (Ed.), *Modern Psychoanalysis: New Directions and Perspectives* (Basic Books, New York, 1968). A book on the research into the newly-wed phase of marriage is in the early stages of writing but the task has only begun of putting together the reports on transition to parenthood.[1]

This study provides another illustration that research strategies aimed at defining continuity and change in patterns of marriage or family or other complex human relationships, must be longitudinal and inter-disciplinary.

> It is important to combine a social science approach using brief assessments of large groups of families with a clinical approach which uses intensive assessments of small numbers of families. Without the social science approach, one will not know how significant the patterns are from an epidemiological standpoint; without the clinical approach, one will not really understand what is going on within a family, or group of similar families, which may account for the observed pattern of functioning. By linking the two approaches, by designing studies in which the same families are studied in both, one can compare the data of social science with the clinical evidence. This comparison provides the basis for speculations about the psychodynamic or adaptive significance of relatively inexpensive and brief observations of family functioning in larger groups. . . . It appears that the eight patterns of marriage can provide a tentative baseline for longitudinal studies of middle-class marriage and family development followed up at later stages of the life cycle (c).

REFERENCES

(a) GOODRICH, W., 'Developmental patterns in the infant and in the young family', Bethesda, Md. *Annual Report, Child Research Branch, National Institute of Mental Health* (1961).

(b) RAUSH, H. L., GOODRICH, W., and CAMPBELL, J. D., 'Adaptation to the first years of marriage', *Psychiatry*, 26, 368–80 (1963).

(c) GOODRICH, W., 'Psychoanalytic speculations on a taxonomy of marriage', Unpublished report (NIMH, 1966).

(d) BENEDEK, T., 'Parenthood as a developmental phase', *Amer. J. Psychoan.*, 7, 389–417 (1959).

(e) EHRENWALD, J., *Neurosis in the Family and Patterns of Psychosocial Defense* (Harper & Row, New York, 1963).

---

[1] Dr Wells Goodrich – personal communication, November 1967.

(f) BURGESS, E. W. and WELLIN, P., *Engagement and Marriage* (Lippincott, New York, 1953).

(g) KELLY, E. L., 'Consistency of the adult personality', *Amer. Psychologist, 10*, 659–81 (1955).

(h) HANDEL, G., 'Psychological study of whole families', *Psychol. Bull., 63*, 19–41 (1965).

THE CHILD RESEARCH COUNCIL'S STUDY OF HUMAN
   DEVELOPMENT: UNIVERSITY OF COLORADO MEDICAL
   SCHOOL, DENVER

Initiated: 1923, still active.

Directors: Walter Wason (1923–30).
           Alfred H. Washburn (1930–60).
           Robert M. McCammon (1960–).

Aim: The study of (a) changes in structure during growth, development and adaptation;
                   (b) changing physiological functioning through life;
                   (c) personality development.

Subjects: Predominantly, almost homogeneously, children of middle-class volunteer parents from the Denver area. 'It becomes an important consideration that a child once entered stays in the program for a long period' (d). Until 1930 children aged 8, 9, or 10 years; from 1930 enrolled at birth or during pregnancy.

At present five children at each year level; some 180 subjects followed from birth to present, of whom forty-six are second-generation children.

The largest part of the psychological programme was initiated in 1946 and oriented towards the longitudinal evaluation of psychoanalytical concepts with a small number of children whose life-history was well remembered by the investigator – with the hazard of 'contamination' of interpretation. A new programme began in 1960 on the development of perceptual and cognitive styles in children and their relation to functioning in other areas; it is currently concentrated on 'field dependence'.

REFERENCES

(a) BENJAMIN, J. D., 'Prediction and psychopathological theory', in Jessner, L. and Pavenstadt, E. (Eds.) *Dynamic Psychopathology in Childhood* (Grune and Stratton, 1959).

(b) BENJAMIN, J. D., 'Some developmental observations relating to the theory of anxiety', *J. Amer. Psychoanal. Ass.*, 9, 652–68 (1961).

(c) BEAL, VIRGINIA A., 'Nutrition in a longitudinal growth study', *J. Amer. Dietet. Assoc.*, 46 (6), 457–61 (1965).

(d) HILDEN, A. H., 'A longitudinal study of intellectual development', *J. Psychol.*, 28, 187–214 (1949).

(e) LEE, VIRGINIA A., 'Individual trends in the total serum cholesterol of children and adolescents over a ten-year period', *Amer. J. Clin. Nutr.* 20(1): 5–12 (1967).

(f) MCCAMMON, R. W., 'Are boys and girls maturing physically at earlier ages?' *A.J.P.H.*, 55(1): 102–6 (1965).

(g) MCCAMMON, R. W., 'The concept of normality', *Ann. N.Y. Acad. Sci.*, *134* (Art 2): 559–62 (1966): presented at conference entitled 'The Biology of Human Variation' held by the New York Academy of Sciences, 1965.

(h) RICCIUTI, H. M. 'Use of the Rorschach Test in longitudinal studies of personality development', *J. Proj. Tech.*, 20, 256–60 (1956).

(i) WASHBURN, A. H., 'The child as a person developing', *A.M.A.J. Dis. Chn.*, 94, pp. 46–53 and 54–63 (1957).

(j) WASHBURN, A. H., *Relations of Development and Aging*, Chapter 3: 'Influences of early development upon later life', compiled and edited by James E. Birren (Charles C. Thomas, Springfield, Ill., 1964).

(k) YARROW, L. J., 'The relationship between nutritive sucking experiences in infancy and non-nutritive sucking in childhood, *J. Genet. Psychol.*, 84, 149–62 (1954).

CHILD TO ADULT STUDY: INSTITUTE OF CHILD
  DEVELOPMENT, UNIVERSITY OF MINNESOTA

Initiated: 1925, still active.

Director: John E. Anderson (1925–).

Subjects: Children who had attended the Institute's nursery school. None observed after 5 years or before 2 years except Shirley's babies (e) until they reached (on average) the age of 28 years for the current study of adult adjustment. Born in Minneapolis and St Paul and their suburbs, they formed a stratified sample of all socio-economic classes. Less than 1 per cent of the parents were foreign born or non-Caucasian.

Not strictly longitudinal, the project is a follow-up of two small samples of these 4,500 children for whom the Institute had nursery school records over the intervening period, and constitutes an extensive study of the problems of predicting adult adjustment from data acquired in early childhood. The measures of adjustment devised, 'the relation between the person and the demands of life', are of particular interest and fall into three broad types: first, the 'pay-off' in terms of success in school, community and occupation; second, the subject's feelings about himself and his perception of his own relation to life; and third, the impression he creates on other people who know him and his circumstances well. 'Preliminary work indicates that the subjective feelings of men about their own adjustment are very closely related to their work and vocation, while the subjective feelings of women are very closely tied in with the way in which their family life is going forward' (c).[1]

REFERENCE

(a) ANDERSON, J. E., 'The effect of change in the social context upon the design of longitudinal research', *Amer. Psychologist*, *12*, 377 (1957).

(b) ANDERSON, J. E., 'The relation between adult adjustment and early experience over a 28-year interval', *Amer. Psychologist*, *15*, 385–6: abstract (1960).

(c) ANDERSON, J. E., 'The prediction of adjustment over time', in Iscoe, I. and Stevenson, H. W. (Eds.), *Personality Development in Children* (University of Texas Press, 1960).

---

[1] Alphabetical references in brackets are keyed to the list of references at the end of the description of this study.

(d) HURST, J. G., 'A factor analysis of the Merrill-Palmer with reference to theory and test construction', *Educ. Psychol. Measmt.*, 20, 519–32 (1960).

(e) SHIRLEY, M., *The First Two Years*, Vols. I–III (University of Minnesota Press, 1931–3).

(f) WERNER, E., 'Personality characteristics of men and women who successfully assimilated stress during their formative years': paper to the 1961 biennial meeting of the Society for Research in Child Development, Pennsylvania State University (March 1961).

THE STUDY OF HUMAN DEVELOPMENT: FELS RESEARCH
  INSTITUTE, YELLOW SPRINGS, OHIO

Initiated: 1929, still active.

Director: Lester W. Sontag (1929).

Subjects: Initially between six and eight newborn infants annually enrolled; from 1944 to the present the number increased to ten. The active sample currently consists of about 300 subjects ranging from birth to 39 years of age, from volunteer middle-class families within a 40–mile radius of the Institute: 25 per cent rural, 50 per cent from small towns, and 25 per cent from two large cities. The population is mainly from native-born Protestant parents of northern European extraction, 60 per cent of whom have two or three children in the study at the present time. Each child is observed in the Fels experimental nursery school for three weeks twice a year from $2\frac{1}{2}$ to 6 years of age.

Aim: From the outset an interdisciplinary study of the physical and psychological growth of children.

'Obtaining a longitudinal record for each child is not neglected but is not the major activity' of the scientists engaged on the study (i). The type of information recorded has constantly changed and the data collection redesigned to obtain additional information. The initial 'shotgun' approach was early abandoned in favour of concentrated work in areas judged more promising or practicable, while changes in staff brought changes in interests. Problems, too, went 'out of fashion' during the conduct of the survey and new problems arose requiring different types of information. Procedures, however, of proven utility 'such as mental tests, home visits or soft-tissue X-ray' have not been interrupted. 'Many of the earlier publications are in fact more or less self-contained short-term studies[1] related to various problems of pregnancy and fetal behavior' (h). The stability and co-operation of the subjects in the longitudinal sample ensure a reservoir for cross-sectional or short-term longitudinal investigations even when the latter require a certain load of additional tests related to biochemical questions, performances in threat situations, and automatic responses to stress. Though the Institute draws on the general population for cross-sectional inquiries attempts are made to utilize the study group so that findings may be related to anthropometric information already assembled. Furthermore, a study may be initiated with a cross-sectional approach which is later changed to a longitudinal one when this seems appropriate. Efforts toward integrating the data from the several fields are made by reviewing a variety of data, such as home visit, nursery and play-school records, and observations obtained from projective techniques, to explain striking individual differences in longitudinal IQ growth curves. Policies developed over the years show a strong tendency to organize a set of more or less self-contained 'short-term' longitudinal studies, one after the other, partly of the group enlisted early, partly of subjects added lately. Current interest in a particular problem rather than concern about long-term continuity and homogeneity of records determines the activities (h).

---

[1] Furthermore, 'the Institute carries out . . . experimental laboratory investigations which are felt to alleviate further the handicaps of mere record keeping over long periods and to stimulate scientific thought amongst the staff.' (h).

The Continuation Study

So called 'because it re-examines in adulthood those who as infants and growing children were subjects of Fels study' (j). The findings are reported by Kagan and Moss (f) and demonstrate the accuracy of the prediction of patterns of adult emotional behaviour from the patterns formed before the age of 10 years.

An extension is now under way which will relate longitudinal information originally collected on seventy-five parents of Fels children to a fresh assessment of these same parents now that their children have reached maturity.

The Fels longitudinal data have also made possible

(i) an analysis now in progress of possible relationships between foetal activity in the eighth and ninth months and emotional behaviour and physiological function beyond the age of 15 years;

(ii) studies in the genetics of growth (under Garn) using sibling and parent-child pairings, in particular the genetic control of the sequence and timing of a child's bone ossification and rate of bone loss in adults.

The longitudinal programme has at present three main emphases:

(i) the relation of behaviour during the first twelve months to functioning during the subsequent three years, with special reference to activity level, and autonomic and behavioural response to frustration and to a variety of sensory experience;

(ii) analytic conceptual preferences in children – reflective and impulsive tendencies: the tendency to reflect before choosing an alternative, the beginning of reflective judgement, can be identified in children as young as 6 to 8 years.

(iii) achievement motivation in school-children and its parental and personality correlates (in conjunction with children other than the longitudinal population).

REFERENCES

(a) CRANDALL, V. J., et al., 'A conceptual formulation for some research on children's achievement development', *Child Development*, *31*, 787–97 (1960).

(b) CRANDALL, V. J., 'Personality characteristics and social and achievement behavior associated with children's social desirability response tendencies', *J. Pers. & Soc. Psychol.*, 4, 477–86 (1966).

(c) GARN, S. M., et al., 'Parental body build and developmental progress of the offspring', *Science, 132*, 1555–6 (1960).

(d) GOLLIN, E. S., 'A developmental approach to learning and cognition' in Lipsitt, L. P. and Spiker, C. C. (Eds.), *Advances in Child Development and Behavior*, Vol. 2 (Academic Press, 1965).

(e) HEATHERS, G., 'Emotional dependence and independence in nursery school play', *J. Genet. Psychol.*, 87, 37–57 (1955).

(f) KAGAN, J., and MOSS, H. A., *Birth to Maturity: a study in psychological development* (Wiley, New York, 1962).

(g) KAGAN, J., 'Change and continuity in development' in Birren, J. E. (Ed.), *Relations of Development and Aging* (Thomas, Springfield, Ill., 1964).

(h) KODLIN, D. and THOMPSON, D. J., 'An appraisal of the longitudinal approach to studies of growth and development', *Monogr. Soc. Res. Child Development*, 23, No. 1 (1958).

(i) SONTAG, L. W., 'History and progress of the Fels Research Institute': paper read to Child Development Conference, Chicago, 1955.

(j) SONTAG, L. W., The Fels Research Institute: report published by Samuel S. Fels Fund covering its activities for the two years ended 31 December 1963 (Antioch College, Ohio, 1964).

(k) SONTAG, L. W., 'Implications of fetal behavior and environment for adult personalities', *Ann, New York Acad. Sci.*, 134, 782–6 (1966).

(l) SONTAG, L. W., BAKER, C. T. and NELSON, V. L., 'Mental growth and personality development: a longitudinal study', *Monogr. Soc. Res. Child Develpm.*, 23, No. 2 (1958).

(m) WATERS, E. and CRANDALL, V. J., 'Social class and observed maternal behavior from 1940 to 1960', *Child Development*, 35, 1021–32 (1964).

THE GROWTH STUDIES AT THE UNIVERSITY OF CALIFORNIA: INSTITUTE OF HUMAN DEVELOPMENT, BERKELEY

These three longitudinal studies are administered within the Institute of Human Development and have now been in progress for more than thirty-five years. Two of the studies have accumulated records from birth or early infancy, the third from early adolescence. For about 500 cases in the original samples data are becoming available on more than two-thirds who are now in their thirties and forties and were enrolled in one of the three projects: the Berkeley Growth Study, the Guidance Study, and the Oakland Growth Study. An important contribution to their success has been the continuity of the principal staff member over the long period of data collection and the personal relationship between permanent staff and study members (l).[1]

Each project 'is an interdisciplinary approach to the study of individual development in a normal sample, with records of health, physical growth, mental development, personality, and of the physical and social environment . . . Although involving different emphases and different groups of subjects, the three investigations have been carried forward with some overlapping of staff and of research procedures. Proposals for further work imply that the three studies will be brought into an increasingly close association in adult follow-ups' (k). To obtain, for example, a large enough sample to assess the influence of family variables and certain intervening experiences upon personality change during and after adolescence, data from the Berkeley and Oakland Studies are pooled or analysed in parallel with the same techniques.

The Berkeley Growth Study
Initiated: 1928 and still in progress.
Directors: Nancy Bayley (1928-   ).
           Dorothy H. Eichorn (1954-   ): for the follow-up of fifty-four (73 per cent) of the main sample at age 25 to 30, the collection of data on their spouses, and the longitudinal study of seventy-eight of their children.

[1] Alphabetical references in brackets are keyed to the list of references at the end of the description of this study.

Subjects: Sixty-one children (half boys, half girls) from volunteer families in the Berkeley area, predominantly (67 per cent) Protestant, professional or white-collar, and of northern European extraction. With the dropping out of a small number of cases the total sample was expanded to seventy-four.

'The plan of the Berkeley Growth Study was to test and measure the mental, motor, and physical development and the health of a sample selected as full-term healthy newborns. The scheduled testing periods, at each of which most of the subjects were seen, to date have occurred at fifty-six ages, the first at three to four days of age, the most recent at thirty-six years' (d).

The Guidance Study
Initiated: January 1929, and still in progress.
Director: Jean W. Macfarlane (1928–   ).
Subjects: A representative selection of 248 cases (half boys, half girls) from an earlier survey which had enrolled every third child born in Berkeley from January 1928 to July 1929; the subjects are, consequently, more representative of an urban population than most longitudinal samples. At the beginning of the study they were divided into two matched groups – Guidance and Control – on the basis of socio-economic factors. Of the parents 80 per cent were born in the U.S.A. and were generally of northern European extraction. The fathers represented the entire occupational range: 25 per cent professional and executive, 40 per cent white-collar, 28 per cent skilled and semi-skilled manual, and 7 per cent unskilled and 'miscellaneous'.

Developmental records have been maintained from 21 months to 18 years, with the emphasis on personality variables and their correlates. Twelve years later a follow-up began of 169 individuals at the age of 30 constituting 68 per cent of the original sample. In general terms the follow-up sought 'evidence as to what combinations of biological and social factors – at what ages, and in what relative weightings – best predict adult status . . . and a body of fact pointing to important new questions to be asked about personality, and forming a basis for a schema of variables relevant to mental health' (k), and the sharpening of personality theory.

Macfarlane (d) has defined the aims of the Guidance Study as follows:

(1) To delineate physical, mental and personality growth and development in a normal group and to ascertain the variations among and within individuals at different developmental periods over a long time span; (2) to see the relationship of these findings (i) to the biological facts (constitutional make-up, sex, health and rate of maturity), (ii) to environmental facts – physical, socio-economic, intellectual and social, including interpersonal relationships to family members, playmates, classmates, teachers and important others, with their varying personalities and impacts upon individual children; (3) to throw light upon critical combinations of facts whereby some individuals are able to realize their full potentials while others fall far short of such realization; some individuals develop mature and sturdy personalities whereas others rigidly or neurotically cling to immature or ineffectual patterns; some individuals under stress gather new strengths and others give up the struggle or disintegrate; and (4) to assess how much confidence we should have in the predictive usefulness of our tools of appraisal of personality characteristics, mental ability, etc., of the child.

The Oakland Growth Study

Initiated: 1932 and still in progress – originally termed 'Adolescent Study'.

Directors: Herbert Stolz and Harold E. Jones (1932–60).
John A. Clausen (1960–)

Subjects: Initially about 200 children (half boys, half girls) ranging from $10\frac{1}{2}$ years of age in the 5th and 6th grades of five Oakland elementary schools, of whom 150 remained in the study some six years later at graduation from high school, and over 100 were available for a follow-up study when they were between 38 and 40 years of age. The children had varied social and economic backgrounds but, in accordance with the basic socio-economic structure of the schools' catchment areas, were all Caucasian, native-born, urban, and predominantly middle class. The initial selection of the subjects by school, and their community of acquaintanceship and experience over the junior and senior high school years, 'provided a unique situation for the observation and recording of social interactions' (e). An assessment of the follow-up sample of survivors at age 38 showed that they differed in no significant way from the original sample of twenty-five years earlier on measures of socio-economic status, intelligence, and adjustment.

The project has provided for two periods of intensive data-collection – adolescence and middle age; a lighter assessment was made of some eighty subjects in their early thirties. The Oakland Study is a three-generation project, with interview data (from 1932) on the mothers of the principal sample and latterly mental test information and related assessments on the children of the third generation. A major cycle of data-collection was completed for each subject in the main sample by 1960 which required twenty to twenty-five hours of interviewing, individual psychometric testing and psychophysiological experimentation. Since these subjects are nearest the age to supply candidates for gerontological research every effort is being made to preserve continuity with as many as possible to provide a study of individual patterns of ageing in normal subjects (k, l).

The 'locus classicus' for the directing ideas of the Oakland Study is perhaps found in Clausen's description (g) of the plans for the data analysis:[1]

---

[1] Cited by Jones, M. C. (l).

In viewing the adolescent subject, one tends to see his development as the resultant of the interplay between genetic potentiality, general patternings of relationship and expectation surrounding him, and salient experiences of self and others, all within a social-cultural matrix that provides general definitions of individual experience. Stature, physical attractiveness, rate of maturing, intellectual potential, and temperament interact with family structure, parental personalities, and the subcultural and ecological correlates of position within the social structure. As individuals mature, the constraints of their original social matrix become less compelling. They not only respond to environmental pressures and potentialities, they select them. They commit themselves to lines of activity and to other persons, as well as to conceptions of themselves. As a consequence, one expects not only changing personal attributes and changing saliences of attitudes and values but also a changed relationship between the way the person sees himself and the ways that he is seen by others.

Under the direction of Professor Mary Cover Jones an investigation is also in progress into differences in activities, interests and attitudes of adolescents separated in time by two decades. Members of the Oakland Study have provided the age-trend data through the tests they had taken from 1932 to 1938, and are being compared with later cohorts of pupils in the 9th grade of the high schools which they had themselves attended some twenty to thirty years earlier. This study is one of a series involving the comparison of different cohorts of adolescents that will make possible an evaluation of secular trends (k).

REFERENCES
(a) BAYLEY, N., 'The accurate prediction of growth and adult height', *Mod. Probl. Paediat.*, 7, 234–55 (1962).
(b) BAYLEY, V., 'The lifespan as a frame of reference in psychological research', *Vita Humana*, 6, 125–39 (1963).
(c) BAYLEY, N., 'Research in child development: a longitudinal perspective', *Merrill-Palmer Q.*, *11*, 3, 183–208 (1965).

(d) BAYLEY, N., 'Methodological problems in longitudinal research' in *Symposium on problems of research and methodology*, *Proc. VIth Int. Cong. Child Psychiatry, Edinburgh*, pp. 24–9 (1966).

(e) BAYLEY, N., 'Behavioral correlates of mental growth: birth to maturity', *Amer. Psychologist*, *23*, 1–17 (1968).

(f) BRONSON, W. C., 'Central orientations: a study of behavior organization from childhood to adolescence', *Child Development*, *37*, 125–55 (1966).

(g) CLAUSEN, J. A., 'Personality measurement in the Oakland Growth Study' in Birren, J. E. (Ed.) *Relations of Development And Aging*: Springfield, Ill., C. C. Thomas (1964).

(h) JONES, H. E., 'Consistency and change in early maturity', *Vita Humana*, *1*, 43–51 (1958).

(i) JONES, H. E., 'Problems of method in longitudinal research', *Vita Humana*, *1*, 93–99 (1958).

(j) JONES, H. E. and BAYLEY, N., 'The Berkeley Growth Study', *Child Development*, *12*, 167–73 (1941).

(k) JONES, H. E., MACFARLANE, J.W. and EICHORN, D. H., 'A progress report on growth studies at the University of California', *Vita Humana*, *3*, 17–31 (1960).

(l) JONES, M. C., 'A report on three growth studies at the University of California', *The Gerontologist*, *7*, 49–54 (1967).

(m) LIVSON, N. and PESKIN, H., 'Prediction of psychological health in a longitudinal study', (based on longitudinal data from the Guidance Study), *J. Abn. Psychol.*, *72*, 509–18 (1967).

(n) MACFARLANE, J. W., 'From infancy to adulthood', *Childh. Educ.*, *39*, 336–42 (1963).

SUMMARIES OF THE FINDINGS OF MAJOR LONGITUDINAL STUDIES IN THE U.S.A.

The issue of *Child Development* for March 1964 contained a report by Jerome Kagan, of the Fels Research Institute, entitled 'American Longitudinal Research on Psychological Development' (39a). The report was the result of a survey conducted by the author in 1962 and commissioned by the Social Science Research

Council of the U.S.A. Consisting though it did of 'brief descriptions' of ten of the major programmes in the U.S.A., it ran to thirty-two pages in the close print of the journal. The author writes:

Although most social scientists are aware of the existence of these programs, there is little awareness of the characteristics of the sample, the kinds of data they have collected, or the degree of inter-project comparability of tests and observational material. The Committee on Socialization and Social Structure of the Social Science Research Council [U.S.A.] initiated a survey of some of these programs in order to assess the information available at these institutions. This survey was not exhaustive, and the criteria for selection were determined, in part, by the Committee's interest in the effect of early socialization experiences on the child's behaviour during the preadolescent and adolescent years. Thus, there was a preference for contacting those programs that began study of the child during the first decades of life and had followed the child at least through the first decade.

To his description of each of the following ten studies, Kagan appends a valuable selected bibliography of publications up to 1962. Other publications have, of course, appeared since that year, and it is clear that longitudinal research has taken on a new significance with the emergence of findings from investigations conducted by these and other centres that have used the life span from early childhood to the middle years as a frame of reference.

Centre	*Title of Study*	*Project Initiated*
— Institute of Human Development, University of California	Oakland Growth Study (Adolescent Study)	1931, still active
— Institute of Human Development, University of California	Berkeley Growth Study	1928, still active

Centre	*Title of Study*	*Project Iniated*
— Institute of Human Development, University of California	Guidance Study	1928, still active
— University of Colorado Medical School	Child Research Council's Study in Human Development	1923, still active
— Fels Research Institute	Study of Human Development	1929, still active
— Institute of Child Development, University of Minnesota	Child to Adult Study	1925, inactive
— Harvard School of Public Health	Longitudinal Study of Child Health and Development [the 'Fourth' Harvard Study]	1929 – ended 1961
— Department of Psychology, Stanford University	Study of the Gifted Child	1921, still in progress
— Menninger Foundation	Infancy, Coping, and Mental Health Studies	1948, still active
— School of Medicine, New York University	Study of Behavioral Development	1956, still in progress

All but one of these studies have been described earlier in this Appendix, and an account specially prepared for us of the seventh study in the list, the 'Fourth' Harvard Growth Study, is reproduced in Appendix IIA. Kagan's survey of these ten major programmes was 'intended as a general source of information for social scientists'. Each summary describes clearly and in very adequate detail the populations studied, the methods employed, the sort of data collected, and the general nature and scope of each project. One aim of the survey, it would seem implied, was to identify 'important similarities' in the major programmes: in his conclusions to the report he notes, first, that measures of intellectual functioning are standard across most of the projects[1] and, second, the presence of

> a core set of behavioral variables which, although measured by different instruments, may have sufficient comparability to justify the pooling of selected aspects of the longitudinal information from different projects. Moreover, if a relation is discovered in one sample, it would be possible to use data from other programmes for replication purposes. The longitudinal use of the Rorschach and TAT stimuli by many of the projects provides the opportunity to study the stability of content and style variables during development and the relation between these two kinds of interpretative responses.

He notes also that while all studies found significant relationships between family variables and child behaviour, the data are far richer on the child than on the parent-child interaction, on the mother than on the father (especially in the early studies), and that across the projects the most common variables are maternal affection, restriction, rejection, and type of discipline. He instances the extensive anthropometric data collected by the major studies and the suggestions they offer for research into relations between variables in physical growth and dimensions of personality. The greater rigour in measurement and the clearer definition of problems in future research will have been possible only because of the early pioneering studies which, with all their limitations, 'established some guides for those who chose the difficult task of unravelling the enigma of human development'.

Major Programmes of Research on Personality Consistency and Change
A symposium on consistency and change in personality arranged by Dr Leon J. Yarrow, of the Washington Infant

---

[1] 'Perhaps the progress made in research on intellectual growth might be partially attributed to the use of a limited number of standard methods that correlate highly with one another.' Schaefer (336).

Research Project, was held at the annual meeting of the American Psychological Association of 1963. Four distinguished investigators discussed the conceptual and methodological issues involved on the basis of recent findings from the major study which each represented: the Berkeley Guidance Study by Bayley; the California Guidance Study by Macfarlane; the Fels Study of Human Development by Moss; and the Coping Study by Murphy. *Vita Humana* devoted a complete issue, No. 2 of 1964, to the papers read to this symposium, which must constitute a principal source of reference for contemporary preoccupations and perspectives in this difficult field. An introductory paper by Yarrow (348) examined the issues and problems raised, while Honzik (36) surveyed the distance research has so far covered in predicting the occurrence of stability and change, in eliciting factors that determine them, and in 'learning something' about 'the probable importance of internal or constitutional factors', and the impact of stress and of maternal and other social pressures on the behaviour of children. A requirement for further progress, she insisted, is a more sophisticated methodology for analysing growth data: 'Correlations and case histories help, but what is needed is a highly complicated prediction equation which will take into account many time series, interaction effects, and the combining and partialling of variables simultaneously. We have just begun to travel, but the road ahead looks very exciting.'

The symposium concluded with an attempt by Schaefer (336), of the National Institute of Mental Health, to work out a consensus of findings and viewpoints, undertaken, he stressed, rather for its relevance to the design of future longitudinal studies than from any expectation of reaching his objective. An evaluation of consensus is hampered at the outset by differences in the ages of subjects for whom findings had been presented and 'the situations in which, and the roles of the persons by whom, data were collected. . . . Persons playing different roles – mother, father, teacher, interviewer etc. – perceive the child differently and probably elicit different behavior.' Other sources of variation are methods of data collection; in these four major studies of personality consistency the primary methods have been observations or interviews with varying degrees of structuring. 'Since we do not know what

142

values might be expected for intercorrelations of measures derived from these methods at approximately the same time, we cannot say whether the obtained correlations through time reflect primarily differences in methods or whether they reflect true changes in the subjects.' In the absence, too, of a standard set of personality constructs, comparisons of findings of the different projects are dependent upon 'an interpretation of the probable equivalence or similarity of concepts', or of their operational definitions.

Inevitable and desirable as were these differences among the pioneering projects, Schaefer suggests:

> ... future longitudinal studies might profitably be co-ordinated for the solution of a limited number of important problems. This co-ordination might consist of an agreement to use a set of common situations, constructs, and methods that would permit comparison, while the broader design of each project would allow creative innovation by the individual or research team. If our current conceptual and methodological sophistication would not justify such standardization, then a co-ordinated program of basic research that would lead to standard methods for personality research should be initiated.[1]

Nevertheless, despite the differences which have been outlined, areas of agreement do exist in the findings of these studies. The highest is found on the consistency of a dimension of active, expansive, extraverted behaviour, and on its interpretation as possessing a genetic, innate, biological basis. Schaefer found relatively high consistency in achievement behaviour, and points to the broad implications for education in the findings that consistency in response to intellectual tasks is established in the pre-school period.

'Perhaps the greatest contribution of these studies', he concludes, 'is their clear demonstration that an adequate theory of personality can only be derived from information on the entire process of development from birth to maturity.'

In a personal communication, Professor Bloom has informed us

---

[1] For information on the scope and design of a group of co-ordinated studies already initiated he draws the attention of the reader to Falkner, F. (Ed.) (24).

that probably the best summary of the use of longitudinal studies in the U.S.A. is found in Stone and Onqué (340). The publication is an annotated bibliography with abstracts, compiled during the course of an extensive study of all the literature on longitudinal research in personality development up to 1955. The project had been approved as a joint thesis by the authors for the M.D. at the Yale School of Medicine, and was limited to longitudinal studies primarily concerned with emotional and social behaviour in infants and children, including other areas 'notably physiolog- ical, motor, and intellectual . . . only when there is a specified explicit or implicit relation to social and/or emotional factors.' The authors selected 297 papers for abstraction.

Professor Bloom's own work, *Stability and Change in Human Characteristics* (12), already referred to on pp. 10–12, was 'in large measure based on the longitudinal studies conducted by many investigators' in the U.S.A. and elsewhere. 'The more detailed investigations and analyses of the relevant published works' took up three years in addition to the sabbatical year during which 'the major outline of the book was completed'.

In view of the shortage of time available for a systematic search of the international literature, the directors of major American centres of longitudinal research had been sounded at an early stage about the availability of something in the nature of a synopsis on the main findings, present situation and prospective developments of their studies. From Dr Robert W. McCammon, the Director of the Child Research Council's Study in Human Development, we received the following information:

> I would delight in being able to send you the information you have requested, particularly as it regards those areas which could not have been adequately investigated without the longitudinal approach . . .
>
> We are about to undertake what we propose as a three-year endeavour to organize, analyse, and publish the data obtained from thirty-five years of longitudinal investigation of healthy human subjects. We regard this as the minimum interval in which even our program can possibly be approached. To attempt this on a world-wide basis is a staggering chore, impossible of accomplishment. I do not wonder that you seek

help, but unfortunately I know of no longitudinal program sufficiently treated to be in a position to answer even part of your questions.

Since I do not want to seem to duck your need because it is a difficult one, I am enclosing a copy of Dr. Washburn's Rachford lectures[1] of some ten years ago. These still represent the best existing summary of our purposes and methods, although both have undergone revision in the intervening decade. I am also sending a list of our publications[2] and if you feel any of these would be of service to you we would gladly forward them if they are still available.

I sincerely regret that I cannot be of more practical assistance to you.

Dr Lester W. Sontag, the Director of the Fels Research Institute, replied in similar terms:

Putting together for you a summary as you have indicated you would like to have is a well nigh impossible feat for me at this time.

I can, however, send you a copy of last year's Annual Report, a descriptive bulletin of the Institute's program, and a bibliography[3]. From these I think you can extract the information you desire.

In the summaries of the last four studies in this Appendix we have contented ourselves with indicating the general nature and scope of the projects and supplementing each account with a brief selection of its publications as illustrative material. We apologize for the palpably inadequate treatment of these very considerable themes, but can only plead that this has been forced on us by scarcity of time. This must also be the excuse for not providing, as we attempted to in the first seven accounts in this Appendix, anything in the nature of a synopsis of the principal findings of

---

[1] Washburn, A. H., 'The child as a person developing', *A.M.A. Journal of Diseases of Children, 94,* 46–53, and 54–63 (1957).

[2] Numbering 170.

[3] *Publications from the Fels Research Institute for the Study of Human Development*: on the Campus of Antioch College, Yellow Springs, Ohio. [A bibliography listing 670 titles.]

each Study.[1] The volume of publications that these centres in particular have produced over the past three decades might well tax the speed and stamina of a Macaulay in the time available for the preparation of this report, or require, at the least, for thorough digestion, the long months and undisturbed seclusion of the voyage by sail to India on which the omnivorous historian of England performed such prodigies of reading. Another prerequisite would have been the immediate accessibility of the literature. No single library in the U.K. contains anything like the entire range, and inevitable delays in borrowing from libraries outside those in one's immediate vicinity add considerably to the labour of following up references and upset the orderly planning of work when time is limited. Our reconnaissance of the field has necessarily varied in depth, but the selection of titles that follows each study will, it is hoped, be found to be reasonably representative.

---

[1] Neither will these be found in Kagan's summaries of the major American longitudinal studies (op. cit.): but this task did not come within his terms of reference. Throughout this Appendix we have drawn heavily on his report, and take this opportunity of gratefully acknowledging our debt to his work.

APPENDIX IIA

LONGITUDINAL STUDIES OF CHILD HEALTH AND DEVELOPMENT, DEPARTMENT OF MATERNAL AND CHILD HEALTH, HARVARD SCHOOL OF PUBLIC HEALTH[1]

BACKGROUND

In 1929 Dr Harold C. Stuart initiated studies of mothers during pregnancy, their families, and the infants born to them. Periodic and broadly oriented follow-up studies of these infants and their families were then organized and carried out from birth throughout childhood. The project, which developed from simple beginnings, came to be known as the 'Center for Research in Child Health and Development'. The first mother was enrolled in early 1930, the last in 1939; the last child still being followed was discharged in 1956 after completion of his eighteenth year terminal examination.

The major goal of the longitudinal studies was to explore all major aspects of development and their inter-relationships in the same children and selected environmental forces which may have bearing upon the developmental progress of these children.

Emphasis was upon *progress*, that is: the growth and developmental changes. The study was primarily concerned with changes which occur in the same individual from birth to the eighteenth year. It was also concerned with different patterns of progress which emerge among groups of individuals.

The needs of paediatricians in providing health services to those children in their practice and of others dealing in health conferences, school, and other services, have been given much thought in planning this research.

THE GROUP UNDER OBSERVATION
Selection of Families for Study
Enrolment was secured as early in the mother's pregnancy as

---

[1] We are deeply indebted to Dr I. Valadian who provided this account for the report.

possible – early enough to allow for six months under observation before delivery.

The mother was required to be a patient at the Boston Lying-in Hospital – no mother was enrolled who did not give assurance that she would come regularly for prenatal care at the Boston Lying-in and planned to be delivered at that hospital.

Both parents were of white North American or North European family background, to avoid heterogeneous mixing of races which would have complicated the interpretation of individual differences. A majority of the families in the group are of Irish descent on both sides; a considerable number whose forebears lived in the United States or Canada for several generations came originally from Northern Europe.

Parents had to be reasonably certain of residing around Boston. For the most part, the heads of families enrolled had steady occupations such as policemen, firemen, managers of chain stores, etc.

The families belonged to the lower-middle economic group since they availed themselves of the services of the regular pre-natal clinics, but could afford to pay for ward services.

Parents had to be interested in having their child in the group and willing to co-operate in many ways, particularly through frequent and lengthy visits to the study centre, and extensive interviews. In return for this co-operation they were provided with health supervision.

Number of children and duration of follow-up
A total of 309 children were enrolled in the study and observed up to and including birth. The initial enrolment was on a tentative basis, with the understanding that follow-up would continue only if mutually acceptable to the parent and the staff of the study.

Of the early losses, fifteen infants were not continued after birth because of still birth, neonatal death, premature birth or gross defect. An additional thirty-five cases were dropped before their first birthday, usually because the mother proved unreliable when giving information, lost interest, or found it more difficult than expected to come to the clinic, or meet requirements in other ways.

The entire project was interrupted for a period of somewhat

over a year in 1942 and 1943 because of absence of staff on war assignments. As a result, all children missed one examination, and a few children two, for the most part at ages ranging from 7 to 13.

For purpose of analysis, the cases have been placed in three series according to the duration of follow-up:

The 'Prenatal Series' includes the original 309 cases
   (152 boys and 157 girls).
The 'Preschool Series' is made up of 228 children
   (111 boys and 117 girls followed to their sixth year).
The 'Maturity Series' consists of 134 children
   (67 boys and 67 girls followed to their eighteenth year).

All children were studied periodically until their 'discharge'. But the more intensive work was with children in the 'Maturity Series' – both in terms of extent of examinations, especially at 18 years, and in terms of evaluation and comprehensive studies of individual children.

FIELD OF STUDY – SOURCES OF INFORMATION
Study areas were selected to reveal some aspects of each child's health, growth, development, and dietary habits, as well as physical and psychological experiences and certain aspects of family composition, home environment or social circumstances.

I. *The family*
Background: Socio-economic, education of parents.

Health and physical characteristics of grandparents, uncles and aunts – information through parent interviews.

Health and physical characteristics of parents. Health histories and physical examinations of both parents taken by the staff at the Study Centre.

II. *The mother's childbearing period*
All mothers experienced a consistent and uniform programme of prenatal care at the Boston Lying-in Hospital. Management of labour and delivery was carried out by the staff of the hospital. All mothers had a two-week period of hospitalization after the

baby's birth. Information of the entire course is available through the hospital records; this has been further summarized and included in the 'Medical Summary' of each child, according to the general topics of:

1. Prenatal care (extent of).
2. Pregnancy events.
3. Labour.
4. Delivery.
5. Condition of the placenta.
6. Postpartum course.

In addition, a medical member of the study staff was admitted as an observer during delivery. He made direct observations upon the duration and characteristics of labour delivery, and the condition of the infant at birth. The study staff also took a special health history and, at intervals, kept a record of postpartum weights of the patients.

A detailed dietary history was taken at the first visit by the nutritionist. Records of usual daily food consumption were made on the basis of dietary interviews at least once during each trimester of pregnancy. A special nutrition history was also taken during the postpartum period.

THE CHILD UNDER OBSERVATION
Neonatal period
The Boston Lying-in Hospital records provided considerable information. Observations, examinations and measurements were made by the paediatrician and the orthopaedist of the study in the Newborn Nursery on the first and fourteenth day after birth. All available information has been summarized and incorporated in the 'Medical Summary' under the headings of:

1. Condition at birth, birth weight and birth length.
2. First examination – time – findings.
3. Neonatal course.
4. Second examination – time – findings.
5. Condition on discharge.

From infancy to maturity

Routine visits to the Study Centre were scheduled at 3, 6, 9 months, one year, every 6 months to 10 years, and every year from 10 to 18 years. To supplement these the Centre held a clinic one afternoon each week. Mothers had been urged to bring their children to this 'well' child conference at least once between routine examinations for weighing, for recording general progress, and for securing health histories at shorter intervals. In addition to this, they had been allowed to come any week at the time of the conference at their own discretion, if they felt the need for further check-up.

Paediatric Interviews and Examinations

Continuous health histories and repeated paediatric examinations have been considered fundamental to the study. Great thought was given to making the history adequately complete, reliable, and useful for research purposes. All important items have been covered routinely. The paediatricians have been primarily responsible for the completeness and accuracy of the information. The director of the study, assuring continuity of research throughout twenty-five years, had taken great care in training his supervisors and assistants to conduct these interviews so that leads which routine questions unfold were adequately explored through further questioning.

The information obtained was recorded in narrative course notes rather than on prescribed forms. These course notes were taken regularly at every visit to the Centre; they were amplified at times and served as a continuous health history for each child. They include specified subjects such as illnesses and feeding, and in addition occasional observations as to the mother's attitudes, the physician's opinions, as to certain occurrences and other interpretative comments. They also include statements as to advice given and reports on certain common habits such as enuresis, thumb-sucking, routine, training, and behaviour. The course notes frequently included summaries of telephone conversations with the mother, and information obtained from physicians who have cared for the child during illness, or transcripts of hospital or clinic records. They also included notes by the nurse, nutritionist and social worker, reporting information concerning the child's health.

The paediatric examinations were concerned with the detection of abnormality in disease, and with an evaluation of health status. The observations made by the paediatrician during his examination were recorded systematically on a printed record form. This form provided specific graded answers to certain chosen questions, and additional space for descriptive comments; such narrative notes which were added clarified or amplified stereotyped entries.

Anthropometric measurements
All measurements were carried out by each of two examiners and recorded separately; it has been required that the measurements of the two examiners check within five millimetres for large structures and three millimetres for small ones. The two examiners had been working continuously together and developed a co-operative technique; it has been routine for one to hold while the other measured, and then for the two to change positions.

The measurements chosen for routine determination were those which contributed most to the evaluation of a child's physical status and growth progress, and which at the same time could be taken on children.

Roentgenographic examinations
A series of roentgenograms had been taken at all routine examinations. The films have been used to study structural abnormalities or changes brought about by disease, and for this purpose have been reviewed by a roentgenologist or by other clinicians on the staff. However, these films were taken primarily for:

1. The determination of the size and form of various skeletal structures.
2. The determination of the relative maturity of the skeleton as observed in the various osseous centres, and in the contours of certain of the bones.

3. The recognition of qualitative variations in the tissues.
4. The recognition of developmental changes in muscle and other soft tissues.

The interest had always been in discovering changes which have taken place from one period to another and in detecting individual differences between children of the same age. The techniques for different measurements were selected to obtain sufficient accuracy to justify using the films for this last purpose; consistency of technique has been kept rigidly.

The body parts visualized were the following:

Skull and face	Lateral	36 in. distance
Jaws	Oblique lateral	14 in. distance
Forearms (to show wrist and elbow)	Lateral and antero-posterior	36 in. distance
Hand and wrist	Antero-posterior	36 in. distance
Chest	Antero-posterior	36 in. distance
Heart	Antero-posterior	72 in. distance
Abdomen	Antero-posterior	36 in. distance
Legs (to show ankle and lower end femur)	Lateral and antero-posterior	36 in. distance
Foot and ankle	Lateral and antero-posterior	36 in. distance
Both legs	Antero-posterior	72 in. distance
Both thighs	Antero-posterior	72 in. distance
Spine	Lateral	72 in. distance

The following are the main measurements taken from the x-ray film:

1. Length of femur, antero-posterior view
2. Length of shaft of tibia – lateral view.
3. Length of tibia – antero-posterior view.
4. Length of shaft of radius.
5. Skeletal chest breadth.
6. Heart breadth.
7. Breadth of muscle and subcutaneous fat tissue at the level of the calf.

Photographic records
Since the third year of the study a series of photographs was taken in standard fashion of all children at each examination.
The following photographs were taken at 14 feet distance.
Antero-posterior – full length.
Lateral standing No. 1 (arms at sides) – full length.
Lateral standing No. 2 (hands folded on chest) – full length.
At the final eighteenth-year examination special photographs for somatotyping were carried at the Forsyth Dental Clinic, and somatotyping was done by Dr Dupertuis.

Dental examinations
During infancy the paediatrician recorded dental observations relating to the time and sequence of eruption and to the gross appearance of the teeth and jaws.
At about the second birthday and at routine examinations thereafter dental examinations were carried out by dentists from the Forsyth Dental Infirmary for Children.
The dental examinations performed consisted of:

1. Inspection, with notation of data relating to the adequacy and character of the processes of growth of the jaws and face, and the eruption of pattern of teeth.
2. Observations on the character and health of the teeth and gums, and the efficiency of the function of mastication.
3. At selected ages, impressions and special roentgenograms have been taken.

Dietary observations
All data relating to the diet of the infant until the age of 9 months were recorded by the paediatricians. After that age a nutritionist obtained continued and reliable information on the customary daily dietary intakes of each individual child. She assessed the average daily food intake, appetite, and dietary management, through dietary histories taken at each routine visit, and each covered the preceding interval of time.

Social studies
Social studies of the families began when the mothers were enrolled.

154

The families were visited

1. Descriptions were made about the backgrounds of the parents:

   Place of birth.

   Socio-economic and socio-cultural aspects of their earlier life.

   Educational and work experience.

   Relationships with family members.

2. Child's family.

Home visiting continued through

Changes occurring in family composition.

        type of dwelling.

        socio-economic and family relationship.

Information about father:

   occupation

   income

   work history   } obtained from mother

   interests, activities

   relationship with children

Family problems such as unemployment or marital discord were carefully described.

Child behaviour

Behaviour described in the records by all members of the staff, 1932–36: major responsibility for the studies of child behaviour assigned to two psychologists.

– measurement of intelligence (nursery school).

– personality studies.

Observations of children in as many typical, usual life circumstances as possible, and careful records in narrative form of their behaviour.

Several members of the research staff interviewed mothers about the child's behaviour during routine examination.

Eighteenth year

Psycho-social team conducted studies of the family and the behaviour of the children.

In order to avoid bias, no access was allowed to previously collected longitudinal data.

Socio-cultural aspect.
Socio-economic.
The child at the eighteenth year
In addition to all the routines described above special examinations were:

1. Photographs for somatotyping: these were taken at the Forsyth Dental Infirmary for Children, and the typing done by Dr Dupertuis.
2. *Special psycho-social evaluation*
   Social worker interviewed the mother, relating both to the child at 18 years, and to the child's development as seen in retrospect by the mother. Phrase association tests were applied by a psychiatrist.

Results
The intensive studies of each of these 134 individual children contributed towards a better understanding of growth and certain developmental processes in childhood and their relation to problems of health.

The original study placed emphasis primarily upon progress as expressed by growth and developmental changes. Concern was with the differences encountered between children in the rates and nature of these changes, as well as the consistencies in them at successive age periods. These studies revealed patterns of human growth, development and adaptation. Patterns of growth in height and weight, patterns of skeletal development of the hand, patterns of caloric and protein intake, as well as patterns of illness experiences have already been published. This constituted the first phase of the evaluation of the data collected during twenty-five years.

The second phase of the evaluation is presently being carried out. It consists of studies of the interrelationships between patterns of growth, of illness experience, and of dietary intakes, as manifested by individuals, relating these variables to overall health and fitness in childhood and at maturity.

A strong association between high protein intake and vigorous growth is found during all three age-periods.

The amount of illness is also related to growth. The group with high illness had the greater proportion of large children at maturity; during pre-school period high illness was associated with rapid growth, while during adolescence this relationship was slightly weaker.

There is no evidence that high protein intake prevents illness or that illnesses reduce dietary intake.

Association of protein intake and illness with progress in skeletal development is not so strong as with growth in height and weight.

FOLLOW-UP

Sixty-seven boys and sixty-seven girls were studied periodically from birth until they reached their eighteenth year, and this group is referred to as the 'Maturity Series'. Additional children were followed for shorter periods but are not dealt with in this report.

These individuals have now reached the age period of 25 to 34 years. They were recalled to Boston for a follow-up study entitled:

1. 'Adult Health Related to Child Health and Development.'
2. 'Adult Social Functioning Related to Child Development.'

The purpose of the present research is to investigate current medical examination data, health and dietary histories, and social behaviour data, in relation to the detailed longitudinal developmental data.

The general objective of this study is to determine the extent to which certain characteristics of young adults can be predicted from a knowledge of their patterns of health and development during childhood. The characteristics of the young adult which it is desired to predict have been selected in part because of their importance for the health of individuals and in part because of the type of information available concerning the childhoods of the study group. The attempt will be made to predict:

1. Level of social functioning.
2. Physique, with particular attention to obesity.
3. Amount of illness and level of health.

    4. Pattern of dietary intake.
    5. Utilization of medical care.

Methods of obtaining data

1. Health history

Two health histories were taken (one by the paediatrician who has worked in the longitudinal study and knows the childhood history of each individual) covering the period after the subject's last examination at 18. The second history by the internist who had no access to the longitudinal record covered the entire childhood. This was the kind of health history a physician would take seeing a patient for the first time. This would allow us to check history information as recalled by the individual with actual events as revealed by the longitudinal data.

2. Physical examination

Conducted by system and including abdominal and internal examinations as well as vision and hearing examinations.

3. Laboratory examination

Included routine examinations such as blood, urine, EKG, and in addition, when indicated, to bring in further information, based on the internist's judgement, special tests were requested.

4. Anthropometric studies

Included body dimensions and somatotype photographs.

5 Dental studies

Included clinical examination of dental health, impressions for dental casts, full mouth radiographs, standardized head radiographs, colour photographs of the dentition.

6. Nutrition studies

The methodology developed by Mrs Burke for the longitudinal study was adapted to the fact that most subjects could not remember very well their food consumption for a long period of time. An attempt was made to get the food pattern for the previous three months, with any striking differences season, vacation or travel might involve.

7. Social studies

A study of the social functioning of the young adult based on an interview with the subjects (in the office and at their homes), their spouses and their mothers.

158

COMMENT

Our search of the literature has revealed little information on the psychological data acquired by the study conducted by the Harvard School of Public Health.

From Kagan's specifications of the sampling for the major American studies initiated between the wars it would seem that the two principal Harvard Growth Studies contained the highest proportion of subjects in the lower socio-economic groups.[1] The 'third' Harvard Growth Study aimed at an adequate sampling of 'public school children of the New England section of the U.S.A.' and considered it had been secured by taking all children (3592 in number) in the first school grade in three cities in Massachusetts

At least four 'growth' studies based on longitudinal[2] data have originated at Harvard University. The first was reported in 1872 by the professor of physiology, who compared the average measurements of the height of twelve males and twelve females made annually over a period of twenty-five years, finding evidence of increases of growth up to that age. The second study, from 1910–20, secured monthly measurements of the height and weight of Boston school-children. The third study was initiated in 1922 by Dearborn and his associates in the Psycho-Educational Clinic of the Harvard Graduate School of Education. This was the largest American study of child development that took simultaneous measurements of physical and mental growth in

---

[1] Kagan, J., 'American longitudinal research on psychological development', *Child Development 35*, 1–32 (1964). Kagan's review covered only the fourth Harvard Study where the families, as Dr Valadian says, 'belonged to the lower middle economic group since they availed themselves of the services of the regular prenatal clinics, but could afford to pay for ward services'.

[2] This use of the term became current in the 1930s. Dearborn and Rothney consider its choice an unfortunate one but describe the data of their (the 'third') Harvard Study as such for the reason they quote from a paper by Stuart, the director of the 'fourth' study: 'because of its wide adoption to denote continuing or repeated studies of the same children in contrast to "cross-sectional" studies of different groups of children at specified ages'. Stuart, H. C., *Monogr. Res. Child Development 4*, 1 (1939).

children from age 6 to 18. An extensive review of the findings forms the subject of Dearborn and Rothney's *Predicting the Child's Development*, which appeared in 1941 (79). The fourth Harvard Growth Study, of which pages 147–158 in this Appendix provide a condensed account, began in 1929 on 309 children from birth, of whom 134 were followed for eighteen years.

The problem of the relation between mental and physical development was a potent influence in initiating the third study. The motives were in the main practical ones, state the authors, but 'it must now be recognized that the practical values have been less than expected'. The correlations between the physical and mental measurements in the study were 'so low that the knowledge of one does not enable us to predict the other'.

Two principles emerge from the findings:

1. Marked individual differences may be found among any age, sex, ethnic or maturity group at any period of measurement, and
2. Marked variability in individual growth curves appears throughout the course of the growth period.

These cannot be considered as new, comment the authors, 'since the first has been demonstrated (although never as consistently, and over as long a period) many times, and the second has been the subject of much discussion. Our results put the principle of variability throughout the growth period on a more secure foundation than was possible by cross-sectional data. . . . We have established the fact that variability rather than consistency in growth is the rule, that prediction except for averages of groups is extremely hazardous (and even this is hazardous at the adolescent period) and that comparison-with-average procedures have little value in the study of individuals'.

The detailed findings may conveniently be summarized as follows:

Mental growth
1. Each mental test used over the period of the study is 'characterized by its own single and peculiar differences with respect to the problems of practice effect and its relation to

individual test problems'. The amount of practice effect is related to the ability of the subject, smaller gains being observed at the lower and larger gains in the upper part of the distribution.[1] The general effect with the majority of tests is to produce increased IQs, the largest gains appearing in the first repetition, but with noticeable gains occurring for as many as four trials.

2. Children tend to remain throughout (to age 16) in the same category as they were at age 8, and to perform at the same level on verbal and non-verbal items in group mental tests. The substitution of non-verbal for verbal material in mental tests could result in handicapping as many children as does the use of tests composed of verbal material exclusively. The group mental tests used in the study gave higher IQs than the Stanford-Binet.

3. Mental growth as measured by the type of group mental tests used in the study continues much beyond the age of adolescence, although with a marked decrease in rate after the age of 20.[2]

4. Neither performance on mental tests nor scholastic attainment shows significant positive relations with the pre-pubescent growth spurt. 'The rapid growth at adolescence need no longer be offered as an excuse for a slump in school performance.'

5. The study demonstrated the advantages in educational guidance of using individual growth curves based on the estimated maximum growth of the individual, or of an

---

[1] 'Some, but not all of these results are confirmed by British investigations, and we would suggest that the difference lies in the greater degree of "test-sophistication" among American children and adults. . . . It is a nice theory that the most intelligent, because of their intelligence, improve most. But all our evidence . . . shows the greatest rises among those scoring least. . . . The conclusion is, in fact, based on changes in test norms, not on rises among actual pupils.' Vernon, P. E. and Parry, J. B., *Personnel Selection in the British Forces* (University of London Press, 1949).

[2] Dearborn and Rothney 'are assuming an indefinite continuation of schooling'. Vernon and Parry (op. cit.).

unselected group, in preference to the technique of 'mental age', and the inadequacy of the commonly employed intelligence quotient as an index of mental growth.

Physical growth

1. The prediction of stage of anatomic growth from chronological age is hazardous. The same individual can display wide differences in the development of various segments of the body at any age, though body weight can effectively be predicted by a method produced by the study.
2. The pre-pubescent spurt is more abrupt than cross-sectional studies had demonstrated, and its timing is closely related to but not coincidental with the onset of puberty: about 50 per cent reached the highest point at puberty; 45 per cent had this jump before or after the date of menarche, but individual cases showed a range of seven years in which this spurt may occur. In general the growth spurt tends to be at or after puberty (90 per cent); only 10 per cent have their spurt before.

Attrition

Dearborn discusses the importance of a careful consideration of this factor in view of the 'emphasis which is placed on age in longitudinal studies'. At age 10, 25 per cent of his original population were lost from the study, at age 15, 50 per cent, and at 17, 75 per cent had left school. A trained social worker 'is needed especially at the age at which students begin to leave school to go to work'. The bulk of the subjects who left the study were in the lower groupings of his occupational scale since their parents seemed 'less likely to be fixed in a geographical area than those of the upper levels. . . . We have, therefore, in our populations, taken age by age, a series of mutilated distributions the causes of which are, at least, uncertain and which, therefore, are not of particular value for use in studies of relative position in terms of the original population. It should, however, be noted that certain published and unpublished studies . . . indicate that samplings of our material, even in its mutilated form, warrant the assumptions of normality usually found in statistical procedures'.

Plans for a continuation of the Third Harvard Growth Study
No follow-up has been made of the Third Growth Study since 1935. A proposal has recently been made for following up the original 3,592 individuals. 'Considering the importance Americans attach to formal education and the use that educators make of intelligence tests, scholastic achievement tests and academic performance (grades) it is remarkable,' say the proposers,[1] 'how few comprehensive follow-up studies have been carried out to determine the relationships between the variables considered important within the American educational system and the degree of success attained by students in coping with the complexities of modern industrial society'. Their principal aims are as follows:

1. to determine the relations between the occupational status attained by the subjects and the mental, scholastic and anthropometric measurements which had been repeated on them annually until graduation from high school or for the duration of their stay in the school systems that had provided them as subjects at age 6;
2. to compare the developmental data of subjects who are now parents with similar data to be acquired for their children;
3. 'to analyse the demographic changes that have taken place in the study population in order to assess the genetic and cultural consequences of the social practices that prevailed up to the end of the reproductive period for this population within a modern industrial society';
4. to examine the relations between rates of physical growth, age at physical maturity, health and longevity in the study population;
5. to make more complete the analyses of the original data in the light of current social theory and with the employment of present-day technology and statistical techniques.

---

[1] DeLong of Grand Valley State College and Bajema of the University of Chicago Research and Training Centre.

APPENDIX III

EUROPEAN LONGITUDINAL STUDIES

A LONGITUDINAL STUDY OF POST-WAR GERMAN
  CHILDREN

Initiated: In 1952 and conducted up to 1961 with the main
sample. A sample of 126 cases was interviewed and
retested in 1964.

Directors: Professors C. Coerper, W. Hagen and H. Thomae.

Aim: A public-health survey initiated by Professor Hagen,
former President of the Federal Health Office of West
Germany, to give school medical officers up-to-date
information on the physique and mental health of
children born in the immediate post-war period.

Subjects: A reasonably representative sample of 2,800 children
aged between 6 and 7 years on their entry to school from
six contrasting areas of Western Germany, 1,500 of
whom were tested for the last time when aged 15 to 16
years. The attrition of almost 50 per cent is attributed to
the subjects' voluntary participation and loss of motivation as they grew older or left school, combined with
the looseness of contact between parents and staff
members of the study, at least at its inception.

An account of the methods and early findings of the study is
published in:

(a) COERPER, C., HAGEN, W., and THOMAE, H. (Eds.), *Deutsche
Nachkriegskinder* (Thieme, Stuttgart, 1954).

The findings on the personality development of the main
sample are reported in Thomae (342). The paper also provides a
valuable list of references to publications arising out of all
aspects of the study up to 1965.

The data for the study of personality development fall into two
broad categories: sociological and psychological. The former
include socio-economic status, size of family, order of birth,

164

parental education and occupational grouping, breast-feeding, 'integration' of family, displacement of family, and country of origin; the latter derive from ratings on a nine-point scale for the following eight aspects of behaviour during the annual psycho-metric testing sessions of one to two hours duration: overt activity in the test situation, mood, general responsiveness, emotional responsiveness, flexibility of adjustment to changes in the test situation, ego-control, 'differentiation', and feeling of security. The scales were based on a personality model outlined by Thomae as early as 1951 which anticipated many trends of recent 'activation' theory.[1] The principal constituents of the model are degree, form, and direction of the individual's activity, type of orienting, regulating and stabilizing mechanisms employed and a kind of 'g' factor called 'differentiation' (capacity for variety of adjustments and behaviour which are meaningful in the situation and display symptoms of 'creativity'). An examination in detail of the relations between socialization variables and emotional adjustment demonstrated the overriding influence of socio-economic status in the data for the main sample – without prejudice, Thomae emphasizes, to the findings of contemporary research elsewhere which stresses the importance of parent-child relationships. The data of the German study in this area are still being analysed, as well as those for aspects such as leisure-time activities and personality and the impact of mass media and technological change (in a series of cross-generational comparisons begun by Thomae and his associates in 1949). The latter investigation may well suggest, it is conjectured, the dominance in the structuring of the personality of family roles and relationships over social and political change: the latter may be less powerful than the emotional relationships stressed by socialization theory, but the influence exerted is nevertheless appreciable.

A factor analysis (Thurstone) of the behaviour ratings for 240 elementary school children produced two factors: Social- and Task-Related Activity, and Ego-Control. Their extraction left enough variance for the individual description of the different aspects of behaviour rated, though level of intelligence clearly

---

[1] Duffy, E., *Activation and Behavior* (Wiley, New York, 1962).

emerged as important in the evaluation of the latter. The analysis is reported in:

(b) ESSING, W., 'Untersuchungen zu einem Beurteilungssystem der Persönlichkeit', *Archiv. für die gesamte Psychologie, 118,* 73–85 (Frankfort, 1966).

A STUDY OF ADJUSTMENT, BEHAVIOUR AND PROGRESS IN SCHOOL: THE INSTITUTE OF PSYCHOLOGY, THE UNIVERSITY OF STOCKHOLM

Initiated: 1964 – probable duration ten years.

Director: Assistant Professor David Magnusson.

Aim: To provide a better basis than is at present available for:
1. the early diagnosis of unsatisfactory adjustment;
2. instituting preventive measures;
3. school counselling.

Subjects: All pupils (approx. 3,300) in Grades 3, 6 and 8 (ages 10–15) of schools in Örebro, a city selected for offering adequate numbers for experimental groups, a well-developed educational system, variety of industrial occupation, developed school psychological services, abundance of leisure activities for young people, and a co-operative attitude on the part of the administration.

Operationally, the study is aimed at:

1. an analysis of the factors that determine adjustment, behaviour and educational attainments, and their relations to success and satisfaction in later training and employment;
2. an appraisal of eventual measures of rehabilitation.

The youngest of the subjects will be followed up for ten years. A feature of the inquiry is the combination of intensive studies of well-defined sub-groups against the background of the entire group of 3,300 from which they have been drawn. The background data comprise: school environment, factors in adjustment, difficulties at school as seen by children and parents, school adjustment as judged by teachers, school attainment, peer relations, self-evaluation, abilities, interests, choice of courses of study, vocational interests and information, with medical and other data on the children from official sources.

The first phase of the investigation is now completed. The success and speed of the operation are attributed by the Director to the active role taken by representatives of the National Board of Education, the local education authorities, teachers' organizations, parent associations, and the close co-operation of the local press.

The collection of data for the intensive studies began in the spring of 1966 of pupils in the following categories of maladjustment: the aggressive and emotionally disturbed, the inhibited, the tense and over-active, the deficient in motivation or in inter-personal relationships.

Reports on eight aspects of the study were in active preparation in 1966.

A STUDY OF GROWTH IN TWINS AND COEVALS AGED 9–16 YEARS: STOCKHOLM

National Board of Education and School of Education, Stockholm

Initiated: 1964 – to be concluded during the academic year 1969–70, with the departure of the pupils from the comprehensive school.

Director: Professor Ingre Norinder.

Subjects: 1,500 children (600 twins contrasted with 900 non-related children who are members of the same classes at school).

Aim: To ascertain the extent to which the secular trend of accelerated physical growth in children is reflected in mental growth, personal relationships, general behaviour, and educational attainments, with special reference to differences in growth between boys and girls.

In connection with the study's special emphasis on sex differences in growth, it was considered that the information of the greatest value would be that acquired from intra-pair comparisons between twins of different sex as they grow up together during adolescence. The comparison envisaged of identical and non-identical twins of the same sex 'is still one of our most promising techniques in obtaining at least a glimpse of the so-called "nature-nurture" relationships in growth processes'.[1] The study of twins also 'has the great advantage that the method in itself forces one to consider and examine individual differences, whereas in mass cross-sectional studies such differences are liable to be overlooked. In fact, the twin method is based upon the study of individual differences. When following up the twins and their coevals, however, we are naturally interested in intra-individual differences as well, as a means of detecting any marked discrepancies in the individual's pattern of growth, as, for instance, between physical and mental development'.[1]

The investigation began with a study of twins in Grade 3 of schools in nearly forty towns, contrasted with one or two children of the same sex in the same classes and born in the same month or at least in the same quarter of the year. To avoid drawing undue attention to the twins the educational and psychological tests are given to all members of the classes containing twins.

The twins are to be followed up to the age of sixteen if possible and, in addition to the educational and psychological tests, anthropometric measurements taken on them and on their matched class-mates twice a year (in April and October) by school nurses. Their health and home circumstances are assessed regularly by school doctors and nurses.

Pupils, numbering around 5,000, in the same classes as the twins and their matched controls, constitute the standardization population for the educational and psychological tests and other instruments used in the study; they comprise: (1) ratings by teachers of the behaviour of the twins and their controls; (2) tests of concentration, attention, and reserve of energy; (3) standardized

---

[1] *School Research: Newsletter No. 12 of 1967* of the National Board of Education (Bureau L4), Stockholm. The Newsletter also cites J. M. Tanner (117): 'we still lack any study in which the material would give us some idea of the relative importance of heredity and environment under various conditions of life', and his opinion that the answer seems to lie in studies of twins: 'It is really very surprising that only recently have longitudinal growth studies been set up using monozygotic and dizygotic twins and their siblings as chief material.'

attainment tests of Swedish and mathematics – the primary object of the latter being to ascertain the pupils' ability to assess their own attainments.

From and including Grade 4 sociometric instruments and tests of general intellectual ability have been added to the battery.

The processing of the complete body of data did not begin until 1969–70, and a number of interim reports are expected. Some preliminary results were presented to the Seminar on Growth held in Stockholm in June 1966 under the auspices of the International Children's Centre.

APPENDIX IV

BRITISH LONGITUDINAL STUDIES

'Our experience with cohort studies,' Dr Walker, the Director, wrote to us,[1] 'is based on three main projects. The first is the Mental Survey, which is reported in our Publications No. XXX, XXV, XLI, XLII, XLVI. A final report is at manuscript stage. Mr Maxwell can provide any information which is required.

The second is a minor project, not yet reported, involving a group of young people who were 15 in 1960 and 16 in 1961. It is called 'Permanence of Learning' in our Annual Reports, but is really a survey of basic skills in English and arithmetic, coupled with sociometric data.

The third is our follow-up of the group of young people numbering about 11,000 who in 1962 took the examination for the Scottish Certificate of Education. We are following their progress in higher education, or in some cases in employment. No detailed report has so far been prepared.'

The 1947 Scottish Mental Survey: the Six-Day-Sample
The group intelligence test given to the 11-year-old children of the 1932 Scottish Mental Survey was repeated with the corresponding group of 11-year-olds in the 1947 Survey, and their results compared. Fuller information was recorded for a sample of about 10 per cent (known as the Thirty-Six-Day-Sample) of the 1947 Survey, and a smaller sub-sample (the Six-Day-Sample) numbering 1,208 children were tested individually with the Binet-Simon test. The follow-up of the subsequent careers from age 11 through school and into employment of these 1,208 children – 'our miniature Scotland', as Dr Walker describes

---

[1] In a letter giving his views on cohort studies when arrangements were being made for the symposium on cohort studies held in London in February 1967.

170

them,[1] developed into a major investigation in its own right. 'Many agencies co-operated with The Scottish Council for Research in Education in this project – the Education Authorities, the Central Youth Employment Executive, the Armed Forces, the Post Office (in tracing changes of address), and the Rockefeller Trust and the Nuffield Foundation in financing the inquiry. The most vital co-operation, however, came from the members of the Six-Day-Sample group themselves, who completed quite a considerable number of information schedules, not all of them short, and from the numerous Home Visitors throughout the country who, as their title suggests, kept in touch with the members of the group and gave invaluable assistance in the collection of information about the follow-up group.'[2]

A very brief summary of the findings to date is given here:

1. Progress in school appeared to depend as much on social conditions as on measured intelligence.
2. Examination of the premature leaving or 'wastage' of pupils selected for education in senior secondary schools demonstrated that lack of ability was by no means the sole operative factor.
3. Personal qualities favourable to academic application, and suitable home conditions, were important factors in successful progress at school.
4. Most boys and girls found employment on their own initiative and had sorted themselves out into work that appeared suitable or at least acceptable. 'Follow-up data are specific to a particular time' – but the general picture was 'comparatively reassuring'.[2]
5. Very broadly, stability of employment during the first years after leaving school was related to level of general ability – the lower the IQ the more frequent the changes of job.
6. When aged 18 the members of the Sample reported general satisfaction with opportunities available in their districts for

---

[1] In his preface to Macpherson, J. S., *Eleven-year-olds Grow Up* (University of London Press, 1958).
[2] Maxwell, J., *The Level and Trend of Scottish Intelligence* (University of London Press, 1958).

pursuing their favoured leisure activities; the pattern of the latter varied with IQ and educational level.

The inquiry has been extended to acquiring data on the relations between marriage, fertility, social class, and occupation in the Six-Day-Sample, to be continued, with the assistance of public records, in the form of a demographic follow-up over an extended period of years to record marriages and births. In addition there are plans for collecting – with the financial assistance of the Eugenics Society – demographic data on deaths, marriage and fertility for a sample of 1,000 who had been given group and individual intelligence tests at age 11 in the Survey of 1932.

An additional proposal was formulated recently by the SCRE for a *follow-up over three years of maladjusted children* who had been attending residential schools in Scotland for this category of handicap for not less than two years.

THE PIC (1948) STUDY AND THE NCDS (1968) INQUIRY
These have been discussed in the main body of this book, and the general outcome expected from the next phases of the studies are outlined in Appendix VII.

THE EFFECT OF BACKGROUND AND SCHOOL UPON
INDIVIDUAL MOTIVATION   *London School of Economics*
This is a ten-year follow-up study directed by Professor H. T. Himmelweit of the Department of Social and Industrial Psychology.

Its data derive from the re-interviews of 600 boys, at age 25, whose behaviour, performance at school, and vocational aspirations had been examined for relations between intelligence, schooling and social background. The re-interviews focus on relations to parents and workmates, vocational adjustment, views on role in society, general aspirations and marriage plans.

OXFORD CHILD HEALTH SURVEY
Institute of Social Medicine, Oxford University
Its general aim, as defined by the late Professor Ryle,[1] was 'to

---

[1] Ryle, J. A., *Changing Disciplines* (Oxford University Press, 1948).

study the health and sickness experience, and the growth and development of babies from birth to school age, employing a population representative of all social groups'. Tactically, its plan was:

1. to keep under continuous observation for a period of five years 500 children born in Oxford after 1st January, 1944;
2. to obtain for these children social records of interest to clinicians and social workers;
3. to identify favourable and unfavourable influences in their inheritance and environment.

The subjects were 'volunteers', the investigators considering it unlikely that a randomly selected sample could be kept under continuous observation. It also excluded 'unusual' babies, such as those with weights of under 4 lbs. at birth, gross congenital defects and foreign parents. Attrition over the period of the survey was not considered to have made any appreciable alteration in the composition of the sample with respect to sex, parity or birth-weight.

'It was originally intended neither to undertake treatment nor to offer advice, but it soon became apparent that this counsel of perfection prejudiced a successful relationship with the mother. Thereafter, all questions were freely answered, and when defects came to light which required treatment, the necessary arrangements were made through general practitioners or hospitals.'

Experience showed that precoded schedules, which may be suitable for single interview surveys on a large scale, are quite inadequate for recording observations in a long-term, prospective survey. An alternative method was devised for further systematizing and reducing in bulk the variegated data from subjective assessments of mother, social workers, clinicians and radiologists that 'jostled' with records of objective facts. This dehydrating process for the benefit of the research worker led to the question whether it could

be carried still further to the advantage of workers in health administration who frequently have to digest masses of information of a similar kind. Is it in fact possible to obtain in a single summary figure some useful *measure of the opportunity for health* in infancy, and, conversely, of the claim to special assistance? The ideal measure of this kind would, presumably, take genetic as well as environmental influences into account. But for practical purposes we need only be concerned with the advantages and handicaps which are ever likely to be brought under social control, namely those stemming from the adequacy or inadequacy of the material environment in which the infant lives.[1]

The Registrar-General's classification into five social classes has been shown by Douglas[2] to be relevant to infant as well as to adult life, but distinguishing as it does only five levels and having as its base only one 'fact' – 'the occupation of the chief wage earner – it would hardly be acceptable as a basis of local administrative action'. For these reasons an objective measure of health opportunity was devised which dispenses with evidence on the financial position of the family and is based on readily obtainable answers to eleven simple questions of fact which can easily be acquired even before the birth of a child.

At least since the times of Galen, men have speculated on the relation between physique and temperament. The Oxford Study provided a random sample of fifty boys and fifty girls when they were within six months of their seventh birthday as subjects for an extensive inquiry[3] into the connection in young children between precise measurements of main components of physique and ratings of personality traits, common signs and symptoms of emotional unrest, and psychiatric assessments.

The correlations established 'offer reasonable hope that the somatotyping of children at the age of 7 will make it possible to pick out those who are specially vulnerable. . . . Moreover, the ability to discern proclivities from the measurement of somatic

---

[1] Stewart, A. M. and Russell, W. T., 'Interim report on the Oxford Child Health Survey', *Med. Officer*, 5 July 1952.

[2] Douglas, J. W. B., 'Health and survival of infants', *Lancet*, 2, 440 (1951).

[3] It is reported in: Davidson, M. A., et al., 'The distribution of personality traits in seven-year-old children: a combined psychological, psychiatric and somatotype study', *B.J.Ed.P.*, 27, 48–61, (1957).

components would discourage too exclusive a consideration of historical, social and environmental influences as causes of breakdown'.

THE THOUSAND FAMILY SURVEY

A joint undertaking shared between the Department of Child Health of King's College and the Health Committee of Newcastle upon Tyne, which has borne the main cost, with the continuous assistance of the Nuffield Foundation.

Initiated: 1947.
Time-span: 15 years to 1962.
Subjects: All births in the City of Newcastle between 1 May and 30 June, 1947. 1,142 infants were enrolled: 967 remained on their first birthday; 847 children were observed for the entire period of the first five years.
Aims: The study of the origins and associations of disease in childhood as a basis for preventive measures.

From the need for an accurate record of the incidence and type of infective diseases in infancy, the project broadened into a study of the lives and health of the subjects. That only seven families withdrew from the survey in the first five years is 'an indication of the goodwill and harmony established with the families and their doctors'. Two volumes have appeared which are models of clarity and of presentation.

(a) SPENCE, J., WALTON, W. S., MILLER, F. J. W. and COURT, S. D. M., *A Thousand Families in Newcastle upon Tyne* (Oxford University Press, 1954).

(b) MILLER, F. J. W., COURT, S. D. M., WALTON, W. S. and KNOX, E. G., *Growing Up in Newcastle upon Tyne* (Oxford University Press, 1960).

Some findings for the first five years

1. Parents can expect to rear children who survive the first week of life.
2. Malignant disease excepted, all causes of death in infancy and early childhood have strong associations with adverse

social factors, and further reduction presents social as well as medical problems.

3. The reduction in deaths sets in high relief the considerable residue from the illnesses of infancy and early childhood of permanent disability and handicap: mental deficiency, the complex neurological defects expressed in cerebral palsy, fits, deafness, and defects of vision, and structural damage to essential organs such as the lungs. Genetic or truly congenital factors play a much smaller part in these conditions than had been thought.

4. The prevalence of disturbed behaviour is high in all years in early childhood. Whereas neither the course of development of such disturbance in its different forms nor the degree of permanence is known, it is clear that the origins are deeply rooted in the personalities of children and parents, and in their ideals of family life and standards of behaviour. Only rarely are disturbed children seen or treated by the family doctor; many pass unrecognized.

5. 'The health of children and the outcome of disease are closely related to family environment. The essentials of a stable and happy home are a sound dwelling of sufficient size, a reasonable income wisely used, and parents who enjoy a satisfying relationship with each other and are sensitive to their children's needs. Most families care for their children faithfully and well and material standards are rising; but many still live in unsatisfactory and overcrowded houses and a considerable proportion of parents are beset with illness or instability in their personal relationships. This gives rise to a surprising amount of family disturbance and disruption. Now that most serious illness is coming under control, that primary poverty has almost gone, that standards of hygiene, nutrition, and education have so greatly improved, the major need in society is for increasingly responsible standards of family behaviour.'

6. 'There are still more deaths, illnesses, and disabilities in infancy and early childhood than is necessary in our present state of knowledge. But further inquiry into family life and its relationship to illness is required. This inquiry must be directed towards the reasons for the excellences as well as the inadequacies of family life, and more sensitive indexes of family environments are needed to assist the prevention of disease in the community and the management of a given

illness in an individual child. Nevertheless, the well-founded techniques of medicine are still required and remain dependable; careful attention to the clinical features and natural history of disease; precise clinical classification; recognition of the influence of age and social circumstances upon the severity and outcome of illness; the discriminating use of antibiotics and of special investigations. All these are necessary, and wise family doctoring and specialist care together could do much more to save life, shorten illness, and reduce disability.'

7. 'The people responsible for further improvement in the health and well-being of children are first and foremost their parents, helped when necessary by doctors in family practice, in hospitals, in public health services, in university departments of paediatrics, by nurses and health visitors, children's officers and other social workers. These in their turn must rely upon the members of regional hospital boards, hospital management committees, and local health committees and their administrative officers, and ultimately upon those who determine policy in the Ministries of Health, Education, and Housing. The essential need is for the continuing education and closer association of all concerned in this common task.'

The concluding paragraphs of the introduction to the second volume warrant reproduction in their entirety, if only for their pertinence to the discussion in our report on regional studies:

In England there is one contemporary investigation which also provides a picture of the first five years. In 1946 the Population Investigation Committee instituted a national survey to record the economic and social facts concerning childbirth in England and Wales. With the co-operation of local health authorities nearly 14,000 infants were enrolled at birth, during one week in March 1946, in 424 maternity and child welfare areas. These children formed a representative sample of the population of England and Wales and the Committee, through its director Dr J. W. B. Douglas, has continued to collect and publish valuable information about their development and illnesses.

Such a large group can be used to collect numerical data and smaller special groups with adequate controls can be isolated for particular study.

The two studies are therefore complementary. Considered together they will provide a fuller and more accurate picture for the health and development of children in the first five years of life than will be obtained from either separately.

Throughout this survey we have been increasingly conscious of its effect upon ourselves, how it has deepened our thinking concerning illness in childhood and in particular about the complex interplay of illness and family. The rich experience gained and the observations recorded have permeated and changed our teaching and influenced our approach to the training of medical students, health visitors, and nurses. *Without this wider field of work our concepts of child health would be narrowed to hospital experience* [our italics]. Yet paediatrics, possibly more than any other branch of medicine, must be concerned with the prevention of illness and the attainment of conditions in which healthy children can grow and develop into mature and responsible adults.

ISLE OF WIGHT STUDIES
Dr Michael Rutter, Institute of Psychiatry; Professor J. Tizard, Institute of Education; Dr K. Whitmore, Department of Education and Science; and Colleagues.

Purposes
1. Survey of the prevalence of handicapping conditions in a total population of children aged 8–10+ (N=3,300; three age groups).
2. Follow-up of handicapped children and controls to age 14+.
3. Experimental studies of different forms of remedial reading.

Method
Surveys were carried out in 1964 and 1965, each being in two stages:
(i) screening tests and inquiries about all children in the age cohorts;
(ii) individual assessment of selected children (N=600) – information from interviews with mothers and from records about them. 1,500–1,800 hours of testing and interviewing in each survey.

178

Staff from Institute of Psychiatry, and clinical and educational psychologists and social scientists, carried out fieldwork using tests and schedules which had previously been piloted and found reliable.

Children were retested in reading in October 1966 and backward readers given the Neale Test (individually) before Easter 1697. First reading experiment now starting. Further surveys and experiments planned.

Costs

1964–6　Grant of £16,500 from Department of Education and Science.

1966–72　Grant of £19,054 agreed to from Social Science Research Council.

1967–71　Grant of £22,205 from Nuffield Foundation.

Staff

This has varied since the fieldwork has been carried out by staff employed at the Maudsley and elsewhere who have spent a week or two on the project (costs per week for these average about £50; made up of honorarium – £20, hotel expenses – £20, travel to and from the island and on the island – £10).

Between two and four professional staff work full time on the project – only two of these are paid out of the grants mentioned above. In addition Dr Rutter and Dr Graham (Institute of Psychiatry) both spend about half time on the project, and Professor Tizard about one day a week – to increase shortly. It would be true to say that the budget meets less than half the costs of the project, even allowing for the fact that many teachers and others on the island have voluntarily given much time to the work, for which they have not been paid.

A LONGITUDINAL STUDY OF AGE AND ABSENCE IN
MANUAL WORKERS

MRC Unit for Research in Occupational Aspects of Ageing
Under the direction of Professor L. S. Hearnshaw of Liverpool, the absence records from three different factories are being analysed in retrospect to check the findings of cross-sectional

studies of age and absence. The findings from one factory have been reported in:

> DE LA MARE, G. and SERGEAN, R., 'Two methods of studying changes in absence with age', *Occup. Psychol.* *35*, 245–52 (1961).

Most enquiries into the connexion between age and absence from work have taken a cross-section of people of different ages and compared their records for a particular period. Groups of workers with the same birth dates have, however, characteristics other than age in common. In the study of this factory, in addition to a cross-sectional analysis of records, each group was followed over a period of ten years from 1949 to test whether differences in absence between the age-groups revealed by the cross-sectional method occurred also within the groups as age increased.

The findings of the cross-sectional analysis had paralleled those of similar inquiries elsewhere which had employed the cross-sectional approach: a higher frequency of 'other reasons' absence among younger men, and greater length of certified sickness absence among older men. Longitudinal evidence failed to confirm that high absence frequency is a characteristic of younger people, and demonstrated that, in the case of the youngest group in the study, its nature was determined by attitudes to work; the frequency in this particular group did not decrease with increase in age. Increase in length of certified sickness seemed to indicate a true ageing effect, but variations in frequency of absence were confounded with differences in values or of attitude to work.

It is understood that records over a twenty-year period (1943–63) from a second factory have not confirmed this finding in the first factory studied.

JUVENILE DELINQUENCY IN ONE LONDON BOROUGH
Time permits only a very brief outline of the following study by the MRC Social Medicine Research Unit directed by Professor J. N. Morris.

This study of all juveniles resident in one London Borough and appearing before the courts since 1958 has shown that half of the boys who make a first court appearance go on to make at least a second. Follow-up of the decisions of magistrates at the boys' first appearances revealed that the half who make a subsequent appearance do so irrespective of 'treatment'. A clinical and social investigation of a representative sub-sample of younger first offenders who appeared before the court in 1964–5 forms the basis of a prediction study of future court appearances by these boys.

LONGITUDINAL STUDIES IN PSYCHIATRIC EPIDEMIOLOGY
Professor Rawnsley has compiled for the information of the MRC Committee on the Epidemiology of Mental Disorders lists of research work in psychiatric epidemiology. The fourth list, of August 1966, was prepared with the aim of providing a reasonably comprehensive account of current projects for interested research workers. From it the following identifying details of a few studies are extracted in illustration of the range of prospective and retrospective longitudinal research in one broad field of medicine:

> Professor Tizard: Enquiry into the psychological development of Mongol babies.
>
> Dr B. M. Mandelbrote: Retrospective and prospective study of admissions and discharges treated in a special therapeutic setting at Littlemore Hospital.
>
> Dr B. H. Kirman: Retrospective survey of hydrocephalus and spina bifida cystica in mental retardation.
>
> Professor E. M. Anderson: A long-term study of termination of pregnancy on psychiatric grounds taking social, economic and other factors into account.
>
> Dr Kushlick: A controlled evaluation of a new form of institutional care for subnormal children over three years.
>
> Dr Murray Parkes: A longitudinal study at the Tavistock Institute of the reaction of women under 65 to the loss of a husband.
>
> Dr C. M. Drillien: Longitudinal study of the growth and development of singletons and twins of different birth weight.

For their bearing on the problem of data linkage a few details are given here of the studies directed by:

Professor Carstairs, MRC Unit for Research in Epidemiology of Psychiatric Illness, University of Edinburgh.

A social classification of the City of Edinburgh using a linkage analysis technique and based on census data and variables such as: rent arrears; peace warnings; road accidents; juvenile delinquency; self-poisonings and injury; school absence (other than sickness).

Professor W. M. Millar, Department of Mental Health, University of Aberdeen.

'Formation of a case register of all referrals to the psychiatric services in North East Scotland: a cumulative record of the psychiatric experience of all patients which includes detailed demographic, social, clinical and patient movement data. Semi-automated record matching and linkage experiments are being carried out using data processing machines. The register permits both cross-sectional and longitudinal analysis of total treated psychiatric morbidity which will have application in both epidemiological and operational contexts.'

UNIVERSITY OF LONDON
CENTRE FOR THE STUDY OF HUMAN DEVELOPMENT
Longitudinal research in psychological development
This project directed by Dr C. B. Hindley, is working in close collaboration with a parallel study of the physical development of the same children, under the direction of Professor J. M. Tanner of the Institute of Child Health. There is also collaboration, under the auspices of the International Children's Centre, with five other researches in Europe which are using similar methods and with centres in Africa and the U.S.A. This enables comparison of results to be made.

Subjects of the main sample, numbering 220, were recruited before birth between 1951–3, and were in 1969 aged 15–17 years. The sample is reasonably representative socio-economically of the population of central London, and did not differ significantly from Census data.

The aims of the study have been to obtain information as comprehensive as the small staff permitted on the development of personality and abilities, in relation to social background and parental attitudes and methods, and to relate later characteristics to earlier.

Methods from infancy onwards have included psychological testing, rating of personality qualities, observations, and interviews with the subjects. Their mothers have been regularly interviewed about changes in the family background, the child's behaviour, and her own methods with the child. Apart from the test results, the case-histories contain the kind of information normally obtained by child guidance clinics, but contemporaneously collected.

Over thirty papers have been published, covering methodological questions, social class and sex differences in general ability and language ability in the first eight years of life; personality characteristics and their change with age, as revealed by doll-play techniques; sleep characteristics in infancy: a follow-up of anoxic children; a follow-up of children whose mothers worked during their early life; difficulties of adjustment to school; and collaborative papers comparing maternal methods with infants, and factors associated with age of onset of walking, in five European samples. [Papers have appeared under the names of C. B. Hindley, T. Moore, L. E. Ucko – (35), (49), (50), (51), (156), (157), (207), (208), (279).]

Present research efforts are directed towards:

1. a factorial study of the composition of abilities in infancy and early childhood, and the predictiveness of different aspects of early ability;
2. consistencies in personality qualities in the course of development, and factors affecting them.

THE UNIVERSITY OF NOTTINGHAM CHILD DEVELOPMENT
   RESEARCH UNIT
The Nottingham survey of child-bearing attitudes and practices
A long term study is being carried out by John and Elizabeth Newson at Nottingham University with the general aim of

providing a detailed picture of the way children are being brought up in a contemporary urban setting. In particular, it is concerned to explore the 'moral atmospheres' in the home whereby children's behaviour is evaluated and interpreted to the child in 'good/ naughty' terms, and the eventual effect of such evaluations upon the development of 'conscience' in the child.

The group of 700 children being studied comprises a class-stratified random sample representative of children born in the years 1959–60 and resident within the Nottingham city boundary, recent immigrants, illegitimate children and those with gross handicaps diagnosed by the age of 12 months being excluded. Information is obtained by means of home interviews with the mothers. A report on Phase I, which dealt with the first year of life, has already been published.[1] This phase was undertaken without any financial support, and was only made possible by the use of health visitors, employed by the Nottingham Health Department, to do the bulk of the interviewing. For obvious reasons it seemed preferable to recruit an independent team of interviewers for the later stages of the research, and this was made possible by the Nuffield Foundation's sponsorship of the second and third phases of the project, which focused successively upon the 4-year-old and the 7-year-old child. A detailed study of the children and their mothers at the 4-year-old stage was published in 1968[2]; and the fieldwork for Phase III, the same group of children at seven years, is on the point of completion. The Social Science Research Council has now assumed financial responsibility for the period ending October 1970, and the work is expected to continue until the children reach late adolescence.

A feature of the Nottingham study is that it now makes use of a small team of married women interviewers who have been rigorously selected and trained for this particular work. As far as possible, successive interviews at the different stages are carried out by the same interviewer. A schedule of considerable length

---

[1] Newson, John and Elizabeth, *Infant Care in an Urban Community* (Allen and Unwin, London, 1963).

[2] Newson, John and Elizabeth, *Four Years Old in an Urban Community* (Allen and Unwin, 1968).

and complexity is used as the core of an otherwise flexible interview, and portable tape recorders allow verbatim transcripts to be made. The mothers are encouraged to elaborate or modify their answers to any given question as much as they wish, both in order to achieve a very full picture of parent and child behaviour, and equally to throw as much light as possible upon the motivation underlying behaviour. The project should thus complement the findings from the national surveys by sampling parental attitudes and feelings in considerably greater depth than is possible when data-collection has to be accomplished at a distance and interpreted without reference to special knowledge of local customs and conditions.

LONGITUDINAL STUDIES IN DEVELOPING COUNTRIES
(We are indebted to Dr David Morley, of the University of London Institute of Child Health, for supplying the literature on which the following note is based.)

There is an urgent need for studies of representative samples of families in village and urban communities of the developing countries to identify diseases, to trace their origins, and to measure their effects. In spite of its difficulties the successful longitudinal study incontestably provides the best basis for planning future medical services. Its place in this field of research has been the subject of a WHO publication by Dr F. J. W. Miller: *The principles underlying the design of a family health study* (WHO Report MHO/PA/144.62). For its connection with measures for inducing change in ideas and customs the following work provides a valuable background: Paul, B. D. *Health Culture and Community* (Russell Sage Foundation, New York, 1955).

Only by a long-term study is it possible to discover even approximately the real medical needs of a community. Cross-sectional studies and hospital figures give misleading estimates of requirements. The Newcastle study found that in England roughly one-third of the work of the family doctor is concerned with children, but of the children seen only 2 to 3 per cent will be referred to hospital. This subject is treated in King (Ed.), *Medical Care in Developing Countries* (Oxford University Press, 1966), which gives details of a procedure for using the date of birth in the record number to separate hospital records into age-groups, a technique used in the Imesi Study.

Africa has provided longitudinal studies in:

The Gambia: Malarial research by Dr I. A. McGregor of the MRC Unit at Fajara (References in *B. Med. J.*, 1962, *2*, 386).

Kampala: Dr H. Welbourn.

W. Nigeria: Dr Bromley and associates at Imesi and Ilesha.

S. Africa: Kark, S. L. and Stewart, G. W., *A Practice of Social Medicine* (Livingstone, 1963).

The Imesi and Ilesha studies

The study of morbidity and mortality in 405 African children from before birth to 5 years of age began in the village of Imesi, Western Nigeria, in January 1957, and has been supplemented by data on admissions to the children's ward of the hospital at Ilesha, a town twenty-five miles away. It was designed to find answers to questions relating to:

(a) the incidence of major diseases in childhood;
(b) the rate of growth in height, weight, and a number of other standard aspects of physical growth;
(c) child-rearing practices and their effects;
(d) the effectiveness of a simple form of malaria prophylaxis in one half of the children.

The course of the inquiry led also to two special studies, (i) of measles, and (ii) of the effect on the child community of offering first a curative and secondly a preventive medical service.

The findings of the studies were applied in developing 'The Under-Fives Clinic' at the Ilesha hospital (see King, M., *Medical Care in Developing Countries*, Oxford University Press, 1966).

REFERENCES

(a) CUTHBERTSON, W. F. J., 'A health and weight chart for children from birth to five', *W. African Med. J.*, *11*, (6), 237–40 (1962).
(b) MORLEY, D., 'A medical service for children under five years of age in West Africa', *Trans. Roy. Soc. Trop. Med.* (January, 1963).

(c) MORLEY, D., WOODLAND, M. and MARTIN, W. J., 'Measles in Nigerian children', *J. Hyg. Camb.*, *61*, 115–118 (1963).
(d) MARTIN, W. J., MORLEY, D. and WOODLAND, M., 'Intervals between births in a Nigerian village', *J. Trop. Ped.*, *10* (3), 82–5 (1964).

And some of the important findings:

From (a) above: A previous difficulty in collecting data had been the impossibility of obtaining accurate dates of birth. In the prospective study these are known and as a result the first figures were produced on heights and weights of West African children, arranged in percentile form. Many months, at times over a year, of failure to grow preceded the onset of malnutrition: in developing areas we should seek the positive achievement of 'normal' growth rather than 'prevent' malnutrition.

From (c) above: The disease in West Africa seems to resemble measles as seen in England before the twentieth century, and requires a fresh hypothesis as to its cause.

From (d) above: The possibility of calculating birth intervals in the area and of suggesting reasons for their variation. The population explosion in developing countries emphasizes the value of fundamental information on birth intervals. The 'reasonable' spacing of births would be highly advantageous to child health. In the developing countries the rearing of young children is fraught with danger, and the inopportune arrival of a younger sibling may be disastrous for the nutrition and health of the older.

APPENDIX V

COHORTS, STAGES AND EPOCHS
by G. F. Peaker

> 'Gather ye rosebuds while ye may,
> Old Time is still a-flying:
> And this same flower that smiles today,
> To-morrow will be dying!'

Cohorts pass through stages as the epoch advances. Herrick's contemporaries are the cohort of 1591; Shakespeare's the cohort of 1564. Survivors of both cohorts made the population of England in 1600. Thus if we label successive cohorts, C_1, C_2, C_3, etc., we have:

Stage	*Epoch*			
	1	2	3	4
4	C_1	C_2	C_3	C_4
3	C_2	C_3	C_4	C_5
2	C_3	C_4	C_5	C_6
1	C_4	C_5	C_6	C_7

The investigator can choose his course through the diagram, according to his needs and his resources. If his race must soon be run he can take the first column, look at each of the cohorts in that column at the beginning and the end of the first epoch, and assume that each cohort is rather like those that come before and after. Given a sensible choice of cohorts, stages and epochs this is likely to be roughly true. In the same school fourth forms do not vary *much* from one year to the next. On the other hand they will vary *somewhat*, and if he is interested in this, and his resources permit, he can find out how much they vary by continuing with the next year (column or epoch). Further, if his resources permit, he can continue with the next year, and the next after that. If he is able to do this he can group his results by stages at the same epoch (columns), by epochs at the same stage (rows), and by cohorts (diagonals). Columns give the contemporary scene. Rows give trends. Diagonals, like Herrick, follow the individual through stages and epochs.

If time is short there is nothing for it but to take a single epoch, representing the available time, and to follow successive cohorts across it. This is not the same thing as a cross-sectional study, which would take the beginning, the middle or the end of the epoch, or some other point of time within it, and make the observations then, taking them to represent progress from birth, the beginning of schooling, or some other starting-point which may be rather vague. If more time is available there is a choice between following a single cohort and spreading the effort over several cohorts.

In principle the latter is to be preferred, unless there are strong grounds for supposing that trends are unimportant. A light sampling of several cohorts can give information about trends which cannot be obtained if the sampling is concentrated on a single cohort. At a time like the present when changes are occurring with great rapidity, trends seem likely to be important for most inquiries. If so this is a strong argument for light sampling of several cohorts rather than intensive sampling of one. An example of extreme concentration is provided by the case where the cohort sampled consists of the children born in a particular week of a particular year, and where the sample is identical with the population. Since this plan abandons at the outset the possibility of obtaining any information about trends, or indeed about differences arising from birthdays at different times of the year, very strong grounds of convenience are needed to recommend it, in comparison with the alternative of taking the children born on the nth day of each month, or every other month, or every third month, and so on.

Defining the population under scrutiny as those born on certain fairly widely spaced days, over two, three, or more years, has two further advantages. In the first place, the field work can be uniformly spread. Secondly, it can be changed if the early results show that part of it is to be fruitless, and general experience suggests that this is likely to be the case, however carefully the original plan is made. This also applies to the computations. All experience shows that it is unlikely that the plan adopted at the outset for summarizing the results will be altogether satisfactory. If the work proceeds by the light sampling of several cohorts instead of by the intensive sampling of one, the computations, like the field work, can be improved in the light of experience as the work proceeds. There is no difficulty about planning a computer programme to aggregate, or to differentiate between, different stages, trends, and cohorts. Both the aggregations and the differences may turn out to be important.

Although it seems unlikely that there will be a balance of advantage in concentrating the cohort into a particular week of birth there may be, for some inquiries, a decided net gain in concentration by structure. Thus for school inquiries it is generally advantageous to make the primary sampling unit the school, rather than the individual pupil. This is likely also to be the case for colleges, hospitals, firms and other organic units. When the sampling is on this basis it is important to discover the design effect, which is that ratio of the number of pupils (or doctors, or nurses, or employees, or what not) actually drawn in the sample to the number needed in a simple equivalent sample that would give standard errors of the same size. Although the formulae for the design effect are usually complicated, and frequently unknown, the effects themselves can always be found, with enough accuracy, by the comparison of sub-samples which can easily be done automatically on the computer. In the case of the school enough is known already to enable efficient designs to be made, in the sense of securing the optimal distribution of the sample between and within schools. In other cases there is probably enough information to make quite a good first shot, which could be improved for subsequent samples by making use of the comparisons available from the first. On experience so far it appears that design effects, though by no means negligible, are usually small enough, if full use is made of stratification, to secure major economies from structural or complex sampling. It is a further fortunate circumstance that they appear to be rather generally smaller for multivariate than for univariate analysis.

The argument about structure also applies to localities. Thus for school inquiries the simple rule of taking 3 per cent of the variation among stratified local authorities, 7 per cent among stratified schools, and the remaining 90 per cent among pupils within stratified schools has been found to give good prior estimates of the sampling variation, in the sense that these prior estimates agree closely with the posterior estimates made after the fieldwork has been done. If the work is to be done in only one or two localities it would be better to select them by judgement rather than at random from within strata. The object of the judgement would be to exemplify the full range.

In brief, the argument of this short paper is that to concentrate on a single narrowly defined cohort is rather unlikely to give an optimum return for the labour expended. It would be better to spread the effort over a succession of lightly sampled cohorts. On the other hand when the inquiry is largely concerned with organic structures, such as schools, hospitals, firms, or localities, concentration to the extent of using complex sampling designs based on these structures will usually pay off.

APPENDIX VI

THE VALUE OF SMALL-SAMPLE, INTENSIVE LONGITUDINAL STUDIES
by C. B. Hindley

LARGE-SAMPLE SURVEYS

There is no doubt that large-scale surveys of the type of Douglas and Pringle and Butler are of great value (see p. 37). Their main virtue lies in the fact that they are able to use a sample which is as representative as possible of the population being sampled at a particular time. This permits of maximal generalization of their findings.

Such surveys should be regarded as longitudinal epidemiological studies, in which the focus of attention is on the broad incidence of various characteristics in a population, with the added factor of change through time. Data tend to be analysed in terms of sociological categories, and conclusions of an actuarial kind are often reached. While the point of departure is usually practically rather than theoretically orientated, the findings have undoubted relevance to many theoretical expectations.

The main limitation of such surveys comes from the same characteristic as their advantage, namely sample size. So far as psychological development is concerned this necessarily includes the use of crude indices of behaviour characteristics. Thus, reliance has to be placed on the assessment of abilities on easily administered pencil and paper tests; personality characteristics also either have to be assessed by such techniques, or from assessments made by many judges (often unskilled), or simply from such concrete facts as attendance at clinics, appearance before a court, etc.

INTENSIVE SMALL-SAMPLE STUDIES

These are called for where the main focus of interest lies in the study of processes of development. The ultimate aim is naturally to produce generalizable findings, but reliance is placed not so much on having a strictly representative sample, which may be impossible to attain, as on the possibility of replicating important findings.

192

This is the normal procedure in scientific inquiry, in which it is by no means assumed that any one investigation will produce conclusive answers.

By means of such comparisons from a number of American longitudinal studies a substantial body of evidence exists on the consistency of the development of intelligence from infancy onwards – see Bloom (12); on the increasing association of IQ during early childhood with social class; on the relative persistence of personality traits during early childhood and from childhood to adulthood – Kagan and Moss (40) and Bronson (302, 303).

A second means of replication lies in the deliberate use of similar methods. Thus the five European studies (and others) whose collaboration the International Children's Centre is sponsoring, are using a common base-line of methods for the study of both psychological and physical development – Falkner (24). It cannot be too heavily stressed that a survey will be successful to a large degree to the extent that there is already in existence a considerable body of fundamental knowledge, and suggestive evidence, which will guide the planners of such a survey in the selection of variables likely to be of significance.

AREAS OF RESEARCH FOR WHICH INTENSIVE STUDIES
ARE VALUABLE

General Studies from Birth to Maturity: Characteristic of these is the attempt to obtain a fairly comprehensive coverage of the different aspects of physical and psychological development.

These have proved their value both in studying particular aspects of development through time – such as intelligence, stability of personality traits, aspects of physical growth – and in the study of inter-relationships among such aspects.

Noteworthy in the U.S.A. have been the study at the Fels Research Institute (see p. 129), and the Guidance Study at Berkeley (see p. 134). In Britain the one example is the joint study of the University of London Institutes of Education and Child Health, which is collaborating with the European studies through the International Children's Centre (see p. 182).

SPECIAL STUDIES

Topic orientated: If it is desired to know the course of development in individuals of any function, longitudinal study will be necessary. This applies for example to the study of conceptual development, specific abilities, personality traits, anatomical dimensions, physiological and biochemical functions.

Special group orientated: Here the questions will be about the course of development of spastic or premature babies, the illegitimate, or, at the other end of the spectrum, of specially bright groups of children.

Experimental Studies: Systematic experimental manipulation of certain variables may be carried out, and the subsequent long-term effects followed up.

APPENDIX VII

LIKELY OUTCOMES OF LONGITUDINAL STUDIES

This appendix gives, in more detail than would be suitable in the main body of the report, the general outcomes expected from the third phase of the PIC (1946) Study, the first and second phases of the NCDS (1958) Study, and a statement, by way of illustration, of what a Ministry (in this case the Home Office) might expect to gain from longitudinal studies. Each section has been prepared for us at our request by its author, at very short notice.

For comparative purposes, we give below the actual costs of similar studies currently in progress.

1. *The National Child Development Study, 1958*
   First 3-year sweep: Tracing and survey of 16,000 children; cross-sectional and longitudinal analysis.
   Staff: Co-Directors (2) part-time.
   Senior Research Officer.
   Average Annual Cost: £20,000
   Second sweep (4 years): Tracing and survey of 16,000 children; cross-sectional and longitudinal analysis.
   Staff: Co-Directors (2) part-time.
   Senior Research Officer.
   Research Officers (2) Medical and Sociological.
   Average estimated Annual Cost: £23,000

2. *The Streaming Inquiry (NFER)*
   Schools: Age-group studies and Cross-sectional surveys.
   Staff: Research Officers (3)
   Technical Assistants (2).
   Average Annual Cost: £13,000.

3. *French in Primary Schools (NFER)*
   Staff: Research Officers (3).

Technical Assistants (2).
Average Annual Cost: £13,500.

4. *Isle of Wight Studies*
3 age-groups of children totalling 3,300.
The costs are given in Professor Tizard's report within studies reproduced in Appendix IV.

THE PIC (1946) STUDY

by J. W. B. Douglas

We intend to have a major sweep at 25 to provide information that will allow us to assess in terms of leisure interests, job satisfaction and personal adjustment the results of the whole process of education. We chose this age because by that time the majority of the young people will have finished their full-time education, and their future careers will be relatively well defined. In the intervening period we are taking specific topics of special interest to ask them about. For example, last year we collected information on smoking and on respiratory troubles in addition to keeping up with their occupational histories and use of the medical services.

I find it very difficult to know what will happen after these young people are 25. The problems of keeping contact with them are certain to increase, and from many points of view the sample becomes in any event unsatisfactory. For example, marriages and births are so widely spread that it would be very many years before we would have an adequate return, and it would be a very complex and rather messy administrative problem to arrange, for example, that the mothers were seen and the infants assessed at a specific date after the confinement and thereafter at various intervals.

I think it is likely that after these young people are 25 we will be content to get as much information fed back to us as possible from official sources. There appears to be no difficulty in getting information on criminal activities that are known, but so far we see no certain means of getting routine reports of visits to general practitioners, attendances at hospital out-patient and in-patient

196

departments, etc.; nor of job changes. The whole situation would, of course, be changed if record linkage came in.

While it is unlikely that we will keep close personal touch with all the individual members of the sample after 25 there may well be some special groups which we will follow.

NATIONAL CHILD DEVELOPMENT STUDY (1958 COHORT)

by Ronald Davie

As with most longitudinal studies, the value of the National Child Development Study is directly related to its duration; the analysis of long-term effects is potentially the most rewarding. However, at each successive 'sweep', three kinds of analysis become possible: first, current, or cross-sectional, analyses; second, longitudinal analyses relating current data to currently obtained retrospective data, and third, longitudinal analyses relating current data to data gathered prospectively at some earlier stage.

Cross-sectional analyses

It is as well to have in mind that each 'sweep' when carried out on a national cohort of a substantial size produces valuable normative data, many of which are not available from any other source at the present time.

The first report of the study contained a large number of such descriptive statistics on, for example, educational retardation at the infant stage, contacts between school and home, mobility, school attendance, anomalous parental situations, children's behaviour and adjustment, and a wide range of medical conditions. The second report, planned for the autumn of this year, will contain similar data on height and weight and the utilization of medical services, and will also incorporate the results for Scotland and Wales.

In addition to the descriptive statistics it was possible in the first report to examine the 'effect' of social class upon educational attainment and adjustment in school, of parental situation and parental interest upon reading attainment; and to investigate sex differences over a wide field of developmental characteristics.

The second report will contain a few more social analyses and also broad regional comparisons.

It is realized that the social-class analysis, whilst a useful first step, does not carry us very far. Thus it is planned to examine the effects of particular aspects of the environment upon attainments and health, although pressure of time precludes the possibility of including this in the second report. The comprehensive nature of the current data also lends itself to the later exploration of many other interesting and potentially fruitful avenues such as the relationship between minimal physical inco-ordination, perceptual difficulties, particular kinds of behavioural difficulties and educational retardation; and the effect of type and size of school and size of class upon attainment and adjustment.

Longitudinal analyses utilizing retrospective data
Retrospectively-gathered information inevitably carries with it an element of unreliability. For this reason the amount of retrospective data collected in the seven-year-old sweep was minimal. However, where such information covers events in the recent past and is of a more or less objective nature, its utilization becomes a viable proposition.

In the first report of the study it was possible, for example, to examine and reach important conclusions about the effects of length of schooling upon reading, arithmetic and adjustment at the age of 7. Although the effect of nursery schooling upon attainments and adjustment has not yet been tackled the data lends itself to an investigation of this question.

Longitudinal analysis utilizing prospectively gathered data
The comprehensive nature of the perinatal information, prospectively gathered, is one of the study's most important features. Nowhere else in the world has comparable data been collected on a national cohort.

Much is known about the conditions at birth which are associated with increased risk of death during the perinatal period. However, our knowledge of the risk of handicap in surviving children is much more fragmentary.

Thus, the potential value of the analysis of relationships

198

between perinatal conditions and current status is great both in terms of preventive medicine and also in relation to the prediction of adverse outcomes, so that available medical and educational resources can be most effectively – and economically – deployed in the early detection of handicapped children.

The value of such analyses is, however, matched by its complexity. The principal difficulty is the intercorrelation of the perinatal factors. Thus, babies who are born early also tend to be lighter in weight than those born at term; the mothers of such children tend to be of lower socio-economic status and to have less adequate ante-natal care; and such births are more frequently accompanied, or preceded, by some obstetric complication. If, then, low birth-weight children are found on follow-up to be handicapped one must be satisfied that this cannot be explained in terms of early gestation, low socio-economic status, poor ante-natal care or obstetric complication. Or, perhaps, some other factor. Clearly, some form of multivariate analysis is called for.

The perinatal variables which it is planned to consider first are: birth weight; duration of pregnancy; birth order; maternal age; maternal height; maternal blood pressure; bleeding in pregnancy; method of delivery; single/multiple pregnancy; maternal smoking; and sex. Socio-economic variables will also be utilized in the analyses in order to partial out their effect.

The outcome variables which will be used at this stage are: reading ability; social adjustment; physical co-ordination; activity level; height; vision; speech; hearing; and enuresis.

Severe handicaps such as cerebral palsy may need to be examined in a rather different fashion. The number of children involved in specific categories of severe handicap will be small in a normative cohort, even when the total number of children in the cohort is as high as 16,000. Some investigation of such conditions may, then, more fruitfully be of a descriptive rather than statistical nature. However, many severe handicaps represent extremes of continua and differ in degree rather than in kind from minimal dysfunction. Where this is the case, numbers should be large enough to permit statistical analysis.

Clearly, the result of the perinatal analyses will be of particular importance and relevance to those concerned with the early detection of handicap: obstetricians, paediatricians and general practitioners. Local health authorities maintain 'At Risk Registers' at the present time, but the proportion of births entered on such registers varies widely from one authority to another.

Guidance is urgently needed, and the National Child Development Study is in a unique position to provide it.

NOTES ON HOME OFFICE NEEDS IN RELATION TO LONGITUDINAL STUDIES

by W. H. Hammond[1]

1. The Home Office has wide responsibilities for the care and upbringing of those children for whom normal family arrangements are either not available or are unsuitable, and who as a consequence are adopted, fostered or taken into care in residential homes. For these the Home Office has statutory charge, jointly with the local authority of the area concerned. Additionally the Home Office is responsible for penal measures which the courts may order as a result of delinquent acts and, through the police, for bringing such acts to the notice of the courts.

2. The Home Office's main need is therefore for multi-disciplinary longitudinal studies which will help to suggest community or individual preventive measures, in the first place, and which will also inform Home Office policy in devising the most appropriate measures to take with the children in its residential or penal institutions or subject to the other disposals of the courts.

3. Any treatment involves a time sequence and a preliminary diagnostic process or classification, and in the present instance it includes the identification of the special needs which distinguish the children under Home Office care from other children. This implies a knowledge of children's normal behaviour and development; hence the Home Office must rely heavily on what have become known as longitudinal cohort studies, to identify the factors which are common to children in other groups of the

---

[1] Dr Hammond has asked that it should be made clear that these are personal and not necessarily official views.

population and those which are specific to the particular groups for which the Home Office has sole or joint responsibility.

4. Cross-sectional studies of the population undertaken at different ages could provide much of the information needed, but for diagnostic and predictive purposes the information should include developmental concepts which take account of the *relations* between different events, and in particular their sequence.

5. The examples below of the specific contribution which longitudinal survey-type studies could provide are concerned with predicting, preventing and dealing with juvenile delinquency, but the same principles apply to other fields within the Home Office responsibility, especially the child-care field.

6. The basic difficulty about the application of information from longitudinal cohort studies to treatment problems and to administration is that, whereas the most effective form of information-gathering in longitudinal studies is contemporaneously (so as to avoid the selective distorting influence of memory), it is not possible to obtain this information in the same way in the special groups, except for the few children who form part of the longitudinal studies themselves, because the handicaps, etc., may occur at some point in the child's development subsequent to the events being recorded. In the same way information of a kind which needs special expertise to collect can be used to advance knowledge, but before much of this information can be used in practical situations it will be necessary to develop objective indications of underlying syndromes.

This suggests that the most immediately useful information is of the hard factual kind which can be recalled with least distortion and which can be checked upon if necessary. In general, the simpler and more widely ascertainable the information in cohort studies, the more useful it is for administrative purposes.

7. The following list indicates the sort of information which could best be obtained from longitudinal studies (it does not claim to be in any way exhaustive).

   1. Concomitants of crime or other handicaps; to increase

theoretical knowledge about incidence and causation of these conditions.

2. Simple objective precursors of crime which can be applied retrospectively in a diagnostic way. Specifically, it would be desirable to identify 'social underprivilege' in a wider sense than poverty (by analogy with under-nutrition) and social malfunctioning or maladjustment (analogous to nutritional imbalance).

   In either case we would then have grounds for tackling the associated social inadequacy or social malfunctioning or distortion, in behaviour other than the delinquency itself.

3. *Predictive information.* By identifying the characteristics which subsequently differentiate delinquents from non-delinquents, or those with subsequent handicaps from those without, we can recognize the sectors of the population which are at the greatest risk – hence preventive educational or other measures might be directed specially to these groups. This is probably the main value of longitudinal surveys to the Home Office.

4. Cohort studies could also be used to provide estimates of fringe anti-social behaviour or 'unofficial' delinquent conduct which would possibly be more relevant than actual court cases for identifying 'at risk' groups and deciding what preventive or remedial educative measures should be initiated by the community.

5. Community programmes applied to the whole of defined social groups so as to change their attitudes or behaviour fall within the scope of longitudinal cohort studies, and these would require longitudinal (follow-up) investigation to assess their value.

6. Some of the above information might have to be undertaken anonymously within the cohort, using certain *group* identification such as social-economic grouping, type of school, family size and so on. The purpose of such an exercise would be to supplement the knowledge of official delinquency which is contained in Home Office statistical records. It would also enable us to see how far the attitudes towards delinquency and acceptance of different standards are

paralleled by the observed delinquency rates. Any differences might indicate the extent of social factors in the identification process itself.

The place of special registers and official records in longitudinal studies

7. A series of age samples (cohorts) might have basic statistical information assembled together among the various official records kept by the General Register Office, Department of Education and Science, and Divisions concerned with crime, child-care, etc., in the Home Office. The data would consist of material collected for administrative purposes, without any special survey being undertaken, and without the individuals being aware that they were the object of a follow-up study. Theoretically such a scheme would involve all children in so far as most of the General Register Office information and most of the educational returns would apply to everybody within the age group. Information about ESN children, notifiable diseases, Children's Department records of children coming into care, etc., and data on convictions would, of course, only apply to special sub-groups. The identification of special handicapped groups would be treated mainly as sorting criteria when studying the information common to all children, with the object of producing syndromes corresponding to the categories.

8. Census-type data for providing sampling framework for short-term follow-up studies.

Special studies might be laid on from time to time rather like census collections, but related to individuals and not households as the unit. These could well be cross-sectional, undertaken mainly for establishing the prevalence of different conditions in the community. They could then be used to provide a sampling framework for mounting relatively short-term follow-up studies (possibly with cyclical overlap) which could together cover a wide age-range, but without the time-lag necessary for individuals to pass through the whole cycle from birth to maturity.

9. The most critical gap in present knowledge so far as the

Home Office needs are concerned consists of the detailed information about the early years of children's upbringing, since this information had to be obtained too late in the NCDS (1958 Cohort) Study, and it is critical to decisions on adoption and boarding out.

10. Longitudinal studies have mostly been concerned with samples of children within a narrow age-range, but the family follow-up studies have a most important part to play in the future.

APPENDIX VIII

A PROPOSAL FOR AN INSTITUTE FOR THE STUDY OF HUMAN DEVELOPMENT AND SOCIAL CHANGE

In the main text (p. 64) we have set out some of the tasks to be discharged as we see them, and proposed the alternatives of a central committee working through existing agencies and having no executive functions of its own, and some form of permanent executive agency or institute. Since our terms of reference specifically charged us to make proposals for organization and finance, we went carefully into the idea of an executive agency – particularly since we believe that certain essential aspects of longitudinal data-gathering and analysis are unlikely to be undertaken by highly-motivated individuals or even by universities without clear-cut institutional support. We therefore set out below proposals for an *Institute for the Study of Human Development and Social Change*, together with some inevitably tentative suggestions as to its finance, affiliation and control.

The conduct of follow-through studies of large samples requires widespread co-operation from many services. There is no reason to suppose that any one type of organization will obviate this entirely, and it is undesirable that it should. The two British national studies in existence have been outstandingly successful in gaining and keeping this co-operation, largely because the principal professional organizations concerned have been closely associated and identified with the projects. It seems important too that the work should be manifestly independent of government so that its findings can be free of any appearance of subjection to official censorship. Hence, the present practice of having a consultative committee representing all the organizations, public and voluntary, should be preserved. Such a body is, however, too unwieldy to decide upon policy and, by and large, not likely to be sufficiently expert to consider scientific questions.

It is suggested, therefore, that the Social Science Research Council should set up a small policy-making and policy-controlling *executive* body as the government of the proposed Institute, and that this body should be served by a scientific advisory committee. These two might come into being at the earliest possible moment, in order that they should undertake the detailed planning and sponsoring of the negotiations necessary to set up the Institute. The executive body, under its chairman, would be responsible for the management of the Institute's affairs, especially for its finance and representation on the SSRC. On it would be represented the consultative committee, and the staff of the Institute. The scientific advisory committee would be appointed from among the members of the executive, with some co-options. It should consist of scientists from all the relevant disciplines (the medical and biological as well as the social sciences); and have the power to set up, as necessary, small research planning groups, or to employ and pay consultants.

Finance

The cost of such a project depends directly on what its scope and final design are decided to be, and only the bare outline can be given here. This is based on what appear to be the reasonable assumptions: (a) That the Institute's programme should be viable in itself, but open-ended in the sense that it can act as a focus and co-ordinating agent for related work conducted and financed by others; (b) That light sampling is all that is strictly necessary for national groups if they are supported by larger regional samples; (c) That full co-operation can be ensured from official statistical sources; and (d) That some at least of the regional groups will in part be financed regionally. It further assumes that, nationally at all events, there will be a number of overlapping age-groups, with the present NCDS study maintained as a long-range one, and a further one started in 1970. Partial age-range groups timed to straddle critical periods of growth would be fitted into this pattern, particularly to study problems of adolescence, middle life, ageing and retirement, if these were thought to be important.

A central office to maintain the national studies, a study in its adjacent region, and to assure the task of liaison with official bodies, other regional studies and related work, would probably require a director and five professional staff with ancillary clerical

206

and data-analysing facilities. This suggests an *annual* budget of between £35,000 and £40,000. The costs of further regional studies would vary according to the extent and intensity of the data sought, the size of the sample chosen, and the degree to which they achieved local financial support. We may venture the estimate – based upon a scientific staff of two with clerical, administrative and statistical support – that each might cost annually not more than £17,000 in all.

The cost of detailed, intensive longitudinal studies of samples of particular groups of children is very difficult to estimate, and depends almost entirely upon the number and kind of the special examinations undertaken. Careful planning in advance would probably reduce costs since many categories overlap, and might well lead institutions with special interests to undertake from their own resources longitudinal studies on subjects selected from regional or national samples. Similarly, such studies or aspects of them seem to be of the kind which appeal to benevolent foundations and charitable bodies with particular interests. We might expect a study of a single group of, say 200–300 subjects to require three research staff. On this basis, rough estimates of annual costs would be £9,000 (one study) and £15,000 (two related studies). A sum of £18,000–£20,000 annually should enable a suitable unit to study three or even four related groups.

Affiliation

So far we have spoken as though the central Institute were to have a completely independent existence. This assumption needs exploring. The 1946 study was originally housed in the Usher Institute of Edinburgh University, and has subsequently become an MRC unit affiliated to the London School of Economics. The Child Development longitudinal study (Institute of Education, Institute of Child Health, London University) was an enterprise of the University of London, and its staff belonged formally to one or other of the sponsoring institutes. The NCDS (1958 Cohort) is formally sponsored by four medical, social and educational institutions and is administered by the National Bureau for Co-operation in Child Care, whose director is co-director of the study.

The important considerations, after the assurance of financial stability and viability, are those of administrative and scientific continuity, administrative economy, and the possibility for staff to have contacts outside their immediate field. We must expect intermediate and junior staff – even when basic security of tenure is guaranteed – to wish to move in and out of projects. It is, on the other hand, highly desirable that the over-all direction of a long-term inquiry should be stable. Small independent units tend to be administratively more expensive, to become somewhat claustrophobic, and to be over-dependent upon the stability of their staff. Hence – at least in its early years – the proposed Institute should, we think, be set up in association with an existing organization concerned with related fields of work and able to supply at least an institutional continuity. Best of all, it should have as its director someone of distinction in the behavioural sciences and who is likely himself or herself to be prepared to consider long-term commitment to it.

If, as was suggested earlier, the NCDS 1958 Cohort becomes the nucleus of the Institute's programme, then it would seem both practical and just to affiliate the Institute to the parent body, the National Bureau for Co-operation in Child Care. The staff of the study, the NBCCC, and the co-directors have gained a most valuable experience of this kind of work which should not be lost. The NBCCC is a relatively small, independent, but in the main publicly financed body with a considerable range of research projects in the social field, a small but highly competent staff, a wide range of contacts in the social, educational and medical services, both statutory and voluntary, and the usual range of information and documentation services. In spite of its brief existence, it has a highly creditable record of activity, publication and research. Its director has been responsible for the psychological and social aspects of the NCDS study, and is herself one of the two or three outstanding workers in the disciplines of child development and educational psychology. Her commitment to the NCDS study is undoubted.

There are, of course, other possibilities, but none which so highly commends itself. One of the other three sponsoring bodies might be prepared to house and administer the Institute. One of these, the Institute of Child Health of the University of London, has been closely associated with growth studies and has rendered considerable direct assistance of a general and statistical kind to the present one. The National Birthday Trust Fund conducted the 1958 Perinatal Survey on which the NCDS was based, and its Director of Perinatal Studies, Professor N. R. Butler, is co-director of the NCDS. The third is the National Foundation for Educational Research, which assisted considerably in the later educational phases of the 1946 Study, in the educational aspects of the NCDS, and conducts longitudinal studies of its own in the educational field. Each of these three bodies has a special relationship to the NCDS which should be recognized, but none has, like the NBCCC, a declared policy of wide interdisciplinary co-operation. It is possible, too, that a university would be a suitable host, if it were prepared to guarantee an interdisciplinary (i.e. interdepartmental) affiliation.

APPENDIX IX

SELECTED BIBLIOGRAPHY

Titles are grouped in the following broad categories and listed in alphabetical order of authorship. In a number of instances the classification has inevitably been arbitrary, especially when a publication could appropriately fall into more than one category, as is frequently the case with entries in categories E and G.

Major publications arising out of British longitudinal studies are not included in the Selected Bibliography; when reference is made to them in the review full bibliographical details will be found in footnotes to the text.

    A. Problems and Methodology in Longitudinal Research.
    B. Physical Growth.
    C. Growth and Decline of Abilities.
    D. Language Development.
    E. Behaviour Tendencies – Development, Consistency, and Variability.
    F. The Critical Period Hypothesis.
    G. Personality Development.
    H. Attitudes and Interests and Vocational Adjustment.
    I. Longitudinal Research in Education.
    J. Early invention.
    K. Papers basic to the Statistical Treatment of Human Growth Data – prepared by J. M. Tanner.

A. PROBLEMS AND METHODOLOGY IN LONGITUDINAL RESEARCH

1. ANDERSON, J. E., 'The effect of change in the social context upon the design of longitudinal research', *American Psychologist*, *12*, 377 (1957).
2. ANDERSON, J. E., 'Dynamics of development: system in progress', in D. B. Harris (Ed.), *The Concept of Development*, pp. 25–46 (University of Minnesota Press, 1957).

3. ANDERSON, T. W., 'The use of factor analysis in the statistical analysis of multiple time series', *Technical Report No. 12, School of Aviation Medicine, Brooks A. F. Base.*

4. BALDWIN, A. L., 'The study of child behaviour and development', in Mussen, P. H. (Ed.), *Handbook of Research Methods in Child Development* (Wiley, London, 1960).

5. BAYLEY, N., 'The life span as a frame of reference in psychological research', *Vita Humana*, 6, 125–39 (1963).

6. BAYLEY, N., 'Research in child development: a longitudinal perspective', *Merrill-Palmer Quarterly*, 11, No. 3, 183–208 (1965).

7. BELL, R. Q., 'Convergence: an accelerated longitudinal approach', *Child Development*, 24, 145–52 (1953).

8 BELL, R. Q., 'An experimental test of the accelerated longitudinal approach', *Child Development*, 25, 281–6 (1954).

9. BENJAMIN, J. D., 'Methodological considerations in the validation and elaboration of psychoanalytical personality theory'. *American Journal of Orthopsychiatry*, 20, 139–56 (1950).

10. BENJAMIN, J. D., 'Prediction and psychopathological theory', in Jessner, L. and Pavenstadt, E. (Eds.), *Dynamic Psychopathology in Childhood* (Grune and Stratton, New York, 1959).

11. BLOCK, J., *The Q Sort Method in Personality Assessment and Psychiatric Research* (C. C. Thomas Springfield, Ill., 1961).

12. BLOOM, B. S., *Stability and Change in Human Characteristics* (Wiley, New York and London, 1964).

13. CHESS, S., BIRCH, H., HERZIG, M. E., KORN, S. and THOMAS, A., 'Issues in longitudinal studies', in *Behavioral Individuality in Early Childhood*, pp. 8–22 (New York University Press, 1963).

14. CHESS, S., et al., 'Distortions in developmental reporting made by parents of behaviorally disturbed children', *J. Amer. Acad. Child Psychiat.*, 5, 226–34 (1966).

15. CHIPMAN, S. S., et al., 'Research methodology and needs in perinatal studies', *Proceedings of the Conference on Research Methodology and Needs in Perinatal Studies held in Chapel Hill, N. Carolina* (C. C. Thomas, Springfield, Ill., 1966).

15a. CHIPMAN, S. S., et al., Bethesda Independent National Institute of Child Health and Human Development, Colloquium on

Longitudinal Studies, Feb. 7–10, 1965, Fort Monroe, Va., *Preliminary draft* (1965).

16. DAMON, A., 'Discrepancies between findings of longitudinal and cross-sectional studies in adult life: physique and physiology', *Human Development*, 8, No. 1, 16–22 (1965).

17. DANFORD, M. B., HUGHES, H. M. and MCNEE, R. C., 'On the analysis of repeated measurements experiments', *Biometrics*, 16, 547 (1960).

18. DAVIES, J., *Survey of Research in Gestation and Developmental Sciences* (Williams and Wilkins, Baltimore, 1966).

19. DINGHAM, H. F., Review of *Handbook of Mental Deficiency* (Ellis, N. R. (Ed.,) McGraw-Hill, 1963) [on need for developmental studies of handicapped] *Amer. J. Ment. Def.*, 70, 491–2 (1965).

20. DOLL, R. and HILL, A. B., 'Mortality in relation to smoking', Pt. 1. *Brit. Med. J.*, 30 May 1964, pp. 1399–410; Pt. 2. *Brit. Med. J.*, 6 June 1964, pp. 1460–7.

21. ELSTON, R. C. and GRIZZLE, J. E., 'Estimation of time-response curves and their confidence bands', *Biometrics*, 18, 148 (1962).

22. EPSTEIN, F. H., 'Some uses of prospective observations in the Tecumseh Community Health Study', in *Symposium on the value of prospective studies, Proc. Roy. Soc. Med.*, 66, No. 1 (1967).

23. ESCALONA, S. and HEIDER, G. M., *Prediction and Outcome: A Study in Child Development* (Basic Books, New York, 1959).

24. FALKNER, F. (Ed.), *Child Development: An International Method of Study*. Vol. V. *Modern Problems in Pediatrics* (Karger, Basel, 1960). French translation: *Croissance et Développement de l'Enfant Normal* (Masson, Paris, 1961).

25. FALKNER, F. (Ed.), *Human Development, by 29 Authorities* (Saunders, Philadelphia and London, 1966).

26. FRANK, L. K., 'Human development: an emerging scientific discipline', in Solnit, A. J. and Provence, S. A. (Eds.) *Modern Perspectives in Child Development* (International University Press, New York, 1963).

27. FURNEAUX, W. D., 'The too few chosen and the many that could be called', *Social Review Monograph* No. 7 (Keele University, 1963).

28. GARN, S. M., 'The longitudinal approach to longitudinal studies', *Colloquium on Longitudinal Studies*, convened by the National Institute of Child Health and Human Development (Bethesda, Maryland 1965).

29. GOLDFARB, N., *An Introduction to Longitudinal Analysis* (*The method of repeated observations from a fixed sample*) (Free Press of Glencoe, Illinois, 1960).

30. GOLDSTEIN, H., 'The detection of errors in data from longitudinal studies', *Proc. Ann. Reunion Child Growth Studies, Brussels, Feb. 1968* (Centre International de l'Enfance, Paris, 1968).

31. GOLDSTEIN, H., 'Longitudinal studies and the measurement of change', *The Statistician*, 18 (2), 93-117 (1968)

32. GRIER, S., 'Methodological problems in industrial ageing research', *Occup. Psychol.*, *33*, 36–45 (1959).

33. GURNEY, M. and DALY, J. F. 'A multivariate approach to estimation in periodic sample surveys', *Proc. Soc. Stat. Soc. Amer. Stat. Ass.*, *242*, (1965).

34. HARRIS, C. W. (Ed.), *Problems in Measuring Change* (University of Wisconsin Press, Madison, 1963).

35. HINDLEY, C. B., 'Some methods and findings in the comparison of data from different longitudinal samples', *Proc. 18th Internat. Cong. Psychol. Symposium 29 Longitudinal Studies of Child Development* (Moscow, 1966).

36. HONZIK, M. P., 'Personality consistency and change: some comments on papers by Bayley, Macfarlane, Moss and Kagan, and Murphy', *Vita Humana*, *7* (2), 139–42, 1964 (Presented at Symposium on Personality Consistency and Change-Perspectives from Longitudinal Research: Annual Meeting of American Psychological Association, Philadelphia, 1963).

37. HONZIK, M. P., 'Prediction of behaviour from birth to maturity' (a review of Kagan and Moss [40]), *Merrill-Palmer Q.*, *11*, No. 1 (1965).

37a. JARVIK, L. F. and ERLENMEYER-KIMLING, L., 'Mental changes and ageing: design of longitudinal studies', *Proc. 18th Internat. Cong. Psychol. Symposium 29 Longitudinal Studies of Child Development* (Moscow, 1966), pp. 116–21.

38. JEFFREY, W. E., 'A developmental dozen', *Contemporary Psychology*, *11*, 100–4 (1966).

39. JONES, H. E., 'Problems of method in longitudinal research', *Vita Humana*, *1*, 93–9 (1958).

39a. KAGAN, J., 'American longitudinal research in psychological development', *Child Development*, *35*, 1–32 (1964).

40. KAGAN, J. and MOSS, H. A., *Birth to Maturity*: A study in psychological development (Wiley, New York, 1962).

41. KESSEN, W., 'Research design in the study of developmental problems', in Mussen, P. H. (Ed.), *Handbook of Research Methods in Child Development* (Wiley, London, 1960).

42. KODLIN, D. and THOMPSON, D. J., 'An appraisal of the longitudinal approach to studies of growth and development', *Monogr. Soc. Res. Child Development*, *23*, No. 1 (1958).

43. KRIS, M., 'The use of prediction in longitudinal study', *Psychoanalytic Study of the Child*, *12*, 175–9 (1957).

44. LAWRENCE, P. S. and TIBBITTS, C., 'Recent long-term morbidity studies in Hagerstown', *Amer. J. Pub. Hlth.*, *41*, 101–7 (1951).

45. LOEVINGER, J., 'The meaning and measurement of ego development', *Amer. Psychologist*, *21*, 195–206 (1966).

46. MANNHEIM, H. and WILKINS, L. T., *Prediction Methods in Relation to Borstal Training* (H.M. Stationery Office, London, 1955).

47. MARE, G. DE LA and SERGEAN, R., 'Two methods of studying changes in absence with age', *Occup. Psychol.*, *35*, 245–52 (1961)

48. MCGRAW, M. B. and MALLOY, L. B., 'The pediatric anamnesis. Inaccuracies in eliciting developmental data', *Child Development*, *12*, 255–65 (1964).

49. MOORE, T. W., HINDLEY, C. B. and FALKNER, F., 'A longitudinal research in child development and some of its problems', *Brit. Med. J.*, *2*, 1132–7 (1954).

50. MOORE, T. W., 'Studying the growth of personality: a discussion of the uses of psychological data in a longitudinal study of child development', *Vita Humana*, *2*, 65–87 (1959).

51. MOORE, T. W., 'The place of longitudinal research in the study of child development' in Miller E. (Ed.), *Foundations of Child Psychiatry* (Pergamon Press, 1967).

52. NETCHINE, S., 'Apports de la méthode longitudinale à l'étude

de la maturation de l'électro-encéphalogramme et de ses relations avec le développement psychologique chez l'enfant normal', *Enfance, 2* (Mars/Avril, 1967).

53. OLSON, W. C., 'Developmental psychology', in Harris, C. W. (Ed.), *Encyclopedia of Educational Research* (Macmillan, New York, 1960).

54. PAGE, E. S., 'A test for a change in parameter recurring at an unknown point', *Biometrika, 42*, 523–7 (1955).

55. RAO, C. R., 'Some problems involving linear hypotheses in multivariate analysis', *Biometrika, 46*, 49 (1969).

56. RAO, C. R., 'The theory of least squares when the parameters are stochastic and its application to the analysis of growth curves', *Biometrika, 52*, 447 (1965).

57. SCHAIE, K. W., 'A general model for the study of developmental problems', *Psychol. Bull., 69*, 84–88 (1965).

58. SECORD, P. F. and BACKMAN, C. W., 'Personality theory and the problem of stability and change in individual behavior: an interpersonal approach', *Psychol. Rev., 68* (1), 21–32 (1961).

59. SOCIETY FOR EXPERIMENTAL BIOLOGY, 'Models and analogues in biology', *Symposia of the Society for Experimental Biology*, No. 14 (Cambridge University Press, 1960).

60. SOCIETY FOR GENERAL SYSTEMS RESEARCH, Papers by Von Foerster, Zoff, A. and McKay, D. M. in *Yearbook* (1960).

61. STANLEY, J. C., 'Studying status vs. manipulating variables', in Collier, R. D. and Stanley, M. E. (Eds.), *Research Design and Analysis: 2nd Annual Phi Delta Kappa Symposium on Educational Research*, pp. 173–208 (Indiana, Bloomington, 1961)

62. STEVENSON, H. W. (Ed.), 'Concept of development': a report of a conference commemorating the fortieth anniversary of the Institute of Child Development, University of Minnesota, *Monogr. Soc. Res. Child Development*, Serial No. 107 (1966).

63. STUART, M. D. and REED, R. B., 'Certain technical aspects of longitudinal studies of child health and development', *Am. J. Pub. Hlth., 41*, 85–90 (1951).

64. TESI, G., 'Some comments on the longitudinal method: Harvard-Florence Research Project', in *Compte rendu de la réunion annuelle des équipes chargées des études* (Centre International de l'Enfance, Paris, 1964).

65. TINBERGEN, J., *L'Econométrie* (A. Colin, Paris, 1954).

66. TUCKER, L. R., 'Implications of factor analysis of three-way matrices for measurement of change' in Harris, C. W., *Problems of Measuring Change* (Wisconsin University Press, Madison, 1963).

67. TUCKER, L. R., 'Determination of generalized learning curves by factor analysis', in du Bois, P. H., et al., *Factor Analysis and Related Techniques in the Study of Learning* (Washington University Technical Report, No. 7, St. Louis, 1963).

68. VANDENBERG, S. G. (Ed.), *Methods and Goals in Human Function* (Academic Press, New York, 1965).

69. WARDWELL, W. J. and BAHNSON, C. B., 'Problems encountered in behavioral science research in epidemiological studies', *Am. J. Pub. Hlth.*, *54*, 972–81 (1964).

70. WEAVER, WARREN, 'Science and complexity', *Amer. Scientist*, *34*, No. 4 (1948).

71. WERNER, H., 'The concept of development from a comparative and organismic point of view', in Harris, D. (Ed.), *The Concept of Development* (Minnesota University Press, 1957).

72. WISHART, C., 'Growth rate determination in nutrition studies with the bacon pig, and their analysis', *Biometrika*, *30*, 16 (1938).

73. ZAZZO, R., 'Les difficultés de la méthode longitudinale', *Psychologie Française*, *10*, 54–62 (1965).

74. ZAZZO, R., 'Diversité, réalité et mirages de la méthode longitudinale: Rapport introductif au symposium des études longitudinales', *Enfance*, *2* (1967). This issue contains important contributions made at the XVIIIth Congress of Psychology, Moscow, 1966, by S. W. Bijou (U.S.A.), D. P. Campbell (U.S.A.), D. B. Elkonine (U.S.S.R.), R. Fischler (U.S.A.), A. J. Harris Lovinger (U.S.A.), C. B. Hindley (G.B.), Jerome Kagan (U.S.A.), S. Netchine (France).

B. PHYSICAL GROWTH

75. AMES, R., 'Physical maturing among boys as related to adult social behavior', *California J. Ed. Res.*, *8*, 69–75 (1957).

76. BALDWIN, B. T., 'The physical growth of children from birth to maturity', *Univ. Iowa Studies in Child Welfare*, *1*, 1 (1921).

77. BERENDES, H., 'Factors associated with breech delivery', *Amer. J. Pub. Hlth.*, 55 (May 1965).

78. BRANTHAVER, C., 'The sequelae of prematurity in a school-age child', *Minn. Med.*, 49, 803–9 (1966).

79. DEARBORN, W. F. and ROTHNEY, J. W. M., *Predicting the Child's Development* (Sci-Art, Publishers, Cambridge, Mass., 1941).

80. DOUGLAS, J. W. B. and ROSS, J. M., 'Age of puberty related to educational ability, attainment, and school leaving age', *J. Child Psychol. Psychiat.*, 5, 185 (1964).

81. DREIZEN, S., et al., 'The effects of nutritive failure in the growth patterns of white children in Alabama', *Child Development*, 24, 189–202 (1953).

82. DRILLIEN, C. M., 'A longitudinal study of the growth and development of premature and maturely born children', *Ment. Developm. Arch. Dis. Child.*, Part III, 34–37 (1959).

83. EBERT, E. and SIMMONS, K., 'The Brush Foundation Study of Child Growth and Development', *Washington: Soc. Res. Child Development*, 8, No. 2 (1943).

84. EICHORN, D. H., 'Two-generation similarities in height during the first five years', in Jersild, A. T., *Psychology of Adolescence*, 2nd edition (Macmillan, New York, 1963).

85. EICHORN, D. H., 'Biological correlates of behavior', in Stevenson, H. W. (Ed.) *Yearbook Nat. Soc. Stud. Educ. Part I Child Psychology* (1963).

86. GARN, S. M., 'Fat thickness and growth progress during infancy', *Human Biol.*, 28, 232–50 (1956).

87. GARN, S. M., et al., 'Parental body build and developmental progress of the offspring', *Science*, 132, 1555–6 (1960).

88. HAMMOND, W. H., 'Some aspects of growth with norms from birth to 18 years', *Brit. J. Prev. Soc. Med.*, 2, No. 3 (1957).

89. ILLSLEY, R., 'Preventive medicine in the perinatal period', *Proc. Roy. Soc. Med.*, 59, No. 3 (March 1966).

90. ISRAELSOHN, W. J., 'Description and modes of analysis of human growth', in Tanner, J. M. (Ed.), *Human Growth*, Symp. Soc. Hum. Biol., Vol. 3 (Pergamon, London, 1960).

91. JONES, H. E., 'Consistency and change in early maturity', *Vita Humana*, 1, 43–51 (1958).

92. JONES. M. C., 'The later careers of boys who were early or late maturing', *Child Development, 18*, 113–28 (1957).

93. JONES, M. C., 'The psychological correlates of somatic development', *Child Development, 36*, 899–911 (1965).

94. KROGMAN, W. M., 'A handbook of the measurement and interpretation of height and weight in the growing child', *Monogr. Soc. Res. Child Development, 13* (1950).

95. LAT, J., 'The relationship of the individual differences in the regulation of food intake, growth, and excitability of the central nervous system', *Physiologia Bohemoslovenica, V.* Suppl. (1956).

96. LAT, J., WIDDOWSON, E. M. and MCCANCE, R. A., 'Some effects of accelerating growth: III. Behaviour and nervous activity', *Proc. Roy. Soc. (B) 153,* 347–56 (1960).

97. LAT, J., 'Nutrition, learning and adaptive capacity', *Symposium on the Chemical Senses and Nutritive Processes* (Cornell University, Ithaca, 20 June 1966).

98. LEVINE, S., 'Infantile experience and resistance to physiological stress', *Science, 126,* 405–6 (1957).

99. LIVSON, N. and MCNEILL, D., 'The accuracy of recalled age of menarche', *Hum. Biol., 34,* 218–21 (1962).

100. MARTIN, J. K., 'Follow-up studies in cerebral palsy', *Canad. Med. Ass. J., 94,* 996–8 (1966).

101. NICHOLSON, A. B. and HANLEY, C., 'Indices of physiological maturity: derivation and interrelationship', *Child Development, 24,* 3–38 (1953).

102. NISBET, J. D. and ILLESLEY, R., 'The influence of early puberty on test performance at the age of eleven', *Brit. J. Educ. Psychol., 33,* 106–9 (1963).

103. PASAMANICK, B. and KNOBLOCH, H., 'Retrospective studies on the epidemiology of reproductive casualty', *Merrill-Palmer Q., 12,* 7–44 (1966).

104. PESKIN, H., 'Pubertal onset and ego functioning', *J. Abn. Psychol., 72,* 1–15 (1967).

105. POPPLETON, P. K. and BROWN, P. E., 'The secular trend in puberty: has stability been achieved?', *Brit. J. Educ. Psychol., 36,* 95–100 (1966).

106. PRUGH, D. G., 'Toward an understanding of psychosomatic concepts in relation to illness in children', in Solnit, A. J. and

Provence, S. A., *Human Perspectives in Child Development* (International University Press, New York, 1963).

107. RICHMOND, J. B. and LIPTIN, E. L., 'Some aspects of the neurophysiology of the newborn and their implications for child development', in Jessner and Pavenstadt (Eds.) *Dynamic Psychopathology in Childhood* (Grune and Stratton, 1959).

108. ROBINSON, N. M. and ROBERTSON, H. B., 'A follow-up study of children of low birth weight and control children at school age', *Pediatrics*, pp. 425–31 (1965).

109. SHUTTLEWORTH, F. K., 'The physical and mental growth of girls and boys age six to nineteen in relation to age at maximum growth', *Monogr. Soc. Res. Child Development*, *4*, No. 3 (1939).

110. SIMON, M. D., 'Body configuration and school readiness', *Child Development*, *30*, 493–512 (1959).

111. SONTAG, L. W., 'Psychosomatics and somatophysics from birth to three years', in Merminod, A. (Ed.), *The Growth of the Normal Child during the First Three Years of Life* (Karger, Basel, 1962).

112. STEWART, L. H., 'Social and emotional adjustment during adolescence as related to the development of psychosomatic illness in adulthood', *Genet. Psychol. Monogr.*, *65*, 175–215 (1962).

113. STOTT, L. H., *The Longitudinal Study of Individual Development* (The Merrill-Palmer School, Detroit, 1955).

114. STUART, H. C., 'The search for knowledge of the child and the significance of his growth and development – examples from the Harvard Longitudinal Studies', *Pediatrics*, *24*, 701–9 (1959).

115. STUART, H. C., REED, R. B. and Associates, 'Longitudinal Studies of Child Health and Development – Series II. Reports based on completed case studies: Department of Maternal and Child Health, Harvard School of Public Health', *Supplement to Pediatrics*, *24*, No. 5, Part II, pp. 875–974 (1959).

116. TANNER, J. M., *Education and Physical Growth* (University of London Press, 1961).

117. TANNER, J. M., *Growth at Adolescence*, 2nd Ed. (Blackwell, Oxford, 1962).

118. TANNER, J. M., 'The regulation of human growth', *Child Development*, *34*, 817–47 (1963).

119. TUDDENHAM, R. D. and SNYDER, M. M., 'Physical growth of California boys and girls from birth to 18 years', *Child Development*, *1*, No. 2, pp. 183–364 (University of California Press, Berkeley, 1954).

120. VALADIAN, I., STUART, H. C. and REED, R. B., 'Studies of illnesses of children followed from birth to 18 years', *Monogr. Soc. Res. Child Developm.*, *26*, No. 3 (1961).

121. WIDDOWSON, E. M., 'Mental contentment and physical growth', *Lancet*, *1*, 1316–8 (1951).

C. GROWTH AND DECLINE OF ABILITIES

122. ALEXANDER, M., 'Relation of environment to intelligence and achievement: a longitudinal study', Unpublished Master's Study (University of Chicago, 1961).

123. ANDERSON, L. D., 'The predictive value of infancy tests in relation to intelligence at 5 years', *Child Development*, *10*, 203–12 (1939).

124. BAJEMA, C. J., 'Estimation of the direction and intensity of natural selection in relation to human intelligence by means of the intrinsic rate of natural increase', Ph.D. thesis, Michigan State University, 1963. *Dissert. Abstr.* July 1964, p. 37.

125. BAYLEY, N., 'Consistency and variability in the growth of intelligence from birth to eighteen years', *J. Genet. Psychol.*, *75*, 165–96 (1949).

126. BAYLEY, N., 'Some increasing parent-child similarities during the growth of children', *J. Educ. Psychol.*, *45*, 1–21 (1954).

127. BAYLEY, N., 'On the growth of intelligence', *Amer. Psychol.* *10*, 805–18 (1955).

128. BAYLEY, N., 'Data on the growth of intelligence between sixteen and twenty-one years as measured by the Wechsler Bellevue scale', *J. Gen. Psychol.*, *90*, 3–15 (1957).

129. BAYLEY, N., 'Learning in adulthood: the role of intelligence', Paper to the *Conference on the Analysis of Conceptual Learning* (University of Wisconsin, 1965).

130. BAYLEY, N., 'Learning in adulthood: the role of intelligence', in Klausmeier, H. J. and Harris, C. W. (Eds.), *Analyses of Concept Learning* (Academic Press, 1966).

131. BAYLEY, N. and JONES, H. E., 'Environmental correlates of

mental and motor development: a cumulative study from infancy to six years', *Child Development*, *8*, 329–41 (1937).

132. BAYLEY, N. and ODEN, M. H., 'The maintenance of intellectual ability in gifted adults', *J. Geront.*, *10*, 91–107 (1955).

133. BELL, A. and ZUBECK, J. F., 'The effect of age on the intellectual performance of mental defectives', *J. Geront.*, *15*, 285–95 (1960).

134. BIRREN, J. E. (Ed.), *Handbook of Aging and the Individual* (University of Chicago Press, 1959).

135. BRADWAY, K. P., 'IQ constancy in the revised Stanford-Binet from the pre-school to the junior high school level', *J. Gen. Psychol.*, *65*, 197–217 (1944).

136. BRADWAY, K. P. and THOMPSON, C. W., 'Intelligence at adulthood: a 25-year follow-up', *J. Educ. Psychol.*, *53*, 1–14 (1942).

137. BROMLEY, D. B., *The Psychology of Human Ageing* (Penguin Books, 1966).

138. BURT, C. L., 'The inheritance of mental ability', *Amer. Psych.*, *13*, 1–15 (1958).

139. CHARLES, D. C., 'Ability and accomplishment of persons earlier judged mentally deficient', *Genet. Psychol. Monogr.*, *47*, 3–71 (1953).

140. CHARLES, D. C. and JAMES, S. T., 'Stability of average intelligence', *J. Genet. Psychol.*, *105*, 105–11 (1964).

141. DEMMING, J. A. and PRESSEY, S. L., 'Tests "indigenous" to the adult and older years', *J. Counsel. Psychol.*, *4*, 144–8 (1957).

142. DENNIS, W. and NAJARIAN, P., 'Infant development under environmental handicap', *Psychol. Monogr.*, *71*, No. 7. Whole No. 463 (1957).

143. DUNCAN, D. R. and BARRETT, A. M., 'A longitudinal comparison of intelligence involving the Wechsler-Bellevue I and the W.A.I.S.', *J. Clin. Psychol.*, *17*, 318–19 (1961).

144. EBERT, E. and SIMMONS, K., 'The Brush Foundation study of child growth and development. I. Psychometric tests', *Monogr. Soc. Res. Child Develpm.*, *8*, No. 2, 1–113 (1943).

145. EELS, K. et al, *Intelligence and cultural differences* (University of Chicago Press, 1951).

146. EISDORFER, C., 'The W.A.I.S. performance of the aged: a re-test evaluation', *J. Geront.*, *18*, 169–72 (1963).

147. FALEK, A., KALLMAN, F., LORGE, I. and JARVIK, L. F., 'Longevity and intellectual variation in a senescent twin population', *J. Geront.*, *15*, 305–9 (1960).
148. FOWLER, W., 'Longitudinal study of early stimulation in the emergence of cognitive processes', in Hess, R. D. and Bear, R. M. (Eds.), *Early Education: Current Theory, Research and Practice.* (Aldine, Chicago, 1968).
149. FREEBERG, N. E. and PAYNE, D. T., 'Parental influence on cognitive development in early childhood: a review', *Child Development*, *36*, 887–98 (1967).
150. GEBER, M., 'Longitudinal study and psycho-motor development among Baganda children', in Nielsen, G. S. (Ed.), *Child and Education* (Munsksgaard, Copenhagen, 1962).
151. GOLDIN, M. R. and ROTHSCHILD, S., 'Stability of intelligence quotient of metropolitan children of foreign-born parentage', *Elem. School J.*, *42*, 673–6 (1942).
152. HAAN, N., 'Proposed model of ego functioning: coping and defense mechanisms in relationship to IQ change', *Psychol. Monogr.*, *77*, No. 8 (1963).
153. HARNQVIST, K., 'Relative changes in intelligence from 13 to 18', *Reports from the Institute of Education, University of Gothenburg, No. 4.* Mimeo (1967).
154. HILDEN, A. H., 'A longitudinal study of intellectual development', *J. Psychol.*, *28*, 187–214 (1949).
155. HILL, K. T. and SARASON, S. B., 'A further longitudinal study of the relation of test anxiety and defensiveness to test and school performances over the elementary school years', *Monogr. Soc. Res. Child Develpm.*, Serial No. 104 (1966).
156. HINDLEY, C. B., 'Social class influences in the development of ability in the first five years', *Proc. Int. Congress Applied Psychology.* (Longitudinal studies in different cultures: a Symposium), pp. 29-41 (Munksgaard, Copenhagen, 1961).
157. HINDLEY, C. B., 'Stability and change in abilities up to five years: group trends', *J. Child Psychol. Psychiat.*, *6*, 85–100 (1965).
158. HOFSTAETTER, P. R., 'The changing composition of "intelligence": a study in T- technique', *J. Genet. Psychol.*, *85*, 159–64 (1957).

159. HONZIK, M. P., MACFARLANE, J. W. and ALLEN, L., 'The stability of mental test performance between two and eighteen years', *J. Exper. Ed.*, *17*, 309–24 (1948).

160. HONZIK, M. P., 'Developmental studies of parent-child resemblance in intelligence', *Child Development*, *28*, 21–28 (1957).

161. HONZIK, M. P., 'A sex difference in the age of onset of the parent-child resemblance in intelligence', *J. Educ. Psychol.*, *54*, 231–7 (1963).

162. HONZIK, M. P., 'Environmental correlates of mental growth: prediction from the family setting at 21 months', *Child Development*, *38*, 337–64 (1967).

163. HUNT, J. MCV., *Intelligence and Experience* (Ronald Press, New York, 1961).

164. HUSEN, T., *Psychological Twin Research* (Almqvist and Wicksell, Stockholm, 1959).

165. ILLINGWORTH, R. S., 'The diagnosis of mental deficiency in the first weeks of life', in Merminod, A. (Ed.), *The Growth of the Normal Child during the First Three Years of Life* (Karger, Basel, 1962).

166. JARVIK, L. F., et al., 'Intellectual changes in aged twins', *J. Geront.*, *17*, 289–94 (1962).

167. JARVIK, L. F. and FALEK, A., 'Intellectual ability and survival in the aged', *J. Geront.*, *18*, 173–6 (1963).

168. JONES, H. E. and CONRAD, H. S., 'The growth and decline of intelligence: a study of a homogeneous group between the ages of ten and sixty', *Gen. Psychol. Monogr.*, *13*, 223–94 (1933).

169. JONES, H. E., 'The environment and mental development', in Carmichael, L. (Ed.) *Manual of Child Psychology*, 2nd edn. (Wiley, New York, 1954).

170. JONES, H. E., 'Age changes in mental ability', in *Old Age in the Modern World* (Livingstone, Edinburgh, 1955).

171. KAGAN, J., 'A developmental approach to conceptual growth', in Klausmeier, H. J. and Harris, C. W. (Eds.), *Analyses of Concept Learning* (Academic Press, 1966).

172. KAGAN, J., SONTAG, L. W., BAKER, C. T. and NELSON, V. L., 'Personality and IQ change', *J. Abn. Soc. Psychol.*, *56*, 261–6 (1958).

173. KAGAN, J. and MOSS, H. A., 'Parental correlates of child's IQ and height: a cross-validation of the Berkeley Growth Study results', *Child Development*, *30*, 325-32 (1959).

174. KALLMAN, F. J., 'Genetic factors in ageing: comparative and longitudinal observations on a senescent twin population', in Hoch, P. H. and Zubin, J. (Eds.), *Psychopathology of Ageing* (Grune & Stratton, 1966).

175. KIRK, S. A., *Early Education of the Mentally Retarded* (University of Illinois Press, Urbana, 1958).

176. KOEH, M. L., 'The relation of "primary mental abilities" in 5- and 6-year-olds to sex of child and characteristics of his sibling', *Child Development*, *25*, No. 3 (1954).

177. MAURER, K. M., *Intellectual Status as a Criterion for Selecting Items in Pre-school Tests* (University of Minnesota Press, Minneapolis, 1946).

178. MCHUGH, R. B. and OWENS, W. A., 'Age changes in mental organization – a longitudinal study', *J. Geront.*, *9*, 296-302 (1954).

179. MEYERS, C. E., et al., 'Four ability factor hypotheses at three pre-literate levels in normal and retarded children', *Monogr. Soc. Res. Child Develpm.*, *29*, No. 5 (1964).

180. MILES, C. C. and MILES, W. R., 'The correlation of intelligence scores and chronological age from early to late maturity', *Amer. J. Psychol.*, *44*, 48-78 (1932).

181. MOSS, H. A. and KAGAN, J., 'Maternal influences on early IQ scores', *Psychol. Rep.*, *4*, 655-61 (1958).

182. OSBORNE, R. T., 'Racial differences in mental growth and school achievement: a longitudinal study', *Psychol. Rep.*, *7*, 233-9 (1960).

183. OSBORNE, R. T., 'Factor structure of the Wechsler Intelligence Scale for children at pre-school level and after first grade: a longitudinal analysis', *Psychol. Rep.*, *16*, 637-44 (1965).

184. OWENS, W. A., 'Age and mental abilities: a longitudinal study', *Gen. Psychol. Monogr.*, *48*, 3-54 (1953).

185. FLAVELL, J. H., *The Developmental Psychology of Jean Piaget*: an approved English exposition (Van Nostrand, Princeton, N.J., 1963).

186. PINNEAU, S. R. and JONES, H. E., 'Development of mental abilities', *Rev. Educ. Res.*, *28*, 392–400 (1958).

187. RIEGEL, K. F., et al., 'The prediction of intellectual development and death: a longitudinal analysis', *Sixth Int. Cong. Geront.*, Copenhagen (1963).

188. ROBERTS, J. A. FRASER, 'Birth order, maternal age, and intelligence', *Brit. J. Stat. Psychol.*, *1*, 35–51 (1947).

189. SARASON, S. B., et al, 'A longitudinal study of the relation of test anxiety on intelligence and achievement tests', *Monogr. Soc. Res. Child Develpm.*, No. 98 (1964).

190. SCHOONOVER, S., 'A longitudinal study of sibling resemblances in intelligence and achievement', *J. Ed. Psychol.*, *47*, 436–42 (1956).

191. SIGEL, I. E., 'How intelligence tests limit understanding of intelligence', *Merrill-Palmer Q.*, *9*, No. 1 (1963).

192. SHIRLEY, M., *The First Two Years. Vol. II. Intellectual Development* (University of Minnesota Press, 1933).

193. SKEELS, H. M., 'A study of the effects of differential stimulation on mentally retarded children: a follow-up report', *Amer. J. Mental Deficiency*, *46*, No. 3, 340–50 (1942).

194. SKEELS, H. M., 'Adult status of children with contrasting early life experiences: a follow-up study', *Monogr. Soc. Res. Child Develpm.*, Serial No. 105 (1966).

195. SKEELS, H. M., UPDEGRAFF, R., WELLNAM, B. L. and WILLIAMS, H. M., 'A study of environmental stimulation: an orphanage pre-school project', *Univ. Iowa Studies in Child Welfare*, *15*, No. 4 (1938).

196. SKODAK, M. and SKEELS, H. M., 'A follow-up study of children in adoptive homes', *J. Gen. Psychol.*, *66*, 21–58 (1945).

197. SKODAK, M. and SKEELS, H. M., 'A final follow-up study of 100 adoptive children', *J. Gen. Psychol.*, *75*, 85–125 (1949).

198. SONTAG, L. W., BAKER, C. T. and NELSON, V. L., 'Mental growth and personality development: a longitudinal study', *Monogr. Soc. Res. Child Develpm.*, *23*, No. 2 (1958).

199. TERMAN, L. M., 'The vocational success of intellectually gifted individuals', *School and Society*, *49*, 65–73 (1939).

200. TERMAN, L. M. and ODEN, M. H., *Genetic Studies of Genius : V*

The Gifted Group at Mid-Life (Stanford University Press, 1959).

200a. 'The Stanford studies of the gifted', in Witty, P. (Ed.), *The Gifted Child* (Heath, 1959).

201. TOZER, A. H. D. and LARWOOD, H. J. C., 'The changes in intelligence test scores of students between the beginning and the end of their university courses', *Brit. J. Ed. Psychol.*, *28*, 120–8 (1958).

202. WOLF, R. M., 'The identification and measurement of environmental process variables related to intelligence', *Ph.D. thesis* (University of Chicago, 1963).

203. ZAZZO, R., *Les Jumeaux: le Couple et la Personne*. (Presses Universitaires de France, Paris, 1960).

D. LANGUAGE DEVELOPMENT

204. BELLUGI, V. and BROWN, R., 'The acquisition of language', *Monogr. Soc. Res. Child Developm.*, *29*, No. 1 (1964).

205. BERNSTEIN, B., 'Aspects of language and learning in the genesis of the social process', *J. Child Psychol. Psychiat.*, *1*, 313–25 (1961).

206. BROWN, R. and BELLUGI, V., 'Three processes in the child's acquisition of syntax', *Harvard Educational Review*, *34*, 133–51 (1964).

206a. LOBAN, W., 'Language proficiency and school learning', Krumboltz, J. D. (Ed.), *Learning and the Educational Process* (Rand McNally, Chicago, 1965).

207. MOORE, T. W., 'Language and intelligence: a longitudinal study of the first eight years. Part I', *Human Development*, *10*, 88–106 (1967).

208. MOORE, T. W., 'Language and intelligence: a longitudinal study of the first eight years. Part II: Environmental correlates of mental growth', *Human Development*, *11*, 1–24 (1968).

209. OLIM, E. G., HESS, R. D. and SHIPMAN, V. C., 'Maternal language styles and their implications for children's cognitive development', *Paper presented to Convention of American Psychological Association* (Chicago, 1965).

210. KELLMER-PRINGLE, M. L. and BUSSIE, V., 'A study of deprived

children. Part II: Language development and reading attainments', *Vita Humana*, *1*, 269–87 (1958).

211. KELLMER-PRINGLE, M. L. and TANNER, J., 'The effects of early deprivation on speech development: a comparative study of 4–year-olds in a nursery school and in residential nurseries', *Language and Speech*, *1*, 269–87 (1958).

212. SAMPSON, O. C., 'A study of speech development in children of 18–30 months', *Brit. J. Educ. Psychol.*, *26*, 194–201 (1956).

213. SAMPSON, O. C., 'The speech and language development of 5–year old children', *Brit. J. Educ. Psychol.*, *29*, 217–22 (1959).

214. TEMPLIN, M. C., 'Longitudinal research in articulation and language', *Childhood Education*, *42*, 326–7 (1966).

214a. TOUGH J. and OLIVER B., 'Language and environment, an interim report on a longitudinal study', University of Leeds Institute of Education (mimeo 1969).

E. BEHAVIOUR TENDENCIES – DEVELOPMENT, CONSISTENCY, AND VARIABILITY

215. AMBROSE, J. A., 'The development of the smiling response in early infancy', in Foss, B. M. (Ed.), *Determinants of Infant Behaviour* (Methuen, London, 1961).

216. ANDERSON, J. E., 'Dynamics of development: system in progress', in Harris, D. A. (Ed.), *The Concept of Development*, pp. 25–46 (University of Minnesota Press, 1957).

217. ANDERSON, J. E., 'The prediction of adjustment over time', in Iscoe, I. and Stevenson, H. W. (Eds.), *Personality Development in Children* (University of Texas Press, 1960).

218. ANDERSON, J. E., 'Behavior problems and cerebral dysfunction in children', I and II, *Minn. Med.*, *49*, 305–9 and 473–7 (1966).

219. BECKER, W. C., 'The relationship of factors in parental ratings of self and each other to the behavior of kindergarten children as rated by mothers, fathers, and teachers', *J. Consult. Psychol.*, *24*, 507–27 (1960).

220. BELL, R., 'Relations between behavior manifestations in the human neonate', *Child Development*, 463–77 (1960).

221. BENNETT, S. and KLEIN, H. R., 'Childhood schizophrenia: 30 years later', *Amer. J. Psychiat.*, *122*, 1121–4 (1966).

222. BOWLBY, J., et al., 'The effects of mother-child separation: a follow-up study', *Brit. J. Med. Psychol.*, *29*, 211–47 (1956).

223. BRIDGES, K. B., 'Social behaviour rating scales in mental development', *Brit. J. Educ. Psychol.*, *10*, 233–6 (1940).

224. BUCHLER, C., *The Child and his Family* (Routledge & Kegan Paul, London, 1940).

225. BUCK, C., 'Relationship of prenatal factors to behaviour problems in childhood – a prospective study', *Ann. N.Y. Acad. Sci.*, *107*, Art. 2, 576–86 (1963).

226. BURDEN, S. and NELLEY, K., 'Chronic school failure in boys: a short-term group therapy and educational approach', *Amer. J. Psychiat.*, *122*, 1211–19 (1966).

227. CASLER, L., 'Maternal deprivation: a critical review of the literature', *Monogr. Soc. Res. Child Develpm.*, *26*, No. 2, Serial No. 80 (1965).

228. CASLER, L., 'The effects of extra tactile stimulation of a group of institutionalized infants', *Genet. Psychol. Monogr.*, *71*, 137–75 (1965).

229. CHESS, S., et al., 'Implications of a longitudinal study of child development for child psychiatry', *Amer. J. Psychiat.*, *117*, 434–41 (1960).

230. DACIS, CARROLL, *Room to Grow: A Study of Parent-Child Relationships* (University of Toronto Press, 1966).

231. DE FRIES, J. C., 'Effects of prenatal maternal stress on behavior in mice: a genotype-environment interaction' (Abstr.), *Genetics*, *50*, 244 (1964).

232. DOLL, E. A., 'Growth studies in social competence', *Proc. Amer. J. Ment. Deficiency*, *44*, 90–6 (1939).

233. FISH, WILE, SHAPIRO and HALPERN, 'The prediction of schizophrenia in infancy. II. A ten-year follow-up report of predictions made at one year of age', *Proc. Amer. Psychopath. Ass.*, *54*, 535–53 (1966).

234. FLINT, B. M., *The Security of Infants* (University of Toronto Press, 1959).

235. FLINT, B. M., *The Child and the Institution: A Study of Deprivation and Recovery* (University of Toronto Press, 1966).

236. FREND, A., 'The role of regression in mental development',

in Solnit, A. J. and Provence, S. A. (Eds.), *Modern Perspectives in Child Development* (International University Press, 1963).

237. FRENKEL-BRUNSWICK, E., 'Motivation and behavior', *Genet. Psychol. Monogr.*, *26*, 121–265 (1942).

238. GLUECK, S. and GLUECK, E., 'The uses and promise of prediction devices', *Int. J. Soc. Psychiat*, Special Edition No. 4 (1964).

239. GLUECK, S., 'Identification of potential delinquents at 2–3 years of age', *Inter. J. Soc. Psychiat.*, *12*, 5–6 (1966).

240. GRAHAM, F. K., et al., 'Development three years after perinatal anoxia', *Psychol. Monogr.*, *76*, No. 3 (1962).

241. GREGORY, I., 'Anterospective data following childhood loss of a parent. 1. Delinquency and high school dropout. 2. Pathology, performance, and potential among college students', *Arch. Gen. Psychiat.*, *13*, 99–120 (1965).

242. HEIDER, G., 'Vulnerability in infants and young children: a pilot study', *Genct. Psychol. Monogr.*, *73*, 1–216 (1966).

243. LAPOUSE, R., 'The epidemiology of behavior disorders in children', *Amer. J. Dis. Child.*, *3*, 594–9 (1966).

244. LEVITT, E. E., BEISER, H. R. and ROBERTSON, R. E., 'A follow-up evaluation of cases treated at a community child guidance clinic', *Amer. J. Orthopsychiat.*, *29*, 337–49 (1959).

245. LINDE, R., 'Attitudinal factors in congenital heart disease', *Pediatrics*, *38*, 92–101 (1966).

246. LINDEMANN, E. B. and ROSS, A., 'A follow-up study of a predictive test of social adaptation in pre-school children', in Caplan, G. (Ed.), *Emotional Problems of Early Childhood*, pp. 80–81 (Basic Books, New York, 1955).

247. LUNZER, E. A., 'Aggressive and withdrawing children in the normal school. I. Patterns of behaviour. II. Disparity in attainment', *Brit. J. Ed. Psychol.*, *30*, pp. 1 ff., pp. 119 ff. (1960).

248. MACFARLANE, J. W., 'Studies in child guidance. I. Methodology of data collection and organization', *Monogr. Soc. Res. Child Develpm.*, *3*, No. 6: Serial No. 19 (1938).

249. MACFARLANE, J. W., ALLEN, J. and KONZIK, M. P., *A developmental study of the behavior problems of normal children between 21 months and 14 years* (University of California Press, 1954, 1962).

250. MASSIMO, J. and SHORE, M., 'The effectiveness of a compre-

hensive vocationally oriented psychotherapeutic program for adolescent delinquent boys', *Amer. J. Orthopsychiat.*, *33*, 634–42 (1963).

251. MASSIMO, J. and SHORE, M., 'Job-focused treatment for anti-social youth', *Children*, *11*, 143–7 (1964).

252. MCKINNON, K. N., 'Consistency and change in behavior manifestations', *Child Develpm. Monogr.*, No. 30 (Teachers College, Columbia University, New York, 1942).

253. MEDNICK, S. A. and SCHULSINGER, F., 'A longitudinal study of children with a high risk for schizophrenia: preliminary report', in Vandenberg, S. G. (Ed.), *Methods and Goals in Behavior Genetics* (Academic Press, New York, 1965).

254. MILLAR, T. P., 'Psychiatric consultation with class-room teachers', *J. Amer. Acad. Child Psychiat.*, *5*, 134–44 (1966).

255. MORRIS, D. P., SORROKER, E. and BURRESS, G., 'Follow-up studies of shy, withdrawn children. I. Evaluation of later adjustment', *Amer. J. Orthopsych.*, *24*, 743–54 (1954).

256. MORRIS, ESCOLL and WEXLER, 'Aggressive behavior disorders of childhood: a follow-up study', *Amer. J. Psychiat.*, *112* (1956).

257. MOORE, T. W. and UCKO, L. E., 'Night waking in early infancy', *Arch. Dis. Childh.*, *32*, 333–42 (1957).

258. MULLIGAN, G., et al., 'Delinquency and symptoms of mal-adjustment: the findings of a longitudinal study', *Proc. R. Soc. Med.*, *56*, 1083–6 (1963).

259. MURPHY, L. B., 'The child's way of coping: a longitudinal study of normal children', *Bull. Menninger Clinic*, *24*, 97–103 (1960).

260. MUSSEN, P. H. and JONES, M. C., 'The behavior inferred motivations of late and early-maturing boys', *Child Development*, *29*, 61–7 (1958).

261. OBERST, B. B., 'Preventive care in infants and children. VI. School adjustment problems and their relationship to guided growth', *Lancet*, *86*, 731–4 (1966).

262. O'NEAL, P. and ROBINS, L. N., 'The relation of childhood behavior disorders to adult psychiatric status', *Amer. J. Psychiat.*, *114*, 961–8 (1958).

263. O'NEAL, P. and ROBINS, L. N., 'Mortality, morbidity and

crime: problem children thirty years later', *Amer. Social Rev.*, *23*, 162–71 (1958).

264. PARENS, H. and WEECH, A. A., 'Accelerated learning responses in young patients with school problems', *J. Amer. Child Psychiat.*, *5*, 75–92 (1966).

265. PECK, R. F., and HAVIGHURST, R. J., et al., *The Psychology of Character Development* (Wiley, New York, 1960).

266. PETERSON, D. R., et al., 'Child behavior problems and parental attitudes', *Child Development*, *32*, 151–62 (1961).

267. KELLMER-PRINGLE, M. L. and EDWARDS, J. B., 'Some moral concepts and judgements of junior school children', *Brit. J. Soc. Psychol.*, *3*, 196–215 (1964).

268. SCHAEFER, E. S., BELL, R. Q. and BAYLEY, N., 'Development of a maternal behavior research instrument', *J. Genet. Psychol.*, *95*, 83–104 (1959).

269. SCHAEFER, E. S. and BAYLEY, N., 'Maternal behavior, child behavior, and their intercorrelations from infancy to adolescence', *Monogr. Soc. Res. Child Develpm.*, *28*, No. 3 (1963).

270. SCHAFFER, H. R. and EMERSON, P. E., 'Development of social attachments in infancy, *Monogr. Soc. Res. Child Develpm.*, Serial No. 94 (1964).

271. SCHOEPPE, A. and HAVIGHURST, R. J., 'A validation of development and adjustment hypotheses of adolescence', *J. Educ. Psychol.*, *6*, 331–9 (1952).

272. SCHRAGER, et al., 'The hyperkinetic child and some consensually validated behavior correlates', *Excep. Child*, *32*, 635–7 (1966).

273. SHEPHERD, M., OPPENHEIM, A. N. and MITCHELL, S., 'The definition and outcome of deviant behaviour in childhood', *Proc. Roy. Soc. Med.*, *59*, 379–82 (1966).

274. SHORE, M., MASSIMO, J., et al., 'Object relation changes resulting from successful psychotherapy with adolescent delinquents and their relationship to academic performance', *J. Amer. Acad. Child Psychiat.*, *5*, 93–104 (1966).

275, SPITZ, R. A., 'Hospitalism: an enquiry into the genesis of psychiatric condition in early childhood', *Psychoanal. Study Child.*, *1*, 53–74 (1945).

276. SPITZ, R. A., 'Relevancy of direct infant observation', *Psychoanal. Study Child.*, 6, 5–66 (1950).

277. THOMAS, A., et al., 'Individuality in responses of children to similar environmental situations', *Amer. J. Psychiat.*, *117*, 798 (1961).

278. THOMAS, A., CHESS, S., BIRCH, H. G. and HERTZIG, M., 'A longitudinal study of primary reaction patterns in children', *Comprehensive Psychol.*, *1*, 103–12 (1960).

279. UCKO, L. E., 'A comparative study of asphyxiated and non-asphyxiated boys from birth to 5 years', *Develpm. Med. and Child Neurol.*, 7, 643–57 (1965).

280. ZUNICH, M., 'Child behavior and parental attitudes', *J. Psychol.*, *62*, 41–6 (1966).

F. THE CRITICAL PERIOD HYPOTHESIS

281. AINSWORTH, M. D., 'Reversible and irreversible effects of maternal deprivation on intellectual development', in Harvey, O. J. (Ed.), *Experience, Structure and Adaptability* (Springer, New York, 1966).

282. BRONSON, G., 'Critical periods in human development', *Br. J. Med. Psychol.*, *35*, 127–33 (1962).

283. CALDWELL, B., 'The usefulness of the critical period hypothesis in the study of filiative behavior', *Merrill-Palmer Q.*, *8*, 229–42 (1962).

284. DAVIS, D. R., 'Family environment and mental illness', in Welford, A. T., et al. (Eds.), *Society: Problems and Methods of Study* (Routledge & Kegan Paul, 1962).

285. DENENBERG, V. H., 'Critical periods, stimulus input and emotional reactivity: a theory of infantile stimulation', *Psychol. Rev.*, *71*, 335–51 (1964).

286. FOWLER, W., 'Cognitive learning in infancy and early childhood', *Psychol. Bull.*, *59*, 116–52 (1962).

287. GUITON, P., 'Socialisation and imprinting in Brown Leghorn chicks', *Anim. Behav.*, 7, 26–34 (1959).

288. LEVINE, S., 'The psychophysiological effects of early stimulation', in Bliss, E. (Ed.), *Roots of Behavior* (Hoeber, New York, 1962).

289. SCOTT, J. P., 'Critical periods in behavioral development', *Science*, *138*, 949–58 (1962).

290. SCHNEIRLA, T. C. and ROSENBLATT, J. S., '"Critical periods" in the development of behaviour', *Science*, *139*, 1110–15 (1963).

G. PERSONALITY DEVELOPMENT

291. ALLPORT, G., *Pattern and Growth in Personality* (Holt, Rinehart and Winston, New York, 1961).

292. ANDERSON, J. E., 'The relation between adult adjustment and early experience over a 28-year interval', *Amer. Psychol.*, *15*, 385–6: Abstract (1960).

293. AUSUBEL, D. P., et al., 'A preliminary study of developmental trends in socio-empathy', *Child Develpm.*, *23*, 111–28 (1952).

294. BARRON, F. and LEARY, T. F., 'Changes in psychoneurotic patients with and without psychotherapy', *J. Consult. Psychol.*, *19*, 239–45 (1955).

295. BAYLEY, N. and SCHAEFER, E. S., 'Maternal behavior and personality development: data from the Berkeley Growth Study', *Child Develpm. Res. Rep. Amer. Psychiat. Ass.*, *13*, 155–73 (1960).

296. BELLER, E. K., 'Dependency and autonomous achievement striving related to orality and anality in early childhood', *Child Development*, *28*, 287–315 (1957).

297. BENJAMIN, J. D., 'Some developmental observations relating to the theory of anxiety', *J. Amer. Psychoanal. Assoc.*, *9*, 652–88 (1961).

298. BLOCK, J., *The Q Sort Method in Personality Assessment and Psychiatric Research* (C. C. Thomas, Springfield, Ill., 1961).

299. BLOCK, J, and HAAN, N., *Ways of Personality Development: Continuity and Change from Adolescence to Adulthood* (Appleton-Century-Crofts, New York, forthcoming).

300. BRONSON, W. C., 'Dimensions of ego and infantile identification', *J. Pers.*, *17*, 532–45 (1959).

301. BRONSON, W. C., KATTEN, E. S. and LIVSON, N., 'Patterns of authority and affection in two generations', *J. Abnorm. Soc. Psychol.*, *58*, 143–52 (1959).

302. BRONSON, W. C., 'Central orientations: a study of behavior

organization from childhood to adolescence', *Child Development*, *37*, 125–55 (1966).

303. BRONSON, W. C., 'Adult derivatives of emotional expressiveness and reactivity-control: developmental continuities from childhood to adulthood', *Child Development*, *38*, 801–17 (1967).

304. CRANDALL, V. J. and PRESTON, A., 'An assessment of personal social adjustments of a group of middle-class mothers', *J. Genet. Psychol.*, *89*, 230–49 (1956).

305. CRANDALL, V. J., et al., 'A conceptual formulation for some research on children's achievement development', *Child Development*, *31*, 787–97 (1960).

306. DORFMAN, E., 'Personality outcome of client-centred child therapy', *Psychol. Monogr.*, *72*, No. 456 (1958).

307. EMMERICH, W., 'Continuity and stability in early social development', *Child Development*, *35*, 311–32 (1964).

308. ERIKSON, E. H., *Childhood and Society* (Norton, New York, 1950).

309. ERIKSON, E. H., *Identity and the Life Cycle* (International University Press, New York, 1959).

310. GOLDSTEIN, I. B., 'The role of muscle tension in personality theory', *Psychol. Bull.*, *61*, 6, 413–25 (1964).

311. GOTTESMAN, I., 'Heritability of personality: a demonstration', *Psychol. Monogr.*, *77*, No. 9: whole No. 572 (1963).

312. HONZIK, M. P., 'Personality consistency and change: some comments on papers by Bayley, Macfarlane, Moss and Kagan, and Murphy', *Vita Humana*, *7*, 139–42 (1964).

313. HONZIK, M. P., 'Prediction of behavior from birth to maturity', *Merrill-Palmer Q.*, *11*, 77–88 (1965).

314. HUNT, J. MCV., 'Traditional personality theory in the light of recent evidence', *Amer. Scientist*, *53*, 80–96 (1965).

315. IVES, V., et al., 'The "neurotic" Rorschachs of normal adolescents', *J. Genet Psychol.*, *83*, 31–61 (1953).

316. JONES, H. E., 'Consistency and change in early maturity', *Vita Humana*, *1*, 43–51 (1958).

317. JONES, H. E., MACFARLANE, J. W. and EICHORN, D. H., 'A progress report on growth studies at the University of California', *Vita Humana*, *3*, 17–31 (1960).

318. JONES, M. C., 'The psychology of drinking and abstaining:

a longitudinal study', *Report to the Cooperative Commission for the Study of Alcoholism* (U.S.A., 1965).

319. JONES, M. C., 'Longitudinal studies at the University of California', *Proc. 7th Inter. Congr. Gerontology* (Vienna, 1966).

320. KAGAN, J. and MOSS, H. A., *Birth to Maturity* (Wiley, 1962).

321. KELLY, E. L., 'Consistency of the adult personality', *Amer. Psychologist, 10*, 659–81 (1955).

322. LASKO, J. K., 'Parent behavior toward first and second children', *Genet. Psychol. Monogr., 49*, 97–137 (1954).

323. LOEVINGER, J., 'The meaning and measurement of ego development', *Amer. Psychol., 10*, 659–81 (1966).

324. LUBORSKY, L., 'Intra-individual repetitive measurements (P-technique) in understanding psychotherapeutic change', in Mowrer, O. H. *Psychotherapy Theory and Research* (Ronald Press, New York, 1953).

325. MALAN, D., 'On assessing the results of psychotherapy', *Brit. J. Med. Psychol., 32*, 86–105 (1959).

326. MCKEE, J. P. and TURNER, W. S., 'The relations of "drive" ratings in adolescence to C.P.I. and E.P.P.S. series in adulthood', *Vita Humana, 4*, 1–14 (1961).

327. MEILI, R., 'A longitudinal study of personality development', in Jessner, L. and Pavendstadt, E. (Eds.), *Dynamic Psychopathology in Childhood* (Grune and Stratton, New York, 1959).

328. MURPHY, L. B., 'Factors in continuity and change in the development of adaptational style in children', *Vita Humana, 7* (2) 96–114 (1964).

329. MUSSEN, P. H., 'Some antecedents and consequents of masculine sex typing in adolescent boys', *Psychol. Monogr., 75*, No. 2: whole No. 506 (1961).

330. NEILON, P., 'Shirley's babies after fifteen years: a personality study', *J. Genet. Psychol., 73*, 175–86 (1948).

331. NEUGARTEN, B. L., 'A developmental view of adult personality', in Birren, J. (Ed.), *Relations of Development and Aging*, pp. 196–208 (Charles C. Thomas, Springfield, Ill., 1964).

332. PHILLIPS, E. L., 'Parent-child psychotherapy: a follow-up study comparing two techniques', *J. Psychol., 49*, 195–202 (1960).

333. RICCIUTI, H. N., 'Use of the Rorschach Test in longitudinal studies of personality development', *J. Proj. Tech.*, *20*, 256–60 (1956).

334. ROSENTHAL, D., 'Changes in some moral values following psychotherapy', *J. Consult. Psychol.*, *19*, 431–6 (1955).

335. SCHAEFER, E. S. and BAYLEY, N., 'Consistency of maternal behavior from infancy to pre-adolescence', *J. Abnorm. Soc. Psychol.*, *1*, 1–6 (1960).

336. SCHAEFER, E. S., 'An analysis of consensus in longitudinal research on personality consistency and change: discussion of papers by Bayley, Macfarlane, Moss and Kagan, and Murphy', *Vita Humana*, 7 (2), 143–6 (1964).

337. SECORD, P. F. and BACKMAN, C. W., 'Personality theory of the problem of stability and change in individual behavior', *Psychol. Rev.*, *68*, 21–32 (1961).

338. SONTAG, L. W., BAKER, C. T. and NELSON, V. L., 'Mental growth and personality development: a longitudinal study', *Monogr. Soc. Res. Child Develpm.*, *23*, No. 2 (1958).

339. STEVENSON, I., 'Is the human personality more plastic in infancy and childhood?', *Amer. J. Psychiat.*, *114*, 152–61 (1957).

340. STONE, A. A. and ONQUE, G. C., *Longitudinal Studies of Child Personality*: Abstracts with Index published for the Commonwealth Fund by Harvard University Press.

(Summarizes and gives the essential findings of longitudinal research up to 1955. The primary concern is emotional and social behaviour in infants and children; studies of other aspects of development are included only when they have reference to social and emotional factors.)

341. STOUT, H. M., 'Adaptiveness to the maternal role at age thirty, and stresses and strength in the mother's family during childhood'. Unpublished study of Institute of Human Development, University of California (1965).

342. THOMAE, H., 'Objective socialization variables and personality development: findings from a longitudinal study', *Human Development*, *8*, 87–116 (1965).

343. TUDDENHAM, R. D., 'Studies in reputation: I, Sex and grade differences in school children's evaluation of their peers. II.

236

The diagnosis of social adjustment', *Psychol. Monogr.*, 66, No. 1 (1952).

344. TUDDENHAM, R. D., 'Constancy of personality ratings over two decades', *Genet. Psychol. Monogr.*, 60, 3–29 (1959).

345. WEBSTER, H., et al., 'Personality changes in college students', in Sanford, N. (Ed.), *The American College*, pp. 811–46 (Wiley, New York, 1962).

346. WERNER, E., 'Personality characteristics of men and women who successfully assimilated stress during their formative years', *Paper to meeting of Soc. Res. Child Develpm.* (Pennsylvania State University, March 1961).

347. WORCHEL, P. and BYRNE, D. (Eds.), *Personality Change* (Wiley, New York, 1964).

348. YARROW, L. J., 'Personality consistency and change: an overview of some conceptual and methodological issues', *Vita Humana* 7 (2), 67–72 (1964).

349. YARROW, L. J. and YARROW, R. Y., 'Personality continuity and change in the family context', in Worchel and Byrne, supra (347).

350. YATES, A. J., 'Symptoms and symptom substitution', *Psychol. Rev.*, 65, 371–4 (1958).

351. ZAX, M. and KLEIN, A., 'Measurements of personality and behavior changes following psychotherapy', *Psychol. Bull.*, 57, 435–48 (1960).

H. ATTITUDES, INTERESTS, AND VOCATIONAL ADJUSTMENT

352. ADAMS, F. J., 'A study of the stability of broad vocational interests at the high school level', unpublished Ed.D. thesis. (New York University, 1957).

353. BALLER, W. R., CHARLES, D. C. and MILLER, E. B., 'Mid-life attainment of the mentally retarded: a longitudinal study *Genet. Psychol. Monogr.*, 75, 235–329 (1967).

354. BURGEMEISTER, B. B., 'The permanence of interests of women college students', *Archives of Psychol.*, 36, No. 255 (1940).

355. HERZBERG, F., BOUTON, A. and STEINER, B. J., 'Studies of the stability of the Kuder Preference Record, and a further study

of the stability of the Kuder Preference Record', *Ed. and Psychol. Meas.*, *14*, 90–100, *14*, 326–31 (1954).

356. HIMMELWEIT, H. T., Follow-up study of vocational adjustment. (Department of Social and Industrial Psychology, London School of Economics.)

356a. HUSEN, T., 'Talent, opportunity and career: a twenty-six-year follow-up', *The School Review*, 76, 2, 190–209 (1968).

357. NELSON, E. N. P., 'Persistence of attitudes of college students fourteen years later', *Psychol. Monogr.*, No. 373 (1954).

358. NELSON, E. N. P., 'Patterns of religious attitudes shift from college to fourteen years later', *Psychol. Monogr.*, No. 424 (1956).

359. NEWCOMB, T. H., et al., *Persistence and Change : Bennington College and its Students after Twenty-five Years* (Wiley, New York, 1967).

360. PATTERSON, C. H., 'The Vineland Social Maturity scale and some of the correlations', *J. Genet. Psychol.*, 62, 275–87 (1943).

361. POWERS, M. K., 'Permanence of measured vocational interests of adult males', *J. App. Psychol.*, 40, 69–72 (1956).

362. REID, J. W., 'Stability of measured Kuder interests in young adults', *J. Educ. Res.*, 45, 307–12 (1951).

363. ROE, A., 'Early differentiation of interests', in University of Utah Research Conference on the Identification of Creative Talent (Utah, Brighton, 1957).

364. ROSENBURG, N., 'Stability and maturation of Kuder interest patterns during high school', *Ed. and Psychol. Meas.*, *13*, 449–52 (1953).

365. STORDAHL, K. E., 'Permanence of Strong Vocational Interests Blanks scores', *J. App. Psychol.*, *38*, 423–7 (1954).

366. STRONG, E. K. JNR., 'Permanence of interest scores over 22 years', *J. App. Psychol.*, *35*, 89–91 (1951).

367. SUPER, D. E., et al., *Vocational development : a framework for research* (Teachers College, Columbia University, Bureau of Publications, New York, 1957).

368. THORNDIKE, R. L. and HAGEN, E., *Ten Thousand Careers* (New York, 1962).

369. TIZARD, J., 'Longitudinal and follow-up studies', in Clarke, A. and Clarke A. D. B. (Eds.), *Mental Deficiency* (Methuen, London, 1958).

I. LONGITUDINAL RESEARCH IN EDUCATION

370. ANDERSON, S. B. and MAIER, M. H., '34,000 children and how they grew', *J. Teacher Educ.*, *14*, 212–16 (1963).

371. BARKER-LUNN, J., *Streaming in the Primary School: a Longitudinal Study of Children in Streamed and Non-streamed Junior Schools* (NFER, Slough, 1970).

372. BROWN, R. C. and HENDERSON, E., 'Longitudinal analysis of pupil progress in a public school', Ed. Res. Assocn. (In preparation.')

373. CAHEN, L. S., 'An interim report on the National Longitudinal Study of Mathematical Abilities', *Mathematics Teacher*, *58*, 522–7 (1965).

374. CAMPBELL, D. T. and STANLEY, J. C., 'Experimental and quasi-experimental designs for research on teaching', in Gage, N. L. (Ed.), *Handbook of Research on Teaching* (Rand McNally, Chicago, 1963).

375. CARROLL, J. B., 'School learning over the long haul', in Krumboltz, J. D. (Ed.), *Learning and the Educational Process* (Rand McNally, Chicago, 1965).

376. FLANAGAN, J. C., et al., 'The identification, development, and utilization of human talents: the American high-school student', *U.S. Dept. of Health, Education and Welfare, Office of Education, Cooperative Research Project No. 635* (Project Talent Office, University of Pittsburgh, 1964).

377. HILL, A. H., 'A longitudinal study of attrition among high aptitude students', *J. Ed. Res.*, *60* (4), 166–73 (1966).

378. HILTON, T. L. and MYERS, A. E., 'Personal background, experience and school achievement: an investigation of the contribution of questionnaire data to academic prediction', *Research Bulletin* (Educational Testing Service, Princeton, N.J., 1966).

378a. HUSÉN, T., *Testresultatens prognosvärde* ['The Predictive Value of Intelligence Tests'] (Almqvist and Wiksell, Stockholm, 1950).

378b. HUSÉN, T., 'Talent, opportunity and career: a twenty-six-year follow-up', *The School Review*, *76*, 2, 190–209 (1968).

379. HUGHES, M. M., 'A four-year longitudinal study of the

growth of logical thinking in a group of secondary modern schoolboys' (M.Ed. thesis, Leeds, 1964).

380. KETCHUM, W. A., 'A description and analysis of longitudinal records of development among elementary children at Ferndale, Mich.' *Co-operative Research Project 096*. U.S. Office of Education (in preparation).

381. LEROY-BOUSSION, A., 'Rythme d'acquisition des lettres et niveau de développement mental': XIII Colloque international de l'association internationale de pédagogie experimentale de langue française, pp. 67–86 (Geneva, 1966).

382. MALLESON, N. and HOPKINS, J., 'University student 1953: a longitudinal study of entrants at University College, London, 1953', *University Quarterly*, *13*, 287–98; *14*, 42–56; and *14*, 156–64.

383. MIALARET, G., 'Etude longitudinale de résultats en lecture': XIII Colloque international de l'association internationale de pédagogie experimentale de langue française, pp. 87–100 (Geneva, 1966).

384. MILLER, G. H., 'The effectiveness of the meaning method in learning arithmetic', unpublished doctoral thesis (University of Southern California, 1957).

385. MORRIS, J. M., *Standards and Progress in Reading* (Newnes, for the National Foundation for Educational Research, 1966).

386. OSBORNE, R. T., 'Racial differences in mental growth and school achievement: a longitudinal study, *Psychol. Reports*, *7*, 233-9 (1960).

387. PERRY, W. L. M., 'A study of medical student selection and performance in the Edinburgh Medical School', *Brit. J. Med. Educ.*, *1*, 16–24 (1966).

388. SCOTTISH COUNCIL FOR RESEARCH IN EDUCATION, 'Assessment for higher education': a five-year follow-up (1963).

389. SHAYCROFT, M. F., 'The high school years: growth in cognitive skills', *Interim Report No. 3, Project No. 3051, Contract No. OE-6-10-065* (University of Pittsburgh and American Institutes for Research, 1967).

390. TRENT, J. W. and MEDSKER, L. L., 'Characteristics and backgrounds of high school graduates and their subsequent progress

and development in higher education', *Co-op. Res. Project No. B. 28* (in preparation).

391. WISEMAN, S., 'A longitudinal study of training college students to assess the effectiveness of education, training and learning in the light of subsequent teaching performance': a five-year project (School of Education, Manchester University, 1963).

J. EARLY INTERVENTION

392. BEREITER, C., 'A nonpsychological approach to early compensatory education' in Deutsch, M., Katz, I., and Jensen, A. R. *Social Class, Race, and Psychological Development* (Holt, 1968).

393. EDUCATIONAL TESTING SERVICE, 'Disadvantaged children and their first school experiences', *Interim Report OEO Contract No. 4206* (Educational Testing Service, Princeton, N.J. 1968).

394. DURHAM EDUCATION IMPROVEMENT PROGRAM, *Durham Education Improvement Program 1966–67. Project of the Ford Foundation* (Durham EIP Information Office, Mutual Plaza, Durham, N.C. 1967).

395. DEUTSCH, M. *Institute for Developmental Studies. Annual Report* (New York Medical College, New York, 1965).

396. FROST, J. L. (Ed.), *Early Childhood Education Rediscovered: Readings* (Holt, Rinehart & Winston, 1968).

397. HESS, R. D. and BEAR, R. M. (Eds.), *Early Education: Current Theory, Research and Action* (Aldine, Chicago, 1968).

398. HODGES, W. L., MCCANDLESS, B. R., and SPICKER, H. H., 'The development and evaluation of a diagnostically based curriculum for preschool psycho-socially deprived children' (United States Department of Health, Education, and Welfare, December 1967).

399. HUNT, J. MCV., 'The psychological basis for using pre-school enrichment as an antidote for cultural deprivation', *Merrill-Palmer Q.*, *10*, 209–48 (1964).

400. HUNT, J. MCV. (Ed.), *The Challenge of Incompetence and Poverty: Papers on the Role of Early Education* (University of Illinois Press, 1969).

401. KARNES, M. B., 'The research program for the preschool

disadvantaged at the University of Illinois', *Paper presented at the 1968 American Educational Research Association convention*, Chicago, February 1968.

402. KLAUS, R. A., and GRAY, S. W., 'The early training project for disadvantaged children: a report after five years', *Monogr. Soc. Res. Child Develpm., No. 120* (1968).

403. LONG, E. R. JR., 'The effect of programmed instruction in special skills during the preschool period on later ability patterns and academic achievement', *Cooperative Research Project* No. 1521, Bureau No. 5-0654 (University of North Carolina, 1966).

404. NIMNICHT, G. P. and MEIER, J., 'A first year partial progress report of a project in an autotelic responsive environment nursery school for environmentally deprived Spanish-American children', *Journal of Research Services II, II*, 3–34 (1966).

405. NIMNICHT, G. P., MEIER, J., and MCAFEE, O., 'A summary of the evaluation of the experimental programme for deprived children at the New Nursery School'. Unpub. report. *Far West Laboratory for Educational Research and Development* (1967).

406. ROBISON, H. F., 'Project CHILD: evolution of a curriculum to heighten intellectual and language development', *Paper presented to NAEYC National Convention at Salt Lake City, Utah*, November 15, 1969 (Teachers College, Columbia University, 1969).

407. SMILANSKY, M., *Intellectual Advancement of Culturally Disadvantaged Children* (Wiley, New York, 1967).

408. STODOLSKY, S., and LESSER, G., 'Learning patterns in the disadvantaged', *Harvard Educ. Rev.*, 37 (4) 546–93 (1967).

409. WEIKART, D. P. (Ed.) *Preschool intervention: a preliminary report of the Perry Preschool Project.* (Campus Publishers, Ann Arbor, Michigan, 1967).

The early work in this rapidly expanding field is very fully documented in HELLMUTH, J. (Ed.) *Disadvantaged Child: Head Start and Early Intervention, Volume 2*, 581–604 (Brunner/Mazel, New York, 1968). No reference, however, will be found there to the following major pre-school studies in progress at Harvard:

Jerome Kagan's study of the growth of cognitive dimensions during the first four years of life;

'The Pre-School Project' directed by Burton White, a longitudinal study of children during the first six years of life to trace the development of various abilities which promote educability, and the role of experience in such development.

K. PAPERS BASIC TO THE STATISTICAL
TREATMENT OF HUMAN GROWTH DATA
prepared by J. M. Tanner

(*from: Compte Rendu de la Reunion Annuelle des Equipes Chargées des Etudes sur la Croissance et le Developpement de l'Enfant Normal, Centre International de l'Enfance, Paris 1964.*)

410. BAYLEY, N., 'Growth curves of height and weight by age for boys and girls, scaled according to physical maturity', *J. Pediat.*, *48*, 187–94 (1956).

411. BERTALANFFY, L. V., 'A quantitative theory of organic growth' (inquiries on growth laws, II), *Hum, Biol. 10*, 181–213 (1938).

412. BLACKITH, R. E., DAVIES, R. G. and MAY, E. A., 'A biometric analysis of development', *Dsydercus Fasciatus Sign. Growth*, *27*, 317–34 (1963).

413. BLISS, C. I. and YOUNG, M. S., 'An analysis of heart measurements of growing boys', *Hum. Biol.*, *22*, 271–80 (1950).

414. BOAS, F., 'The growth of children', *Science 19*, 256–7; 281–2; *20*, 351–2 (1892).

415. BRYAN, A. H. and GREENBERG, B. G., 'Methodology in the study of physical measurements of school-children. Part II. Sexual maturation – determination of immaturity points', *Hum. Biol.*, *24*, 117–24 (1952).

416. BRYAN, A. H., 'Methods for analysing and interpreting physical measurements of groups of children', *Amer. J. Publ. Hlth.*, *44*, 766–74 (1954).

417. BURRELL, R. J. W., HEALY, M. J. R. and TANNER, J. M., 'Age at menarche in South African Bantu girls living in the Transkei reserve', *Hum. Biol.*, *33*, 250–61 (1961).

418. COCK, A. G., 'Genetical studies on growth and form in the fowl', *Genet. Res. Camb.*, *4*, 167–92 (1963).

419. COUNT, E. W., 'Growth patterns of the human physique: an

approach to kinetic anthropometry. Part I, *Hum. Biol.*, *15*, 1–32 (1943).

420. DEMING, J., 'Application of the Gompertz curve to the observed pattern of growth in length of 48 individual boys and girls during the adolescent cycle of growth', *Hum. Biol.*, *29*, 83–122 (1957).

421. DOSSING, J., *Determination of individual normal weights of school-children* (Munksgaard, Copenhagen, 1952).

422. EDWARDS, D. A., et al., 'Design and accuracy of calipers for measuring subcutaneous tissue thickness', *Brit. J. Nutr.*, *9*, 133–43 (1955).

423. GARN, S. M., 'Fat, body size and growth in the newborn', *Hum. Biol.*, *30*, 265–80 (1958).

424. HEALY, M. J. R., 'Some statistical aspects of anthropometry', *J. Roy. Statist. Soc. B.*, *14*, 164–84 (1952).

425. HEALY, M. J. R., 'The effect of age-grouping on the distribution of a measurement affected by growth', *Amer. J. Phys. Anthrop. N. S.*, *20*, 49–50 (1962).

426. HOGBEN, H., WATERHOUSE, J. A. H. and HOGBEN, L., 'Studies on puberty: Part I', *Brit. J. Soc. Med.*, *2*, 29–42 (1948).

427. HUNT, E. E., COOKE, G. and GALLAGHER, J. R., 'Somatotype and sexual maturation in boys: a method of developmental analysis', *Hum. Biol.*, *30*, 73–91 (1958).

428. HURME, V. O., 'Standards of variations in the eruption of the first six permanent teeth', *Child Development*, *19*, 211–31 (1948).

429. ISRAELSOHN, W. J., 'Description and modes of analysis of human growth', *Symp. Soc. Study Hum. Biol.*, *3*, 31–42 (1960).

430. JENSS, R. M. and BAYLEY, N., 'A mathematical method for studying growth in children', *Hum. Biol.*, *9*, 556–63 (1937).

431. LEECH, F. C. and HEALY, M. J. R., 'The analysis of experiments on growth rate', *Biometrics*, *15*, 98–106 (1959).

432. MEDAWAR, P. B., 'Size, shape and age', in *Essays on Growth and Form presented to D'Arcy Wentworth Thompson*, edited by W. E. Le Gros Clarke and P. B. Medawar, pp. 157–87 (Clarendon Press, Oxford, 1945).

433. MERRELL, M., 'The relationship of individual to average growth', *Hum. Biol.*, *3*, 37–69 (1931).

434. NOWAKOWSKI, T. K. and PERKAL, I. J., 'The method of Nowakowski and Perkal for determining the relationship between stature, weight and age', Note by Spahler, J. N., *Yearbk. Phys. Anthrop.*, *8*, 196–8 (1952).

435. RAO, C. R., 'Some statistical methods for comparison growth curves', *Biometrics*, *14*, 1–17 (1958).

436. REEVE, E. C. R. and HUXLEY, J. S., 'Some problems in the study of allometric growth', in *Essays on Growth and Form Presented to D'Arcy Wentworth Thompson,* edited by Le Gros Clark, W. E. and Medawar, P. B., pp. 122–55 (Clarendon Press, Oxford, 1945).

437. RICHARDS, O. W. and KAVANAGH, A. J., 'The analysis of growing form', in *Essays on Growth and Form presented to D'Arcy Wentworth Thompson*, edited by Le Gros Clark, W. E. and Medawar, P. B., pp. 188–229 (Clarendon Press, Oxford, 1945).

438. SHOLL, D. A., 'Regularities in growth curves including rhythms and allometry', in *Dynamics of Growth Processes*, edited by Boell, E. J., pp. 224–41 (University Press, Princeton, New Jersey, 1954).

439. SHUTTLEWORTH, F. K., 'Sexual maturation and the physical growth of girls age six to nineteen', *Monogr. Soc. Res. Child Develpm.*, *2*, No. 5 (1937).

440. TANNER, J. M., 'Notes on the reporting of growth data', *Hum. Biol.*, *23*, 93–159 (1951).

441. TANNER, J. M., 'The assessment of growth and development in children', *Arch. Dis. Childh.*, *27*, 10–23 (1952).

442. TANNER, J. M., WHITEHOUSE, R. H. and TAKAISHI, M., *Individual-type standards from birth to maturity for height, weight, height velocity and weight velocity : British Children 1960* (1965).